BETWEEN AUSCHWITZ AND JERUSALEM

PARKES-WIENER SERIES ON JEWISH STUDIES
Series Editors: David Cesarani and Tony Kushner
ISSN 1368-5449

The field of Jewish Studies is one of the youngest, but fastest growing and most exciting areas of scholarship in the academic world today. Named after James Parkes and Alfred Wiener, this series aims to publish new research in the field and student materials for use in the seminar room, to disseminate the latest work of established scholars and to re-issue classic studies which are currently out of print.

The selection of publications reflects the international character and diversity of Jewish Studies; it ranges over Jewish history from Abraham to modern Zionism, and Jewish culture from Moses to post-modernism. The series also reflects the inter-disciplinary approach inherent in Jewish Studies and at the cutting edge of contemporary scholarship, and provides an outlet for innovative work on the interface between Judaism and ethnicity, popular culture, gender, class, space and memory.

Other Books in the Series

Holocaust Literature: Schulz, Levi, Spiegelman and the Memory of the Offence
Gillian Banner

Remembering Cable Street: Fascism and Anti-Fascism in British Society
Edited by Tony Kushner and Nadia Valman

Sir Sidney Hamburger and Manchester Jewry: Religion, City and Community
Bill Williams

Anglo-Jewry in Changing Times: Studies in Diversity 1840–1914
Israel Finestein

Double Jeopardy: Gender and the Holocaust
Judith Tydor Baumel

Cultures of Ambivalence and Contempt: Studies in Jewish–Non-Jewish Relations
Edited by Siân Jones, Tony Kushner and Sarah Pearce

Alfred Wiener and the Making of the Wiener Library
Ben Barkow

The Berlin Haskalah and German Religious Thought: Orphans of Knowledge
David Sorkin

Myths in Israeli Culture: Captives of a Dream
Nurith Gertz

The Jewish Immigrant in England 1870–1914, Third Edition
Lloyd P. Gartner

State and Society in Roman Galilee, AD 132–212, Second Edition
Martin Goodman

Disraeli's Jewishness
Edited by Todd M. Endelman

Claude Montefiore: His Life and Thought
Daniel R. Langton

Between Auschwitz and Jerusalem

YOSEF GORNY

VALLENTINE MITCHELL
LONDON • PORTLAND, OR

First published in 2003 in Great Britain by
VALLENTINE MITCHELL
Crown House, 47 Chase Side, Southgate
London N14 5BP

and in the United States of America by
VALLENTINE MITCHELL
c/o ISBS, 920 NE 58th Avenue, Suite 300,
Portland, Oregon, 97213-3786

Website: www.vmbooks.com

British Library Cataloguing in Publication Data

Gorni, Yosef
  Between Auschwitz and Jerusalem. – (Parkes-Wiener series on
Jewish studies)
  1. Holocaust, Jewish – (1939–1945) – Influence 2. Jews – Israel
Attitudes 3. Jews – Identity 4. Israel and the diaspora
  I. Title
  909′.04924′0825

ISBN 0-85303-419-2 (cloth)
ISBN 0-85303-421-4 (paper)
ISSN 1368-5449

Library of Congress Cataloging-in-Publication Data

Gorni Yosef.
  [Ben Oshvits li-Yerushalayim. English]
  Between Auschwittz and Jerusalem / Yosef Gorny.
    p. cm – (Parkes-Wiener series on Jewish studies)
  Includes bibliographical references and index
  ISBN 0-85303-419-2 (cloth) – ISBN 0-85303-421-4 (pbk.)
    1. Holocaust, Jewish (1939–1945)–Influence. 2. Jews –Israel– Attitudes.
  3. Jews–Identity. I. Title. II. Series.

  D804.3.G6813 2003
  956.94′.001′9–dc21   2003043632

Typeset in Janson 11/13pt by Frank Cass Publishers
Printed in Great Britain by MPG Books Ltd, Victoria Square, Bodmin, Cornwall

Dedicated to the memory of Abraham and Edita Spiegel
who wandered in spirit between Auschwitz and
Jerusalem

Contents

Series Editor's Preface ix

Acknowledgments xii

Introduction 1

1 The Statist Discourse: The Eichmann Syndrome 17

2 The Theological Discourse 52

3 The Academic Discourse 83

4 The Ideological Discourse 125

5 The Pundits' Discourse: The Holocaust as an
Ethnic Mission 196

6 Summary: The Mythic Ethos of Holocaust and State 220

Index 243

Series Editor's Preface

The salience of 'the Holocaust' at the end of the 1990s provoked a great deal of comment, much of it shallow and ill-informed. At its most puerile, this commentary attributed the prominence of Holocaust memorialization and 'post-Holocaust issues', such as restitution and compensation for Nazi slave-labour, to a global conspiracy of Jewish leaders who instrumentalized the history of Jewish suffering for political and financial gain, mainly on behalf of Israel. The repeated assertion of a linkage between efforts to recall the Nazi persecution of the Jews and justification of the policies (and ultimately the existence) of the state of Israel fostered dangerous misconceptions about the origins of consciousness about the Nazi genocide and its relationship to Jewish identity in Israel and the Diaspora. After such a torrent of polemic and misinformation it is a relief to read this wise, calm, and deeply researched analysis of the emergence of 'Holocaust consciousness' in Israel and the USA and its complex, always changing place in Jewish self-perception.

Contrary to the myth that memory of Nazi persecution and mass murder of the Jews was suppressed in the years 1945 to 1967, when it was dredged up and inflated with the intention of justifying Israel's territorial acquisitions in the Six Day War, Gorny shows that the recent history of Jewish suffering was always a subject of argument and research. In Israel past events pervaded everyday life and politics thanks to the 1951 law for the punishment of Nazi war criminals and collaborators, the 1953 law to set up a memorial authority and day of remembrance, the long-running controversy over reparations from West Germany, and a sensational libel case in 1954–56 revolving around the conduct of Jewish leaders in Nazi-occupied Hungary. At a more rarified, but no less influential level, the founding figures of the historical profession, the mentors to a generation of lecturers and teachers, wrestled with the origins of Nazi anti-semitism and reasons for the Jewish catastrophe. It was during these years that, for good or ill, a connection was forged between the destruction of European Jewry and the birth of the Jewish State. Israelis learned that the fate of the Jewish Diaspora was a unique lesson in the dangers of power-lessness, proving the need for a Jewish state that empowered the Jewish people.

In America awareness of the European Jewish disaster was initially restricted to Jewish circles, but Gorny demonstrates that a vigorous public debate was initiated by the abduction of Adolf Eichmann from Argentina in May 1960 to stand trial in Israel. Hannah Arendt's acerbic commentary on the trial, published in 1963, further widened the scope of the debate and the range of participants. The Six Day War in 1967 and the Yom Kippur War in 1973 drew American Jews closer to Israel and heightened the apparent relevance of the Nazi years to contemporary experiences, but within a peculiarly American context. The years of persecution and genocide were summoned up to give American Jews a niche in the pantheon of suffering that increasingly characterised the architecture of American civic culture. By pointing to America's less than urgent response to the wartime plight of European Jewry, American Jews brought the Holocaust home and laid down their own claims against the WASP hegemony, enabling them to join the 'culture of grievance' shaped and sustained by a coalition of immigrants and minorities. American Jewish aspirations for installing consciousness of the horrors perpetrated in wartime Europe in the mind of modern America finally achieved realisation in the United States Holocaust Memorial Museum which Stuart Eizenstat, one of its prime movers, characterised as 'an American museum about a distinctly Jewish event with a universal message'. Indeed, far from promoting a narrow Jewish nationalist agenda, the advocates of 'Holocaust remembrance' wanted to universalize and Americanise its lessons.

Perhaps the most surprising metamorphosis occurred in Israel in the 1980s. There left-wing and liberal academics, intellectuals, and media pundits reacted sharply to attempts by right-wing Zionists, notably Menachem Begin, to draw the most hawkish moral from the era of Jewish defencelessness. They were appalled that Jewish suffer-ing in the past was being summoned up to justify the infliction of suffering on the Palestinians in the present. In an effort to undermine arguments from history some disputed whether there was any connection between the Nazi genocide against the Jews and the founding of Israel and insisted that Jews were not the only victims of Nazi racism. Others were content with the specificity of the Jewish tragedy, but disputed whether it had any bearing on the conduct of Israeli state policy. Even in Israel, then, at no time was there an unchallenged consensus that the Nazi assault on the Jews was linked to the emergence of Israel in any unproblematic fashion or that any prior victimisation of the Jews provided political or moral legitimacy for the use of state power against other peoples.

Gorny suggests that the connection between 'Holocaust consciousness' and Zionism may not only by questionable, but the two may even be mutually exclusive. He illustrates how the rise of 'Holocaust consciousness', especially within the framework of liberal, multicultural societies in England and America, can actually displace Israel as the cynosure of Jewish identity. He cites a string of thinkers who have divined a universal message in the Nazi persecution and mass murder of the Jews, one that enables Jews to cultivate a distinctive sensibility while also having something to share with society at large. Exile, dispossession, and survival provide a badge of identity that is less uncomfortable than the Zionist insignia. Indeed, there were always trend-setting figures, like George Steiner, for whom the Nazi horror was central to their identity, and who saw it as a basis for Jewish particularity, while at the same time vehemently denouncing Zionism and Israel.

In this thoughtful and exhaustive work Yosef Gorny shows that the connections between Jewish consciousness of Nazi oppression and the emergence of an Israeli national consciousness are far from clear. He explodes the simplistic equation of 'Holocaust consciousness' and pro-Zionism amongst Jews in the Diaspora. While not everyone will agree with his taxonomical approach or his categorisations, his rigorous approach displaces the trite explanations that have recently cluttered bookshops and library shelves. In fact, thanks to his analysis we can see how they are merely transient phenomena of a continuing argument over the place of 'the Holocaust' in Jewish life, one that has been going on since the Nazi shadow first fell on the Jewish people.

David Cesarani, Series Editor

Acknowledgments

This book was written between 1994 and 1997. In the course of my work I received assistance and support from various institutions and persons, to whom I owe special thanks. During part of the writing period I stayed in New York as a visitor of the Jewish Theological Seminary of America (JTS) and of New York University (NYU), whose hospitality immeasurably facilitated my work, and for that I thank personally Professor Ismar Schorsch, the president of the Jewish Theological Seminary; Professor Menahem Schmeltzer, Rector of the JTS at that time; Professor Robert Chazan, then Head of the Program of Jewish Studies in NYU and Professor David Engel of the same department. I would also like to thank the manager of the Jewish Memorial Foundation, Dr Jerry Hochbaum, who encouraged me to undertake this research. I owe special thanks to my friend, Professor Daniel Carpi, who replaced me as head of the Institute for the Research of Zionism during my absence, and to Professor Arye Carmon, president of the Israel Democracy Institute. The publication of this book in English was aided by a grant from the Abraham and Edita Spiegel Family Foundation Chair, and the Memorial Foundation for Jewish Culture.

In addition, I wish to express my gratitude to Naftali Greenwood, whose inspired translation of this text into English unerringly succeeds in keeping the inner spirit of this complex subject, and to Sally Green, the devoted editor of this book.

Finally, I am deeply thankful to my wife Geulah, the permanent companion and gifted assistant in all my works, and especially in this one.

Introduction

One ascends to the United States Holocaust Memorial Museum in Washington, a red-brick building that looms awkwardly on a green hill. It stands out from its surroundings, its contents seemingly challenging and daring them: challenging and daring that quadrangle of grass and cherry trees, embellished with white neoclassical buildings; those museums of science and technology; and those museums of history and the arts that display the magnitude of the human intellect.

I do not know whether the symbolism of this clash – between the lofty, the beautiful, and the noble, and the lowly, the brutal, and the murderous in the behavior of humankind – occurred to those who conjured the idea of the museum, who funded its formation, and who sought to place it in this location. In retrospect, however, this contrast is like a mute outcry, not only against the evil that human civilization contains but also against the fate of the Jewish people. This people, which gave the world the one and all-merciful God, whose prophets caused the utopia of justice to blossom, from which came forth the world's great reformers and most important practitioners of the humanities and the sciences – this people is donating to this very society and civilization, at the political navel of the world, its own disaster!

Furthermore, it is making this donation to the great masses, few of whom are Jewish, and means it to represent an act of soul-searching, personal cleansing, and – so to speak – a social lesson that may reinforce the universal dominion of ethics and justice. To wit: to turn the lesson of the Holocaust into a 'New-New Testament' of sorts, a third testament following the Jews' Old Testament and the Christians' New Testament, a possession of all those created in God's image, irrespective of their faith.

Most of the visitors who throng this sad exhibition unquestionably obtain a momentary catharsis. They circulate in the holy silence of a cemetery, their facial expressions and their eyes attesting to their emotions. The outer impression is that the visitors are concerned mainly about matters close to their own hearts and realities. Therefore, viewers are attracted to the exhibit that explains the racial doctrine, and the survivors' heart-rending personal accounts bring tears to many eyes, including those of the young.

One doubts whether the millions who have visited the museum learned a permanent moral lesson there, and whether that the additional millions yet to visit in the years to come will do so. One doubts whether the momentary agitation is not transitory and will leave no imprint on these people's daily lives. However, these masses unquestionably attest that the Holocaust has become part of the American folk culture, at the initiative and with the encouragement of much of the political, media, and cultural elite. In this sense, it serves the Jews as another entry pass into American society. The museum of the Jewish catastrophe, established across the way from the monuments to the founding fathers of American society, has become an emblem of the Jews' normalization in the United States, in the sense that their calamity has become part of this society's historical, spiritual, and moral heritage.

This development is chiefly the result of ideological and psychological changes that American society has experienced over the past generation. In other senses – economics, politics, science – the Jews have for years been important and integral constituents of this society. This change, of course, is linked to the general transformation of American society from the cultural worldview of an Anglo-Saxon melting pot to ethnic multicultural pluralism, whose content is not yet clear but whose public legitimacy has already become unchallengeable.

Thus the United States Holocaust Memorial Museum in Washington, by exhibiting the suffering of a specific ethnic group, by intending ideationally to convert this suffering into a universal and American moral, is the most pronounced emblem of the normalization that American Jewry has attained. However, this emblem comes with two paradoxes. First, it incorporates the suffering inflicted on the Jews outside the United States, by other peoples, into the American heritage. This precedent may turn the United States into a receptacle that carries the heritage of the human suffering of all of its ethnic groups, which represent all of humanity. This is historically absurd and socially pernicious, for it fosters groups that bear an everlasting grievance, their just demands overwhelmed by their aggressive demands.

The second paradox flows from the first: the more the museum acquires general significance, and the more the public at large shows an interest in it, the more its Jewish complexion will diminish. True, its pronouncedly Jewish exhibits will remain dominant even after testimonies about other peoples' sufferings are added, but the Jewish people's painful intimacy with its disaster will be dulled, blurred, and eventually obfuscated. After all, the boulevards of the American capital reserve no place for the Jews' suffering except in its universal American sense. However, this suffering belongs primarily to Jews as Jews. It belongs to them as do their faith and prayers, as does their resurrection movement, as does their struggle for national existence. It is theirs because of the difference between the bearers of the scars and the pain and those who commiserate with them; between a people whose history was fundamentally changed and peoples whose histories continue to follow their ordinary trajectory despite the sufferings and political upheavals that the present century has visited upon them.

At the opposite pole is Yad Vashem – positioned within the perimeter of national particularism, far from the center of world power, in the state of the Jews, in Israel's Jerusalem but outside the bustle of the city, on hillsides of gray stone, in a forest of upright pines.

Those who seek the differences between these two institutions will find them in their aesthetic symbolism: the difference between fertile lawns and gray, exposed stones; between merrily blossoming cherry trees and grave, spiky pines; between proximity to the military cemetery in Washington and proximity to Mount Herzl and the cemetery for the fallen of the Israel Defense Forces; between a museum that overlooks its surroundings and Yad Vashem, which is concealed from them. The former attempts to claim a station of prominence in the panoply of American culture; the latter, in its setting in the historical capital of Jerusalem, next to the graves of those who made national independence a reality, denotes the negative dimension of Jewish existence – the Holocaust.

This symbolic contrast points to a highly meaningful turnabout in cognizance of the Jewish collective identity with respect to its two modern components, the Holocaust and the State of Israel. Until not many years ago, one might have regarded the two as twin players in an inseparable historical fate: the Holocaust justified the struggle for statehood, and its lesson gave the Jews the strength to struggle for the state's existence; the state reinvigorated the people who had experienced the Holocaust and assures its continued collective existence. Now that the museum in Washington has demonstrated its success, the fissure between the two is becoming visible – between perceiving the

Holocaust as part of the national ethos and myth and viewing it as a universal American phenomenon; between its unbreakable interrelationship with the Jewish state and the attempt to assimilate its lesson into the multicultural society of the United States; between the national historical continuum that regards both the Holocaust and Israel as being rooted in the process of development in Jewish–Gentile relations (a process with a causal logic of sorts) and the attempt to shift the phenomenon of extermination to the plane of transnational social processes, thus lending it a universal complexion that dwarfs its particularistic nature. Thus the Jewish people is marching to the brink of a crisis of collective consciousness that may lead to portentous results in view of the cultural–religious and civil–political fragmentation of Jewish society. Until now, this Jewish multifacetedness – advocates and creative artists in various languages, in different religious streams, some pious and others secular, equally entitled citizens in free countries along with citizens of the Jewish nation-state – has had a shared framework of consciousness and pertinence: the state and the Holocaust. Now, as stated, this framework is liable to dissolve.

The nexus of Holocaust and state – or, to use different terminology, of Holocaust and resurrection – has been complex and tense since its inception at the end of World War II. Basically, it originated in the psychologically and historically understandable attempt to forge the negative lesson of the Holocaust, impotence, into a political and spiritual instrument in the struggle for statehood. In metaphorical terms, one may say that the expression 'Masada shall not fall again' was juxtaposed with the expression 'like lambs to the slaughter'. Essentially, however, it was a dialectic tension that preached unity despite contradictions and believed in the elimination of these contradictions by means of positive historical development. According to this perception of the Holocaust-and-resurrection consciousness, the similarities of magnitude and importance between the two facets outweigh the dissimilarities. The tension that evolved and developed in the past decade is different. First, the contradiction is no longer dialectic. Second, it serves as a manifestation of the dissociation that is occurring between the center of Jewish reality – the State of Israel – and the large Jewish collective in the United States.

The transition from the dialectic tension to the post-dialectic tension is the central theme of this book. This is a historical study that does not deal with the history of the Holocaust. It concerns trends of thought pertaining to the Holocaust, but not with moral, theological, or philosophical questions that stem from it. It deals with consciousness, not in its individual and psychological sense but in its collective, national, and social sense. It deals not with the form of collective remembrance but with its public motives. The motives of this remembrance, a public affair that takes on various public forms – ceremonies, symbols, memorial days, pilgrimages, statues, and monuments – are ideational and political and aim to serve national, social, and political needs and interests. This remembrance is always public, unlike the internal, personal, and undirected remembrance of the individual. Therefore, while individuals occasionally need outside intervention to elevate their remembrance from the subconscious to the conscious or from thought to verbal or written expression, in collective remembrance a deliberate effort is sometimes made to evade the motives or to conceal some or all of them from the public.

This work concerns itself with the overt and covert contents of the motives of the public remembrance, including its conceptual and political significance, and with how this remembrance has been shaped to the limit beyond which public remembrance, in its various forms, becomes a factor in its own right in the coalescence of the collective consciousness.

This consciousness is manifested in what I term 'public thinking', which, as stated, is other than theological cerebration although it contains elements of it. 'It is neither a philosophical method nor an ideological doctrine. It is an intellectual cultural phenomenon, publicistic and pluralistic, that attempts to explain reality and steer its development based on historical tradition, moral principles, and religious faith.'[1] This thinking is expressed mainly through the popular press and academic publications. Its participants are intellectuals and academics, rabbis and public figures, journalists and politicians. Thus, there is a close correspondence between the debate and the realities debated, with their changing long-term cultural trends and their immediate political considerations. As such, public thinking has become one of the factors that shape reality, and its weight, of course, varies commensurate with the nature of the historical situation. Thus, for example, the tension between the consciousness of Holocaust and resurrection, which I have defined as dialectic and post-dialectic, corresponds to changes in the changing relationship between Israel and the Diaspora, a relationship derived from developments that do not originate in these two consciousnesses. However, it is the relationship between this special consciousness and objective political and cultural developments that makes them interact. Thus, the Americanization of the Holocaust consciousness may hasten the weakening of the

Israel–Diaspora relationship, whereas emphasis on the uniqueness of
the Holocaust would have the opposite effect. The inception of the
coalescence of Holocaust consciousness as an important component in
the collective Jewish identity does not resemble its conclusion. It began
in the late 1960s and early 1970s for particularistic Jewish motives and
ended in the 1990s with universal trends.

This historical development occurred differently among American
Jewry and in Israel. In the United States, one may discern four phases:
first the phase of repressed knowledge in the 1945–60 period – from
the end of World War II until shortly before the capture of Adolf
Eichmann; then the phase of transitory emotional consciousness, in
which the horrors of the Holocaust were revealed to the public on a
personal level but not discussed profoundly in their pan-Jewish sense.
Later came the national-consciousness phase, between 1967 and the
late 1970s, in which Israel fought its crucial wars and, as the results of
the expansion of historical research began to filter to the masses, the
Holocaust became a fixture in public consciousness; and finally from
the early 1980s to the present time – a direct outgrowth of the previous
phase, in which political developments that some of Diaspora Jewry
finds perplexing, such as the war in Lebanon, and social and cultural
processes that matured, made the Holocaust a state of consciousness in,
and a familiar component of, the Jewish collective identity.

One may explain the repression of the Holocaust at the public and
even the personal level in the Western Diaspora by noting that
survivors or members of *she'erit hapleta* lacked the psychological
strength and the cultural and public stature that would allow and
prompt them to deliver their recollections into the public realm. As for
the Jews, their minds and hearts were not attuned to what their compatriots had endured in Holocaust-era Europe.

For the postwar generation, it was a time of general optimism. The
United States had embarked on a wave of economic prosperity from
which most of the Jewish community benefited. This was manifested
not only in the enrichment of Jews – which transcended the gains of all
other groups and communities – but in other fields from which Jews
had been barred. The most salient and significant example in terms of
the Jews' public status was the breakthrough in the universities, especially the famous, elitist ones, both as students and as faculty members.
The dynamic of this practical social integration made the Jews feel
subjectively and know objectively that their Americanization process
had succeeded. The utopian dream of the late nineteenth-century
immigrants, who sought not only existential security but also social

acceptance, had begun to come true. From now on, American Jews were no longer immigrants who benefited from the mercies of the host country's liberal democratic regime and economic wealth; they had become full-fledged members of this community. They had shed their blood for it in the war and contributed their intellectual capabilities and ethical values to its society. It is not by chance that the universities, in which Jewish students proliferated, and the rabbinates of the modern religious currents spawned the activists who played such a great role in the blacks' struggle, under Martin Luther King, for equal rights. At this time, the Americanization of the Jews took a radical turn not only in sociopolitical terms but in cultural-traditional terms as well. Middle-class Jews were increasingly inclined to integrate into the religious spirit of American society at large. As Jews migrated en masse from cities to middle-class suburbs, they began to organize around synagogues, foremost those of the Conservative and Reform movements. Although this trend had more to do with cultural and social leanings than a strengthening of religious faith, Will Herberg's claim in 1955 – that the Jews had attained a status equivalent to that of the two Christian faiths (Protestant and Catholic) – made the book containing this argument one of the most discussed and influential works among intellectuals of that generation.[2]

In this climate, issues of pronouncedly particularistic Jewish significance were relegated to the fringes of public consciousness.[3] Thus students and some rabbis waged a struggle for equal empowerment of blacks, intellectuals failed to grasp the Holocaust and barred it from the realm of their thinking, and the *she'erit hapleta* survivors still held their silence. Only the political functionaries concerned themselves with this matter – important in itself but devoid of public reverberations – in their discussions on how to apportion the German reparation money between Israel and the Diaspora and among the various Jewish organizations.[4]

The best indication of that climate of public disengagement from and repression of the Holocaust is the Jewish response to the Eichmann affair in 1960–64. To be sure, Eichmann's abduction elicited reactions and disagreements in public opinion. The Jewish and general press covered his trial extensively, and the tumult triggered by Hannah Arendt's book *Eichmann in Jerusalem: A Report on the Banality of Evil* dragged into the affair intellectuals who had been aloof from any Jewish concern until then. All of them attested to the Jews' sensitivity to Israel's good name, to the procedures of correct jurisprudence, and, above all, to the role and intentions of the Jewish leadership in the ghettos during the Holocaust, which Arendt accused of indirectly helping the Germans carry out their extermination campaign. However, this commotion did not set the stage for the onset of a methodical, probing discussion of the Holocaust as a historical phenomenon and a significant event for the Jews. The attitude toward Israel as a singularly Jewish phenomenon was also affected by the Jews' powerful wish and vigorous action to integrate into American society.

The Zionist and non-Zionist public leadership in the 1950s had an interest in stressing the absence of dual loyalty among the Jews, i.e., to the United States and to Israel. Therefore, the World Zionist Organization and other Jewish entities, especially the American Jewish Committee, emphasized that American Jews were, principally and unconditionally, loyal citizens of their country. Philanthropic efforts on behalf of Israel also slackened perceptibly at that time relative to Israel's first few years – precisely when Israel needed generous assistance to absorb socially the masses of immigrants who had arrived in 1948–52 and doubled its population, even as American Jewry amassed wealth. Furthermore, many Jews affiliated with liberal circles had become critical of Israel's policies, especially its 'imperialist conspiracy' with France and Great Britain in the 1956 Sinai Campaign. Hovering over all these circumstances was a cloud of disenchantment with the new Jewish state. Many observers had concluded that the sundry utopian hopes that they had pinned on Israel were not progressing toward fruition and that Israel was becoming just another country. Thus, the normalization of Israel gave a justification of sorts to the Americanization of Jewry.

The situation in Israel was different. In Israel's first decade, its Government acted both directly and indirectly to turn the Holocaust into a public and national affair.[5] Legislation for the prosecution of Nazis and their assistants was passed in 1951, giving the State the status of prosecutor in the name of the Jewish people for the crimes perpetrated against them. In 1953, the Knesset passed the Remembrance of Holocaust and Heroism – Yad Vashem Law, which the Minister of Education at that time, the historian Benzion Dinur, presented on behalf of the government. Thus, remembrance of Holocaust and heroism, coupled with the memorial day for the fallen of the Israel Defense Forces and the independence festivities, became a symbol of state that expressed the Jewish people's resurrection in its homeland.

At the public level, two furors occurred at this time, both of them political. The first erupted after the reparations agreement with Germany was signed, and the second concerned the question of Zionist leaders' collaboration with the Nazis. In 1952, the controversy led to violent street clashes between right-wing demonstrators and police, as an inflamed mob headed by Menachem Begin attempted to storm the Knesset while the reparations debate progressed inside. In 1954, Rudolf (Israel) Kasztner went on trial for collaborating with the Nazis. Together with him in the defendant's dock, in the court of history, was the Zionist leadership for its sins of omission in rescuing European Jews during the Holocaust. Kasztner's assassination by a Jew, after the Supreme Court acquitted him on appeal, added personal tragedy to the political drama that had unfolded against the backdrop of the national disaster. Then, in 1961, Adolf Eichmann went on trial in Jerusalem. Thus it happened that by the 1950s and the early 1960s, the government of Israel, deliberately or inadvertently, had turned Holocaust awareness into Holocaust consciousness. The reconstitution of the Holocaust as a symbol of the state on the one hand and a topic of debate (over relations with Germany) on the other, and criticism of the Holocaust-era Zionist leadership on the one hand and the Eichmann trial on the other – especially the testimonies given during the trial – all reinforced consciousness of the Holocaust in Israel.

It can be said that in Israel, the coalescence of Holocaust consciousness was preceded by an attempt to shape Holocaust consciousness as part of the collective identity. The motives for this were both ideological, to cement the unity of the new society, and political, to undermine the dominion of the Mapai party. Thus, for different motives, the ideology underlying the Holocaust and Heroism law and the political intentions behind the tumultuous debate over the reparations agreement with Germany and the Kasztner trial served the same cause.

The Eichmann trial, ten years later, actually furthered the same intent but had the special effect of eliciting broad public consciousness of the theme of the Holocaust. The testimonies about having been on 'another planet', in the phrase of the author Ka-Tzetnik, and the 'man in the glass booth', as Haim Guri described the defendant, gave the public a better sense and a more profound understanding of what had transpired there. This is not to deny that Israel had gone through a stage of repression, but it lasted only a few years.[6] Statehood had been just proclaimed, a war of independence tantamount to a struggle for survival had just ended, and the country faced immense difficulties in absorbing masses of immigrants, including the recently arrived

Holocaust survivors. Thus issues of the here-and-now superseded the experience of the past. Furthermore, the survivors were unable and unwilling to be reminded of the past at that time. However, the phase of repressed knowledge was shorter in Israel than in the United States, and the border between the two phases, of cognizance and of consciousness, was blurred by the public agencies' ideological and political campaign to instil the lesson of the Holocaust among the people.

In the United States, in contrast, the boundary between the phases of repressed knowledge and public awareness was clearly drawn and marked by three events that originated outside the internal realities of American Jewish society.

The three events that turned knowledge into awareness took place successively within a six-year period: the Six-Day War in 1967, the inception of conflict between blacks and Jews in 1968, and the Yom Kippur War in 1973. These events neither resemble nor bear any relationship to each other. The Six-Day War ended with a stunning Israeli victory and prompted surprising national fervor among Diaspora Jews, transcending even that which erupted when the State of Israel was established. In contrast, the Yom Kippur War, although it too ended in an Israeli victory, came at a heavy cost in lives and challenged confidence in Israel's hitherto unchallenged military might. The tension between blacks and Jews, first manifested in New York, was utterly unrelated to the other two events.

However, they all shared a common denominator: the Jewish existential angst, coupled with a sense of isolation and abandonment. Shortly before the Six-Day War, young Jewish activists in radical movements that sought to transform American society found themselves alone in their concern for Israel's existence. Their comrades in arms, both black and white, abandoned them – arguing that Israel was an imperialist state that had committed an unpardonable injustice against the Palestinian people.

Something similar happened to the political and religious Jewish establishment, which had been entertaining the illusion – born of the Will Herberg doctrine – that theirs was one of three faiths, along with the Protestant and the Catholic, that enjoyed equality of class, partnership, and fraternity in the United States. The leaders of the two Christian faiths spurned the entreaties of Jewish leaders and rabbis to stand beside Israel, beleaguered and threatened with annihilation. This rejection recurred in the Yom Kippur War.

The radical Jewish students who found themselves alone among their comrades in their concern for Israel when the country faced the risk of devastation experienced a similar disillusionment. Consequently, many turned to Jewish nationalist courses of action; some even settled in Israel.

On top of all these was the overt black antisemitism that first erupted in 1968. The event that triggered it was a demand by committees in the black slums of New York to replace white school principals and some white teachers with black educators. This prompted a teachers' strike, and since a majority of the teachers were Jewish, the two communities found themselves in conflict. The anti-Jewish incitement from the blacks' camp took on a racist complexion that included notorious Nazi manifestations. The schism between the two population groups remains unhealed, nearly thirty years later.

Thus, three assaults on Jewish existence – the two wars that threatened Israel with destruction and the troubling phenomenon of black antisemitism – became conductors of Holocaust consciousness.

The combination of protracted outside pressure and a spontaneous internal awakening, such as that following the Six-Day War, reinforced Israel–Diaspora unity. Thus, one may speak of the 'Zionization' of world Jewish society. This applies in two senses: in public identification with Israel, the Zionist state – the embodiment of the doctrine defined by the United Nations as a form of racism – and in adopting the Zionist prescription for Jewish existence, i.e., reliance on strength: political and economic strength in the Diaspora, especially in the United States, and military strength in Israel. Interestingly, the vociferous right-wing slogan, 'never again', also earned the sympathies of left-wing Jewish radical groups that had become disenchanted with the general radical movement because of its hostility toward Israel at its time of distress and its indifference to antisemitic manifestations among blacks.

The fourth period, which we have defined as the consciousness phase, has two markers. On the one hand, one finds the coalescence of a sensitive grass-roots perception of the Holocaust as an object lesson for Jewish existence – a perception that takes on a quasi-ritual complexion on memorial days and in the 'March of the Living' by Jewish youth to the extermination camps and thence to Jerusalem, as if to close a national circle; in the construction of Holocaust museums; and in the role of affluent survivors in funding all this activity. On the other hand, thoroughgoing intellectual debate came into being at this time about the meaning of the Holocaust, both as a particularistic Jewish phenomenon and as an event in universal history. Two types of motives

powered this debate: intellectual-academic and political. In the intellectual realm, the amassing of research and scholarly inquiry on the
Holocaust in the preceding thirty years contributed to it. At the political level, the debate was prompted by political developments in the
Middle East.

Holocaust consciousness as a public emotional phenomenon began
with the 1976 television mini-series *Holocaust*, which told the story of a
Jewish family in Germany during the Nazi era, horrified millions of
Jews and non-Jews, and turned the Holocaust into a legitimate public
issue, and ended in 1993 when the United States Holocaust Memorial
Museum opened in Washington and became a site of pilgrimage for
millions. As for Israel and much of Diaspora Jewry, the accession of the
Likud in 1977 also helped enhance emotional consciousness. Prime
Minister Menachem Begin was the only leader who attempted
consciously to instill the lesson of the Holocaust in the grass-roots
Jewish collective consciousness. On the emotional plane and among
grass-roots circles, Holocaust consciousness created a sense of Jewish
unity between past and present, between Israel and the Diaspora. On
the conscious-cognitive plane, however, the opposite occurred. Here,
in view of the political events in the Middle East, the war in Lebanon,
and the intifada, the schism between persons of liberal worldview who
stressed the moral dimension of Jewish existence, and conservatives
who underscored the need to use force, progressively widened. A rift
developed between those who regarded the Holocaust as a lesson to the
nation – to avoid further reliance on the gentiles' goodwill – and those
who adduced from it a universal lesson and argued that only by
turning Holocaust remembrance into the moral province of the collective would its recurrence be prevented. Thus, the attitude toward the
Holocaust and, with it, toward Israel became a political tool in the
hands of the two radical extremes.

This study focuses mainly on the consciousness phase, during
which the Holocaust became an increasingly important component in
the Jewish collective identity, along with religious faith and the status
of Israel. It traces systematically the development of public thinking in
this respect, stresses the connection between this thinking and the
ideological perceptions of the participants in the debate for influence
over Jewish and general public opinion, and compares Israel with the
Diaspora. In view of this approach and research method this book is, as
stated, a sequel to its precursor, *The State of Israel in Jewish Public
Thought: The Quest for Collective Identity.*

The set of concepts that I invoked in *The Quest for Collective Identity*

– 'general normalization', 'singular normalization', and 'Jewish normalization' – are used again in the present study to show that discussion of the Holocaust and its relationship with Israel is connected with the ongoing historical debate on the normalization of Jewish existence.

The title of this book, *Between Auschwitz and Jerusalem,* carries several theological, historical, and ideological meanings. In the theological respect, the title may symbolize a reference to divine mercy toward a people that experienced a terrible disaster that religious faith cannot explain – a modern, collective Job-like situation, so to speak, in which, though the probing questions about human suffering remain unanswerable, the compensation for this suffering is palpable.

From the historical standpoint, the title expresses the substantive transformation that has occurred in the status of Jewry among the nations: the transition from collective impotence to sovereign might; from nearly total dependency on others to a relative independence that bases the Jews' relations with their surroundings on mutual interests; from a sense of existential isolation among the peoples to recognition of political-ideational partnership with some of them.

In its ideological significance, this pairing also expresses the tension between concepts that originate in the pre-Holocaust and the pre-statehood reality and have persisted to this day, a tension that flows from the struggle in modern Jewish history between universalism and particularism, between Diaspora and Eretz Israel, between Zionism and anti-Zionism, between negation and affirmation of exile, between Zionism and post-Zionism. In this context, Auschwitz may be emblematic of everything negative in Jewish history outside of Eretz Israel, but it may also serve as a signal for the resumption of the Jews' moral mission among the gentiles. Jerusalem, too, may be a symbol of resurgent Jewish nationhood and a harbinger of a future return to Zion, but may also symbolize the advent of aggressive Jewish nationalism.

None of these three senses alone typifies the link between Auschwitz and Jerusalem as discussed in this study, but all three evince themselves in this pairing to different and varying degrees. The symbolic poles of this tension today are Yad Vashem in Jerusalem and the Holocaust Memorial Museum in Washington. After all, the transition to an understandable and inevitable rivalry between a long-standing, high-status institution and a newcomer that wishes to earn its status, and the transition to institutional jealousies in fundraising for their operations, are both indicative of a substantive problem in Jewish existence. The underlying ideology of the museum in

Washington aims to liberate the Diaspora from Israel's custodianship, and to accomplish this it needs its own symbolic ethoses that may unify it despite and beyond its current fragmentation. Remembrance of the Holocaust is the facile ethos. Therefore, Jewish leaders and intellectuals in London, too, have embarked on an effort to establish a Holocaust museum. Community leaders in Berlin have also bruited a plan to build a mammoth memorial to the victims of the Holocaust. The day when these and similar initiatives will be taken in other countries is not far off.

The roots of the discourse discussed in this book lie in an attempt to counterbalance the centrality of Israel through Holocaust consciousness and the ritual attached to this consciousness. Therefore, although the discourse is influenced by public trends and general intellectual and academic thinking, it is foremost an intimate dialogue among Jews. Non-Jewish intellectuals and historians take no part in it; at the most, they serve it as a backdrop. Neither do *haredi* (ultraorthodox) theologists participate in it, because just as they avoid probing the ways of God in view of the Holocaust, so, *a fortiori*, do they avoid exploring the relationship between the Holocaust and the State of Israel. This, of course, stems from their *a priori* rejection of the State as a Jewish entity and their view of the Holocaust as punishment for the Jews' iniquities – which, in greater or lesser part, are associated with the very action that led to the formation of the state.[7]

In this sense, this discourse on the meaning and present and future implications of the Holocaust is not merely a discussion of the dead but a discussion of the living, not only of a world laid waste but of the world that exists today and will exist tomorrow.

Since the original Hebrew version of this book was published, three books have appeared in the United States that deal indirectly and directly with the same problem in different ways and, by so doing, emphasize the uniqueness of this book.

The first of these books is by Shlomo Shaffir: *Ambiguous Relations: The American Jewish Community and Germany Since 1945* (USA, 1999). This is a well-balanced, meticulously documented academic study about the American Jewish establishment's policy toward post-war Germany. Shaffir's traditional opinion on Hannah Arendt's negative attitude toward Zionism and its impact on the Jewish discourse differs, in some ways, from my views from this perspective. The second book is Peter Novick's *The Holocaust in American Life* (USA, 1999); the third is Norman Finkelstein's *The Holocaust Industry* (London/New York, 2000). The two last-mentioned books are intentionally provocative unidimensional academic studies that have an overt ideological and even political mission.

Without concealing its ideological leanings, my book is not about a political conspiracy of the Jewish leadership to make the Holocaust into an instrument of support for the State of Israel. It is a study on the intellectual and spiritual perplexities in what I call 'public thought'. It is concerned not only with American Jewry but also with Israeli Jewish society. Its main topic is not Jews in American society but the Jewish people worldwide and its collective identity. It takes not a unidimensional but a multidimensional approach, showing the various and different views of diverse groups as they are expressed in the Jewish population centers, foremost the USA and Israel, and attempting to draw comparisons among them.

Apart from the introduction, this study comprises six chapters, five of which represent various aspects of intellectual discourse on the Holocaust–Israel nexus.

Chapter 1 – the statist discourse or the Eichmann syndrome – begins the discussion in terms both of time and of contents. The discussion here touches upon the Eichmann trial but does not deal with the way it was conducted or with its results. Instead, it concerns itself with the debate concerning Israel's right to prosecute Eichmann as the representative of the Jewish people. This chapter elaborates on Hannah Arendt's attitude toward this question specifically and toward the state of the Jews generally.

Chapter 2 – the theological discourse, or faith and politics – discusses the trilateral relationship of faith, Holocaust, and Israel. The discussion here moves along three planes: uncertainties concerning God's place in history, the metaphysical and mysterious relationship between the Holocaust and the State of Israel, and the relationship between policy and ethics from a religious perspective.

Chapter 3 – the academic discourse, or history and ideology – deals with the attempts of academics (historians, sociologists, and philosophers) to explain the Holocaust in objective terms. The crux of this discussion concerns the nature of the Holocaust: is it particularistic or universal? The chapter examines how the sundry approaches of the participants in this discourse correspond to their *a priori* ideational worldview. In other words, it attempts to expose the link between methodology and ideology.

Chapter 4 – the intellectual discourse, or ideology and politics – shifts the discussion from the halls of academia to the public domain. This discourse, by its very nature, is not among professional academics who operate within the methodological framework of disciplines. It is a multifaceted discourse in terms of its participants and the themes discussed. The political and ideational complexion of this discourse is not concealed behind the scientific approaches that mask the preceding discourse.

Chapter 5 – the public discourse, or ethnicity and politics – completes the cycle of discourses on the Israel/Holocaust relationship. It revolves entirely around the establishment of the United States Holocaust Memorial Museum in Washington, and its theme is the status of the Jews as an ethnic group in the United States. The pivotal question is whether the Jews' historical experience reflects their singular fate only or whether its principal message is universal. The political dimension is associated with the relationship with other ethnic groups that also carry historical memories of persecution and discrimination.

Chapter 6 – the mythic ethos of Israel and the Holocaust – summarizes the entire problem in view of developments in the past century of Jewish history.

NOTES

1. See Yosef Gorny, *The State of Israel in Jewish Public Thought: The Quest for Collective Identity* (London: Macmillan, 1994), pp. 3–4.
2. Will Herberg, *Protestant, Catholic, Jew: An Essay in American Religious Sociology* (USA, 1955).
3. This survey is based on the following works: Deborah E. Lipstadt, 'The Holocaust: Symbol and "Myth" in American Jewish Life', *Forum W.*, 1980/81; Stephen J. Whitfield, 'The Holocaust and the American Jewish Intellectual', *Judaism*, September 1980; Arthur Hertzberg, *The Jews in America: Four Centuries of Uneasy Encounter* (New York, 1989); Jack Wertheimer, *A People Divided: Judaism in Contemporary America* (New York, 1993); Leon A. Jick, 'The Holocaust: Its Uses and Abuses Within the American Public', *Yad Vashem Studies* (Jerusalem, 1981); Yosef Gorny, *The State of Israel in Jewish Public Thought: The Quest for Collective Identity*, pp. 3–4.
4. Ronald W. Zweig, *German Reparations and the Jewish World: A History of the Claims Conference* (USA, 1987).
5. On this matter, see Charles S. Liebman and Eliezer Don-Yehiya, *Civil Religion in Israel: Traditional Judaism and Political Culture in the Jewish State* (USA, 1983).
6. On this matter, see Yehiam Weitz, 'Shaping the Memory of the Holocaust in Israeli Society of the 1950s', *Major Changes within the Jewish People in the Wake of the Holocaust* (Jerusalem: Yad Vashem, 1996).
7. In this matter, see Eliezer Schweid, 'The Orthodox-Religious Confrontation with the Holocaust', *Mahanayim on the Holocaust* (a), Rabbi Menahem Hacohen, ed. (Jerusalem: Sapir Center), pp. 10–35 [Hebrew]. See also Schweid, *A Struggle Till Dawn*, Chapter 6, 'The Meaning of the Holocaust in Jewish History' (Jerusalem, 1990 [Hebrew]).

1

The Statist Discourse: The Eichmann Syndrome

This world will come back to this story and pause at it. Humanity will
continue to carry inside the recollection of the gas chambers without
defeating it. The 1940s will be the watershed between the eras.
Haim Guri, *Facing the Glass Booth*

The public discourse on the relationship between the Jewish state and
the Holocaust began with the abduction, trial, and execution of Adolf
Eichmann. During those years – 1960–64 – the debate surrounding
this episode took place in three phases and on three planes. The first,
the legal one, dealt with the legality of the abduction and Israel's
competence under international law to prosecute Eichmann. The
second was moral; it concerned the verdict and the implementation of
the sentence. The third was national; it followed the tempest of
emotions that Hannah Arendt unleashed with her book, *Eichmann in
Jerusalem: A Report on the Banality of Evil.*[1]

In the first two phases, the debate spanned the entire population
and attracted the attention of the American, Western European, and
Soviet-bloc media. In the third phase, it was principally Jewish-only.
This debate, in which the most important Jewish intellectuals in the
United States and Europe took part, a cognitive dissonance of sorts –
which one may also term an existential dissonance – came to the
surface. On the one hand, it took place within a Jewish community
that, after World War II, attained an economic, civil, and cultural status
hitherto unknown in the annals of the Diaspora history; thus, this
community had an interest in repressing memories of the Holocaust,
which might unhinge it from its surroundings. On the other hand, the
fervor and fury expressed by Arendt's critics showed that repression
should not be mistaken for indifference, that the tragedy of the
Holocaust was deeply embedded in American Jews' feelings, and that
this collective was still susceptible to a psychology of social besiege-
ment. Arendt's allegation against the Jewish leadership in Europe

might tarnish the individual and collective image of Jews in their surroundings. This may explain the heatedness and centrality of the debate in the Diaspora as against its marginal importance in Israel. The roots of this transcend the fact that Arendt's book was not translated into Hebrew; they are also connected with the very existence of the state, which largely absolved Jews from having to pass the test of non-Jewish surroundings.

Be this as it may, the Jewish institutions' sensitivity to American public opinion inspired the American Jewish Committee to monitor for two years, from May 1960 to June 1962 – the time of Eichmann's abduction to that of his execution – a survey of opinions in the press. The study encompassed thousands of general newspapers but excluded the Jewish press.[2]

The authors of the survey explained their point of departure in a series of questions that added up to an allegation against the enlightened democratic world that had gone to war against fascism – questions that still reside at the forefront of the contemporary public and historical debate. By the very act of phrasing them publicly, the authors underscored the defense brief concerning Israel's action. The questions follow:

- What was the attitude of the United States and the free countries toward the Nazi regime in its initial phases?
- Was the United States government willing to support the opponents of the Nazi regime in Germany?
- What was the attitude of the United States to the appeasement policy toward Germany?
- Did the free world do everything within its ability to give asylum to Jewish refugees who had fled Germany?
- Did the statespeople and public opinion, by refraining from castigating the Nazi regime, not become indirect accomplices in the regime's ascent and survival?
- Has the enlightened world learned a lesson from this miserable episode with respect to its future?
- In other words, to what extent might political silence and popular inertia cause, under certain conditions, a recurrence of the very acts that Eichmann symbolizes?

Of course, no answers were proffered, but the questions show that the American Jewish Committee (AJC) had decided to defend Israel aggressively. This is certainly the result of an agreement concluded in the early 1950s between Prime Minister Ben-Gurion of Israel and Jacob Blaustein, president of the AJC, concerning the totality of Israel–Diaspora relations.[3]

The authors of the survey drew several conclusions from the findings. They noted with satisfaction that most of the press generally evinced sympathy for and understanding of the resolve of the government of Israel in pursuing Eichmann and bringing him to trial. However, the same press that affirmed the abduction objected to the prosecution of Eichmann in Israel, arguing that Israel's refusal to turn Eichmann over to an international court for prosecution represented an affront of sorts to Western principles of law and justice. The authors of the survey considered this belief – that the Eichmann trial should be transferred from a Jewish national setting to an international venue – indicative of a growing editorial tendency to link the Jews' tragedy to the concept of totalitarianism, a concept certainly culled from Arendt's well-known book on the origins of totalitarianism, both Fascist and Communist. In the authors' opinion, non-Jewish molders of public opinion invoked this concept to universalize the meaning of the Holocaust, similar to racial discrimination or persecution and religious or political oppression. In so doing, the opinion-makers disregarded testimonies at the trial – the gist of which was carried in their newspapers – that begged the question: why did this fate strike the Jews in particular?

Pursuant to these remarks, the authors of the survey stressed that the very concept of antisemitism did not appear in most of the newspapers, except in a few editorials. No fact better underscores modern society's special attitude toward Jews in its midst, an attitude both ambivalent and dialectic, endowed concurrently with emancipation and with antisemitism.

The authors of the survey explained this disregard by noting that antisemitism as a political phenomenon was alien to the American political tradition, in obvious contrast to the popular antisemitic sentiments that circulated widely in the US before World War II. Since the end of the war, in the authors' opinion, a political struggle was being waged against all kinds of racial discrimination, which had been invested with general and universal significance. Thus irrational antisemitism as grounds for the extermination of human beings is exceptional in this sense and, therefore, unacceptable. This surely explains, the authors believed, why the general press disregarded several specific agonizing phenomena that the court discussed, such as the uniqueness of Nazism as expressed in its attitude toward the Jews, the fact that the Nazi state had marked six million Jews for death from the outset, and that the Jews 'were permitted to die' by the enlightened Western world.[4]

The thought that arises from these condensed remarks suggests that the border between two approaches to understanding the Holocaust, the universalist and the particularist, was visible by the early 1960s. The universalist view treats the Holocaust as a pan-human phenomenon that belongs to modern society; the particularist approach stresses the Jewish singularity of the Holocaust as part of the general modern phenomenon of mass annihilation. This debate will preoccupy us in the chapters to come, but it is worth emphasizing here that at that phase, in the 1960s, most universalists were non-Jews and their conviction had no implications for the essence of Jewish existence as an ethnic-national collective. This problem is an internal Jewish affair, as we shall see. As for Jewish society's response to the abduction of Eichmann, it was of two minds. On the one hand, Jews expressed amazement about the sophistication, resolve, and boldness of the Israeli government and security services. On the other hand, they were concerned about the international good name of Israel, which had carried out the abduction, and were anxious about the potential effect of the affair on their status as Diaspora Jews and their relations with Israel. The first facet of the response was hidden; the second facet led to sophisticated rejoinders and explanations in the domain of international law; and the third facet evolved into a discussion of principle on the status of the Jewish state among the Jewish people. We shall discuss this here.

The first personality who took up this issue was Joseph Proskauer, president of the American Jewish Committee in the late 1940s. During his tenure as president, Proskauer renounced his opposition to the idea of establishing a Jewish state and became a supporter of it, no other solution to the survivors' distress having been found during those decisive years of struggle for statehood. During the debate concerning the partitioning of Palestine and establishment of a Jewish state, Proskauer formed a personal relationship with Ben-Gurion. Thus, it is no coincidence that immediately after the abduction of Eichmann, Proskauer forwarded an urgent personal letter to Ben-Gurion, expressing his profound concern about the effects this action would have on the status of Diaspora Jewry and of Israel worldwide. With his letter, Proskauer enclosed an article from the *Washington Post* arguing that Israel lacked the competence to represent Jews in other countries and to act on behalf of 'an imaginary Jewish ethnic unit', i.e., a worldwide Jewish nation that, in the author's opinion, did not exist.[5]

These matters undoubtedly reflected Proskauer's outlook, since they matched the views of leaders of the American Jewish Committee ever since Israel had been founded. In contrast to the perspectives of several veteran Zionist leaders, the AJC directors stressed that Jews in the free world were above all citizens of their countries of residence. Accordingly, the government of Israel had neither the right nor the competence to represent them, to speak on their behalf, or even to attempt to protect them from antisemitic attacks. It was on the basis of these guidelines that the Prime Minister of Israel, David Ben-Gurion, and the president of the American Jewish Committee, Jacob Blaustein, had signed their agreement in 1951. The crux of the agreement was separation between Diaspora Jews, citizens of their countries, and Israel at the political and juridical level and an intimate relationship between the two entities in economic assistance, *halutsic aliya* (immigration to Israel in the sense of Zionist pioneering), and spiritual and cultural enrichment. At this juncture, Proskauer found himself in an embarrassing situation, since the *Washington Post* columnist and the heads of the American Council for Judaism – declared and principled anti-Zionists – were liable to attack the American Jewish Committee at its soft underbelly, the compromise posture that it attempted to maintain between a totally American Jewish identity and fealty to Israel's well-being, a combination that could pass the test as long as the two countries avoided conflicts of interest and tensions. Since in the Eichmann affair Israel seemed to be heading toward a confrontation of principle with American public opinion, Proskauer became concerned and sent off his letter to Ben-Gurion.

Oscar Handlin, a professor of American history at Harvard University, made explicit public remarks on this subject and in this spirit. He construed the competence that the government of Israel had arrogated to itself in capturing and punishing Adolf Eichmann in the name of the Jewish people as a menace to the Jews' future well-being. By so behaving, Handlin argued, Israel had, as it were, absolved the enlightened world of the need to concern itself with upholding the rights of Jews as human beings and citizens. For more than a century protests against pogroms, massacres, and lesser forms of discrimination had been noted for the inner conviction of progressive people that 'these were crimes not against Jews or Armenians, the direct sufferers, but against humanity. The appeal to a common conscience and a common stake in human decency.' In contrast to this tradition, Israel's action amounted to a declaration that henceforth it would assume full responsibility for the status, security, and rights of Jews outside its borders. Thus, 'The principle [of liberal-universal responsibility for the Jews' well-being] is thereby abandoned and the line of defense is parochially narrowed.'[6]

These remarks were written less than one generation after the Holocaust, by which time it was already evident that the annihilation of European Jewry had neither shaken the morals of Western society nor inspired its political system, let alone its historic leadership, to take special vigorous action to save those who could have been saved. This may actually have occurred because of the Western liberal universal tradition, which refused to acknowledge the particularistic Jewish problem and take special action against the Nazis before they began to annihilate the Jews.

This is an example of how the anti-national ideology, which was not far from the staunch anti-Zionism of the American Council, blinded as important a historian as Oscar Handlin. However, this did not mark the limit of his web of argumentation against the abduction of Eichmann by the government of Israel.

Continuing, Handlin decried the normalization trend that had surfaced among a majority of Jews, including many members of the American Jewish Committee, with which Handlin was close. As he put it, the Jewish people is unique in that, while other peoples live by the sword, it seeks to use universalist ethics as its shield. As a historian, Handlin traced this trait to the Jews' statelessness, which spared the Jewish people the temptation of resorting to military force. Beyond this political and practical rationale, however, Handlin was convinced that Judaism as a faith, as he perceived it, possessed a set of supreme and binding moral values. Now, the Jewish state had sullied this ideal moral reality, as engendered by the worldview and Western culture of Oscar Handlin. With much lament he contemplated the 'dual morality' of his compatriots, who postured as pacifists but proved to be supporters of Israel's willful belligerence, as in the Sinai Campaign; who ordinarily opposed capital punishment but favored it for those who had attacked their co-religionists; and who expressed support for international moral codes but defended the Jewish nation's right to take the law into its own hands. In Handlin's opinion, these phenomena in themselves mark a tragic turning point that should prompt the Jews to search their souls.

The claim that the Jews as a stateless and unarmed people entrusted their fate solely to universal ethics that they accepted as a supreme value pertains, of course, to the past two hundred years of European history, those of the Jewish emancipation. This, of course, is the truth but not the whole truth. Handlin projected the worldview of liberal Western Jewry, especially that of Germany, onto the entire Jewish people. He overlooked one fact: for millions of Eastern European Jews and hundreds of thousands in Asia and Africa, these universal ethics were devoid of importance and significance. If these grass-roots Jews were allowed to choose between reliance on their own sword or reliance on the universal ethics of their non-Jewish counterparts, they would certainly opt for the former. Handlin's self-assumed right to project the value system of Western Jewry onto Eastern Jewry (Jews of Eastern European and Afro-Asian origin) originates to no small extent in arrogance on the part of Western Jewry, especially its intelligentsia, toward its Eastern co-religionists. However, Handlin is mainly of interest not for his psychology but for his anti-national ideology.

In another article published about a year later – the Eichmann trial now under way in Israel – Handlin clashed swords with his opponents, the Zionist intellectuals who had criticized him for his previous article.[7] It is no coincidence that the article appeared in a publication of the American Council for Judaism, because the opinions expressed corresponded fully with the Council's worldview. Handlin regarded the Eichmann trial not as an isolated event but as an attempt by the government of Israel to impose its dominion over the Diaspora, because of the unexpressed principle on which this political aspiration was based: that only Israel may represent the Jewish people as a national entity.

Handlin's aim in this exposition was to spar with his Zionist rivals, who, he believed, were on the defensive and generally ambivalent in this matter. However, the logic of their worldview carried them back, again and again, to the same approach, to wit: Jews the world over are not mere co-religionists, akin to a Catholic entity, but members of a people who interrelate through national affiliation, and the State of Israel is the only political instrumentality that expresses and actualizes their collective interests.

This American Zionist posture of principle, and the efforts of the government of Israel to actualize it – including through violations of international law – jeopardized the existence of Jews in advanced societies. In addition to the argument he brought up in his previous article – that the policies of the government of Israel diminished the enlightened governments' responsibility for the well-being of the Jews – he now cited the possibility of a further risk to their existence in these countries, which, he believed, might eradicate or diminish the Jews' entitlement to civil equality. In other words, the various states would undertake to grant Jews residency rights and no more. Interestingly, these arguments, expressed by the anti-Zionist segment of British Jewry against the Balfour Declaration, now resurfaced nearly half a century later under totally different historical conditions – after the Holocaust, with the Jewish state in existence, and after Western Jewry had acquired political power and social respectability. The explanation for this phenomenon is rooted in historical factors, political considerations, and psychological situations. In the ideational respect, it flows from the anti-national perspectives of certain segments of the Jewish people. In the political respect, it originates in the fear, widely felt among Jews during those years, of being trapped in a dual loyalty situation. In the psychological respect, it expresses the typical apprehension of a minority group, especially one not yet freed from the sense of being in exile.

The solution mirrored that chosen in the distant past, at the onset of the struggle for emancipation by Jews of liberal or socialist inclinations: acceptance of universal principles and abandonment of tribal and national ones. Otherwise, the action taken by the government of Israel, and similar actions that might yet occur, would not only undermine the Jews' status but also isolate their suffering. By extension, the Jewish people would dwell alone not only in its fate but in its agonies. Then, by no coincidence, Handlin confirmed his universalist stance by mentioning the Mortera affair, the Dreyfus trial, and the Kishinev pogrom, in which enlightened public opinion sided with the Jews, but disregarded contemporaneous events such as those of World War II in which the same public opinion left the Jews to their fate.

Be this as it may, the important point for the purpose of our discussion is that, according to Handlin, the fears expressed by those of like mind before the Balfour Declaration had ominously come to pass because of actions taken by Israel, the bearer of the idea of inclusive Jewish nationhood. Accordingly, he believed, the two Jewish entities must be clearly separated: the religious entity comprising equally empowered citizens in the free countries, and that of the citizens of the Jewish nation-state.

It is worth noting that Handlin's views were neither original nor his alone. First, American Jews, including Zionists, were preoccupied with the question of dual loyalty in the civil–political and national–spiritual senses, as we discuss below. As for defining Jewishness as religion only and staunchly resisting the idea of Jewish nationhood, he was preceded by the American Council for Judaism.[8]

The Council's ideologue, Rabbi Elmer Berger, obviously objected vehemently to the behavior of the government of Israel. Although unlike Handlin he expressed an understanding of the emotions under-lying this behavior, this understanding did not deter him from arguing explicitly that the government, motivated by a Zionist national ideol-ogy that espoused the existence of a Jewish people represented by the State of Israel, was jeopardizing the existence of Jews as equally empowered citizens in the free countries. Berger then addressed a political demand to the Jews: not to submit to Israel's dictates, just as they must not, in the name of their civil freedom, succumb to the dictates of any other government that abused them, even the govern-ment of the United States.[9]

Elmer Berger had been an opponent of Zionism since the 1940s, during which time the organization he headed exerted virtually no influence. Therefore, even if Proskauer in his letter to Ben-Gurion expressed concern that the Eichmann abduction would reinforce this anti-Zionist organization among American Jews, the menace was not great. In contrast, Oscar Handlin, the professor from Harvard, was a respected, apolitical personality whose views might reverberate among the public. Therefore, the Zionist intellectuals reserved most of their vitriol for him.

The essayist and author Marie Syrkin (daughter of Nachman Syrkin, who laid the foundations of the Zionist–socialist synthesis) responded to Handlin's articles from a diametrically opposite point of departure. In her opinion, the competence of the Jewish state to pros-ecute Eichmann stemmed from the fact that the Final Solution, of which Eichmann was a major perpetrator, had targeted the Jews as a people and not as Jewish citizens of France, Poland, or any other country. By implication, paradoxically, it was the Nazis' perception of the Jews as one nation, although dispersed around the world and holding various countries' citizenship, that empowered the State of Israel to represent general Jewish interests. This argument, of course, was aimed at those Jews and non-Jews who did not recognize the exis-tence of a Jewish nation. Marie Syrkin and those of similar views had no need for proofs such as these to reinforce their pan-Jewish world-view. For them, and especially for her, Jews living in the Diaspora belong simultaneously to two entities: the worldwide Jewish collective and the civil entity represented by their country of residence. Therefore, she wrote, the competence that the State of Israel arrogated to itself in prosecuting Eichmann on behalf of the Jewish people does not represent an intervention in the lives of Jews as citizens of the United States or any other country; consequently, it does not endanger their status as such, as Oscar Handlin alleged. Had the government of Israel sought to prosecute someone who had committed crimes on American soil against Jewish citizens, this would be an undesirable and risky intervention. However, as stated, that was not the case.

Because the two entities – two authorities – are separate, Syrkin argued, Israel does not represent Jews such as Handlin and the American Council for Judaism, who do not want this representation. Israel speaks in the name of all Jews against whom the terrible injustice of the Holocaust was perpetrated and who wish to relate to it as Jews. This however, amounts not to political or national intervention in the Eichmann trial, but to a profound emotional and moral connection, which, in her opinion is neither un-American nor un-Jewish, as Handlin believed it was. On the contrary: this connection is at once American and Jewish, i.e., universal, since the support of a majority of American Jews of this Israeli action is not exceptional relative to the behavior of other American ethnic groups that defend their interests. And the capture of Eichmann, Syrkin emphasized with emotion, represents the defense of a Jewish interest and a matter of universal significance, because it urges the conscience of humankind to reassess the Nazi era; because it emits a demand for justice in interpersonal relations; and because Israel, by taking this action, raised the anguish of the Jewish people to the level of an issue in universal ethics, through which people everywhere could learn much about themselves and their world from the Jews' tragic experience. Therefore, concerning the American Jews, 'Their only involvement is moral and that is surely neither un-American nor un-Jewish.'[10]

The well known social historian Ben Halpern of Brandeis University, a member of the Zionist movement since adolescence, came out against the comprehensive argument, expressed by Jews and non-Jews, regarding Israel's lack of judicial competence to prosecute Eichmann. In his opinion this criticism is an inseparable part of the Jewish people's historical relationship with the Christian society that surrounds it. The criticism, Halpern argued, originates not only in the fact that Israel appointed itself the representative of the Holocaust victims but also because Israel is a Jewish state. The society that, in the course of history, had accused the Jews of crucifying the Messiah, poisoning wells, and using Christian children's blood for ritual purposes, finds it discomfiting to watch the Jews prosecute their murderers. Whereas the Jews Halpern said, with direct reference to Handlin, who submit to the good or bad will of their gentile neighbors tremble and protest in view of the possibility that Israel might represent them.

Halpern, assigning historical guilt to the Christian critics and expressing contempt for his Jewish rivals, expressed the activist Zionist stance in this dispute. From this posture he asserted with satisfaction that the times have changed and it is too late to return to the patronage and safety of equal civil status. Now that the State of Israel has been established, the Jewish people can no longer hide behind the ghetto walls; instead, whether a majority of Jews wish it or not, it must defend its right to full equality despite being a distinct people. Because the singularity of its peoplehood lies in its worldwide dispersion, the defense of its rights cannot be confined solely to the sovereign competence of the countries in which Jews live. Since the State of Israel was established, the defense of Jews' rights should be as accepted in international society as defense of the rights of Indians in South Africa by the government of India.[11]

Thus Halpern expanded on Marie Syrkin's locution. Syrkin argued on behalf of a specific Jewish condition, in which the interests of Jews around the world coexist with those of Jews as free citizens in their countries of residence. She also distinguished between a crime committed against the entire Jewish people and an assault against Jews as citizens of these countries. In contrast, Ben Halpern entitled the Jewish state, at least theoretically, to defend the rights of Jews wherever they live, as the government of India is entitled to do with respect to Indian citizens. More broadly speaking, Halpern considered this form of political behavior in international relations – in the context of the status of national minorities – an arrangement that should be pursued worldwide, in view of the shocks and disasters that swept society at large between the two world wars. Thus, for Syrkin, the involvement of American Jews in the Eichmann trial and their identification with Israel's actions were merely emotional. For Halpern, in contrast, Israel's intervention in a Jewish affair that oversteps its territorial and political sovereignty is legitimate from the standpoint of the overall national interest. In a subsequent debate on Jewish identity Halpern drew a distinction between 'the interests of Jews and the Jewish interest',[12] which do not always coincide or overlap. In the case at hand, Halpern spoke in the name of the Jewish interest.

In the midst of this ideological disputation among Jewish intellectuals of the highest stature, which pertained to its own time and, in part, expired upon the passing of that era, a young and little-known intellectual expressed a faint emotional undertone that eventually became a central theme. Paul Jacobs, a journalist who published most of his writings in the non-Jewish press, visited Israel during the

Eichmann trial and reported his impressions of it. He explained that he
had attended the trial as a person estranged from his Jewish origins and
becoming even more estranged. As such he rejected the parochial and
tribal suspiciousness that Israel was developing toward the surrounding world. However, the trial prompted him to re-examine his
worldview in two senses: his attitude toward his Jewish origins and his
criticism of Israel, which was applying political instrumentalities in
defense of Jewish interests. Formerly convinced that Israel was invoking Machiavellian and baneful tactics in its international policy, he
discovered in the course of the trial that these devices, although illegitimate and dangerous *a priori*, are essential under certain historical
conditions. This realization prompted him to acquiesce, to a great
extent, in the parochial, chauvinistic, and suspicious manifestations of
the Israeli government's policies. This, in turn, led him to express what
I called the undertone that over time became a melody: the nexus of
Holocaust consciousness and Jewish identity. Reflections on his
American Jewish identity came to him in the courtroom. Until then,
Jacobs believed confidently that he was an American who by chance
had been born Jewish. From then on, he wondered whether non-
Jewish society had always treated him as a Jew who by chance was also
American.[13]

Thus a radical young Jew tied an emotional Gordian knot between
the Jewish Holocaust and the Jewish state, which, by means of its
tactics, had made the Holocaust an inseparable part of his Jewish identity. The public, as stated, would eventually adopt this nexus in the
form of a progressively deepening consciousness and a surging experience, starting with the crisis of the 1967 Six-Day War.

If so, we have isolated three responses that, for most of Jewish
public opinion, affirmed Israel's right to prosecute Eichmann. Among
the three, that of Marie Syrkin, which reflects the thinking of
American Zionism – identification with Israel – expressed the Jewish
consensus in the Eichmann affair. Ben Halpern's expanded Zionist
perspective on the political competence of the Jewish state was adopted
by a small minority only. The third response, the non-Zionist response
that nevertheless represents the phenomenon of Jewish 'penitence' in
the national sense, expresses the emotion that gripped the Jewish intelligentsia upon the publication of Hannah Arendt's book, which we
shall discuss below.

The questions debated in public thinking in the United States took
on a different complexion in Israel, the sovereign Jewish state. First,
the controversy over Israel's competence to prosecute Eichmann was

not internal but external, and the emotion this controversy provoked was not prompted by criticism of Israel's actions in world public opinion. Israelis had been accustomed to this kind of criticism since the state had been established; it had occurred when the government ordained Jerusalem as its capital, during the military reprisal actions in the 1950s, and in the aftermath of the Sinai Campaign. Thus, Israelis attached the current protests to a general web that was summed up in the popular saying 'The whole world is against us'.

Consequently, the Eichmann affair generated excitement in Israel because of disagreements not between Jews and gentiles but between Jews and Jews, especially the dispute between Ben-Gurion and Nahum Goldmann concerning the composition of the court that would adjudicate Eichmann's case.

The government of Israel, by force of its sovereign competence as the agency that interned Eichmann – an internment that was given a *de facto* international moral endorsement – had three options: to turn Eichmann over to an international court as the perpetrator of crimes against humanity; to add international representatives to the Israeli panel of judges; or to prosecute him before an exclusively Israeli-Jewish court. None of the three – not even the formation of an international court – would impair Israel's sovereign competence, if it were formed through the initiative of the government of Israel and not in response to international political pressure. Such pressure had not been applied to any great extent, for had it been applied the government of Israel under the cautious leadership of David Ben-Gurion would have weighed the matter differently, especially after the Sinai Campaign. What matters in our discussion, however, is not the political vacillation but the question of principle as presented in public.

It was Ben-Gurion who articulated the official stance of the government of Israel on Eichmann, both outwardly – to the world political community and, especially, to the President of Argentina, the country whose sovereignty the abduction had violated – and to Diaspora Jewry and Israeli public opinion.

In each of these responses he sketched the Israel–Holocaust relationship in absolute terms.[14] To the President of Argentina, Arturo Frondizi, Ben-Gurion invoked the history of Jewish martyrology, of which the Holocaust was the horrific climax, and stressed that historical justice could be accomplished only in the State of Israel – the living destiny of those who had survived the Holocaust. To his friend Proskauer, president of the American Jewish Committee, he proved that there is a worldwide Jewish people that expresses its national will

by means of its state. To Israeli public opinion, he explained how
important the trial would be for young people, who through it would
come to know the fate of their people in exile. He also believed that the
trial would point an accusing finger at, and issue a warning to, Arab
rulers who were plotting to annihilate Israel with the help of Nazi
criminals.[15]

Ben-Gurion used all three information tactics in his letter to
Proskauer, whom he addressed as 'my dear friend'.[16] In his missive to
one the most important political figures in American Jewry, Ben-
Gurion, not by chance, set forth several guidelines that are worth
dwelling on. First, he argued that the six million murdered Jews
'believed and felt with every fiber of their being that *they belonged to a
Jewish people* [emphasis in the original] and that there is such a thing as
a Jewish people in the world'. Accordingly, a total identity exists
between them and Israel, since the newly formed state is, according to
its statement of principles, a Jewish state. However, since statehood
was declared only after the war and the Holocaust, 'only the six million
Jews [among all victims of Nazi persecution] did not have a redeemer
at the level of a state until the State of Israel came into being'. The
government of Germany, which had agreed to pay reparations to Jews
who had suffered at the Nazis' hands, also recognized Israel as the
agent of Jewish affairs. Accordingly, Eichmann would be prosecuted in
Israel, the Jewish state, the sole successor of the six million murdered,
because these millions

> regarded themselves as sons of the Jewish people and only as sons
> of the Jewish people. If they had lived, the great majority of them
> would have come to Israel. The only historical prosecuting attor-
> ney for these millions is Israel, and for reasons of historical justice,
> it is the duty of the Israeli government, as the government of the
> Jewish state, whose foundations were laid by millions of
> European Jews and whose establishment was their dearest hope,
> to try their murderers.

Ben-Gurion's remarks, although conceptually clear, require careful
judgment from the historical perspective. It is difficult to agree that all
of those millions murdered in Europe had considered the Jewish state
their object of desire. Many Jews in Western countries, for example,
spurned Zionism in favor of civil rights in liberal countries. The
Bundists believed in the effectuation of Jewish cultural nationhood in
the socialist era to come. The ultraorthodox deemed the actions of

Zionism a heresy and a pre-empting of God's will. Therefore, the millions on behalf of whom Ben-Gurion spoke were the nationalist and Zionist elements in Jewry. Especially dubious is his allegation that had these millions survived, 'a large majority of them would have come to Israel'. This was simply impossible from the practical standpoint, and their very survival in their places of residence was certainly a decisive factor in their continued existence there. Ben-Gurion also showed a lack of precision in arguing that the government of Germany, by consenting to tender reparations to Israel, 'acknowledged that this state speaks on behalf of all the murdered Jews'. The greater portion of reparations money was remitted to individuals; reparation moneys were also tendered to various Jewish organizations, among which Israel garnered the lion's share because it had taken in nearly half a million Holocaust survivors.[17] However, Ben-Gurion was undoubtedly right in arguing that, in the historical test after the Holocaust, the establishment of Israel was the action of a majority among the Jewish people. From this standpoint, that of the dead and living Jews who recognized Jewish nationhood, only the Jewish State of Israel could prosecute Eichmann for crimes committed against individual Jews. Furthermore, if we carry Marie Syrkin's arguments forward, it was the Nazis who had declared war against the Jewish people and murdered millions of Jews in waging this war. By its own criteria and those of the international arena, the Jewish people is alive in Israel as a collective entity, and as such it proposed to prosecute the agent of its annihilation.

Nevertheless, Ben-Gurion's stance, as articulated for domestic and external consumption, evokes a disturbing thought as to his attitude toward the Holocaust. There is no doubt that during the war Ben-Gurion did not invest his full vigor, vehemence, and authority in continual, ongoing efforts to rescue European Jews in every possible way. Some consider this an abandonment of European Jewry, prompted either by hard-heartedness or by ideological motives such as 'negation of the Diaspora' and 'Palestine-centrism'. Some argue that Ben-Gurion did not forsake Diaspora Jewry to its fate; instead, eschewing small daily actions in the belief that they could not change the situation substantively, he pledged himself to the development of grand and complex plans that would bring the Jewish masses to Palestine after the war.[18] Others marshal evidence, painstakingly and methodically, that Ben-Gurion did work intensively and tirelessly for the rescue of European Jewry.[19] I tend to believe that Ben-Gurion, the consummate realist, understood that European Jewry was beyond meaningful deliverance,[20] whereas Ben-Gurion the indefatigable optimist sketched out the post-war emigration to Palestine of the Jewish millions. From his standpoint the calamity of the Holocaust unquestionably vindicated the Holocaust in the historical sense. Thus, just as the disaster had helped Israel come into being after the war, so would it help to reinforce the existence of the state in the 1960s by means of the Eichmann trial. In both cases, in elaborating the million-immigrant plan and assuming the right to speak for the murdered Jewish masses, Ben-Gurion engaged in grand thinking as a utopian. His new utopia was a Jewish state that, by means of the Eichmann trial, brought the murderers of its people to historical justice and rallied Jews around its standard. In discussions in the Mapai Central Committee on 19 May 1960, coinciding directly with the capture of Eichmann but focusing on the future of the World Zionist Organization, Ben-Gurion indeed declared himself a utopian.[21]

The Supreme Court, sitting in judgment of Eichmann, followed Ben-Gurion's lead. Explaining the competence of the state to judge Eichmann for his crimes against the Jewish people, the court noted the topical proximity of the Holocaust and the establishment of the state. Basing itself on the Declaration of the Establishment of the State of Israel and the Nazi and Nazi Collaborators (Punishment) Law, passed in 1950, it ruled:

> the horrible massacre of millions of Jews by the Nazi criminals, which led the Jewish people in Europe to the brink of extinction, was one of the weightiest factors in the establishment of the state of the surviving remnant. The state must not be severed from its roots, among which the European Holocaust is enumerated.

In response to defense counsel Robert Servatius's argument – that the State of Israel is incompetent to judge Eichmann because the crimes against the Jews were not committed on its sovereign soil – the court asserted: 'the people is one and the crime one; the crime attributed to the defendant is "killing millions of Jews with the intent of destroying the Jewish people". The Jewish community in Israel today, and that which dwelled in Palestine then, is part of the Jewish people that the defendant, according to the indictment, sought to destroy.'

The justices elaborated further on Ben-Gurion's formula:

> A people that may be murdered with impunity is in existential danger. Indeed, this was the curse that beset the Jewish people because of its state of exile and lack of sovereignty, [for] any evil-

doer could abuse the Jews without fear of being punished by his victims. Hitler and his accomplices exploited the defenselessness of the dispersed Jewish people to annihilate it in cold blood. If only to correct a small portion of the terrible injustice of the Holocaust, the sovereign Jewish state was established per recommendation of the United Nations to allow the surviving remnant to defend its existence by governmental means. One of these means is to punish the murderers who carried out Hitler's contemptible bidding.

Beyond this, the court, relying on precedents in international law, stated that a crime committed against a nation at a time that it lacked sovereign competence is justiciable *post factum* by the same nation once it attains territorial sovereignty, even if the crime was not perpetrated in that specific territory. Accordingly, in the judges' view,

> The State of Israel, the sovereign state of the Jewish people, discharges by its legislation the function of fulfilling the Jewish people's right to punish the criminals who killed its members with intent to terminate its existence. We are convinced that this competence corresponds to the principles of the existing law of nations.[22]

Although in its preamble to the verdict the court refrained from discussing crucial historical questions that had determined the fate of the Jewish people during the Holocaust, the verdict itself, and the rationale proffered with respect to the state's competence to prosecute Eichmann, were ideationally and ideologically pregnant. The basic assumption – that Eichmann could be tried in Israel because a worldwide Jewish people exists and because the state ordained as that of this people represents it in the sense of international law – is an emphatically Zionist argument. True, the court did not extend this rationale as far as Ben-Gurion had when he argued that the Holocaust claimed millions who would otherwise have become inhabitants of the Jewish state, and that their potential citizenship is tantamount to actual citizenship. Neither did the court address the question of whether the government of Germany, by tendering restitution to the State of Israel, had recognized it as the representative of the Jewish people. Essentially, however, it accepted Ben-Gurion's basic argument of principle: that the Jews have only one instrumentality with which to prosecute their murderers – their sovereign state.

Gershom Scholem concurred, although he objected to the sentence and its implementation. Scholem depicted himself as one who welcomed Eichmann's having been brought to justice, who 'lauds the very existence of the trial and the form the legal authorities gave it', and who 'considers the trial a tremendous moral accomplishment in educating the nation to conduct a great historic reckoning'.[23] However, Scholem sought to conduct the 'historic reckoning' with the German nation by exploring a different question: 'How did what happened happen, and how could it happen?' His purpose was to educate the Jewish nation, a nation that Zionism, in Scholem's view, had returned to history, thereby adding a new dimension to the traditional relationship between Jews and gentiles, one of political normality. For this very reason, he believed it important that the question 'How did it happen?' 'remain current with all of its gravity, its nakedness, and its horrors'. Because his construction of the historical reckoning was primarily moral, both among Jews and between Jews and the world at large, he believed the execution of Eichmann might pollute it.

Therefore, there was a difference of principle between Scholem and Ben-Gurion in the matter of the Eichmann trial. Although both stressed the historical value of the trial for internal and external consumption, Scholem's reference was to a protracted historical reckoning, an intra-Jewish refashioning of the Jewish identity, so to speak, as – according to his well-known point of view – has recurred throughout Jewish history. Outwardly, the purpose of this reckoning is to place German–Jewish relations on a different human plane. Ben-Gurion, in contrast, regarded the trial not as a historical reckoning but as a historical watershed – not only at the political level in relations with Germany, to which he attributed much political and economic importance, but principally as a turning point in Jewish history, engineered by the Jewish state.

It is no coincidence that, precisely as the trial began with a discussion of the relationship between the Jewish people and the Jewish state, Ben-Gurion reignited a dispute with Natan Rotenstreich that had begun in 1957 – after the Sinai Campaign – concerning the state as a *value*.[24] In response to Rotenstreich's allegation that Ben-Gurion takes it for granted that the reality of the state itself carries ideational contents – 'and it does not' – Ben-Gurion replied that 'the state is also an idea, because it is a reality different from that of Jews the world over. It is different, and its difference is the idea. ... The reality is a reality that intrinsically fulfills ideas of revolution. It exists; it has not lapsed.' Vis-à-vis 'the Jewish people in the world, this is the greatest ideational, moral, and spiritual manifestation that we have'.[25]

To sum up the discussion thus far, one may say that the Eichmann affair provided a further opportunity to underscore the principled contrast between two juxtaposed points of view: the anti-Zionist view, which sought to separate the Jewish state and the Jewish Holocaust totally, and the Zionist approach, which regarded them as linked in an inseparable and multifaceted relationship. According to the first approach, Israel is the state only of such adherents of the Jewish faith as dwell there. By implication, there is no Jewish national entity but only a religion. The second approach, in contrast, presumes the existence of a single Jewish nation that derives national unity – beyond religious singularity – from a past, present, and future that all Jews share. According to this perception, the State of Israel represents the overall interest of the Jewish people, as distinct from the limited interests of Jews who enjoy equal rights in free countries, in whose affairs the Jewish state lacks the competence to intervene. Consequently, from this perspective – in which the Israeli leadership acquiesced – Jewish national identity is distinct from civil territorial loyalty. Accordingly, Jewish national consciousness represents a superstructure of sorts that embraces the various nationalities that Jews may hold. To put it differently, the Jewish national consciousness under Diaspora conditions is a harmonizing and unifying ethos. This ethos was given political fulfillment and moral reinforcement in the Eichmann trial. Thus, although different undertones radiated from the Zionist approach – those of Ben-Gurion and Goldmann,[26] those of Scholem and Ben-Gurion, those of Syrkin and Halpern – the basic point of view was one: the competence and duty of the Jewish sovereign entity to prosecute those who had wronged the Jewish people.

The approach of Hannah Arendt, who became famous for her book *Eichmann in Jerusalem: A Report on the Banality of Evil* after having earned a reputation among intellectuals several years earlier, rested between these two basic views, the Zionist and the anti-Zionist.[27]

Paradoxically, although the book generated special excitement among American Jews and ruptured her relations with them – so badly that she avoided further public debate on perceived Jewish issues – Hannah Arendt actually positioned herself between two diametrically opposed views. Logically, the extreme and unequivocal opinions she expressed in *Eichmann in Jerusalem* prompt one to assume that she would side with those who opposed the Jewish state and condemned its behavior. She did not, and her conduct makes one ponder the paradoxes in her personality that explain her attitude toward the Jews and shed light on her general worldview, which continues to fascinate Western intellectuals.

The first paradox has to do with her language. The creator of the pregnant locution 'the banality of evil' now seems, because of her extreme style, to have fallen into the trap of 'the banality of rationalism', as I define it – a dispassionate, pitiless state of mind that originates more in cerebration than in villainy, a condition that, when overdone, also leads to superficiality.

Thus Arendt, who so tellingly describes the estrangement that the totalitarian regime occasions between victim and oppressor, is herself much tainted by this very trait. Consequently, in an absolutist and banal style, she could accuse by generalization the Jewish leadership in the ghettos of *de facto* collaboration with the Nazis; subject these leaders to personal insults – by hinting, for example, that Leo Baeck had behaved in the manner of a German *führer*; mock the Galician origin of Eichmann's prosecutor, Gideon Hausner; depict the policemen who guarded the courtroom as brutal, almost fascist Oriental types; and angrily describe the attack on her in Jewish public circles in almost antisemitic terms: 'In the long run it's perhaps beneficial to sweep out a little of that unique Jewish rubbish.'[28]

Furthermore, in the midst of the trial and despite everything she heard and saw there, she managed to attribute racist traits to Judaism and Israel because of Israel's failure to separate religion and state and, especially, because of Judaism's rejection of intermarriage. Paradoxically it is this approach, stemming from an extreme intellectual arrogance that her critics had noted in the past, that inspired her to take a withered, value-unintensive view – banal although not routine – of a human condition that cannot be probed in depth without warmth and pertinent, comprehensive, and exhaustive judgment, for only thus can the nuances of its complexity be understood. In this context, Arendt may be described as deficient in *ahavat Yisrael*, in Gershom Scholem's famous locution.[29] One may indict her for having been estranged from Jewish history and therefore incapable of understanding such things outside the 'Jewish historical memory',[30] to use Dan Diner's expression. I would say that she was estranged from – or deliberately dealt herself out of – the Jewish *general* memory, since her culture and the course of her life gave her principally a Western-centric vision of Jewish history. However, although Arendt lay outside the Jewish historical memory, she did not dissociate herself from the Jewish nation generally. This is the second paradox in her personality and worldview. Even though her culture and way of life clashed with Jewish national and cultural realities, and even though she may be defined as an existential assimilationist, her national perspective approximated that of the great national historian Simon Dubnow, as we shall see.

Here lies the third paradox concerning Arendt, which surfaces in her attitude toward David Ben-Gurion, prime minister of Israel. Her animosity and hostility toward him were explicit and overt. She accused him of staging the trial in pursuit of self-defined Israeli national goals, irrespective of doing justice with Eichmann as a war criminal under the accepted rules of justice in the enlightened world. She then labeled Ben-Gurion a 'dangerous idealist' who bore guilt for the manifestations of degeneracy that had become visible in Israel. She cited the well-known Lavon affair – which had piqued her interest from the time it began, about two years before the Eichmann trial – as evidence. In her opinion, which was always staunch, his orchestration of the Eichmann trial was meant to counteract the loss of public stature he had suffered following the Lavon affair. Thus she attended the trial with a preconceived notion about its nature.[31] She may even have established a psychological, if not conscious, linkage between the 'plot' concocted by Ben-Gurion, leader of the State of Israel, and that of the leaders of the Judenräte, whom she accused of *de facto* collaboration with the Nazis. Nevertheless, Arendt and Ben-Gurion were much in agreement on the central issue connected with the trial – Israel's right to try Eichmann as the representative of the Jewish people. The reason undoubtedly lies in Arendt's national outlook and her tortuous confrontation with Zionism, in which her multivalent attitude toward the State of Israel also originated.

This, it seems, brings us to Arendt's fourth paradox: her attitude toward Zionism. She joined the Zionist movement in the 1930s, after the Nazi accession, under the influence of a friend, the leading German Zionist Kurt Blumenfeld, and in acknowledgment that Zionism provided the answer to Nazi antisemitism. As a refugee in Paris, she worked for Youth Aliyah. When she went to the United States in the early 1940s, her institutional relations with the Zionist movement were ruptured. To make a living, she worked for Jewish community institutions and wrote for the German-Jewish expatriate newspaper *Aufbau*. However, she remained involved in Zionist politics. In 1948 she attempted to help Judah Magnes disseminate the idea of the binational Jewish–Arab state. Her affinity for the political idealism of Brit Shalom prompted her to write a radical critical article against the perceptions of political Zionists from Herzl to Jabotinsky to Ben-Gurion.[32] However, despite her idealistic views regarding the Jewish–Arab conflict, she was a militant whose outlook verged on

Zionist Revisionism in the matter of the Jewish boycott against
Germany – an outlook in which the Zionist leadership did not acquiesce. She sided with David Frankfurter and Herschel Grynszpan, who,
on their own counsel, had set out to avenge the Jews' trampled dignity
by assassinating Nazi officials; she publicly supported, in articles she
published in *Aufbau* in the early 1940s, the Revisionist emissary Hillel
Kook's idea of establishing a Jewish army that would fight the Nazis.
Her very decision to align herself with Zionism, as she explains it,
came about because only Zionism espoused activism in response to the
Nazi menace. One of the roots of this approach was rejection of the
exilic mentality, an approach with which Arendt concurred even
during the Eichmann trial. To her mind, the exilic mentality was a
historical attribute of the Jewish elite – symbolized by the Rothschilds
on the one hand and community leaders such as Leo Baeck on the
other – marked by willingness to trust and cooperate with the regime
at hand. Trapped in their 'collaborationist' mentality, Diaspora leaders
could not distinguish between enemy and friend among non-Jews.
Since the Jewish religious tradition attributed hostility toward Jews to
all *goyim*, they believed that their security lay in rapprochement and
cooperation with the regime's bureaucracy. Arendt regarded this
Diaspora trait, originating in the abnormality of the Jewish situation,
as the main reason for the cooperation between the Jewish leadership
and the Nazi regime that abetted the Jews' annihilation.

Importantly, she aimed her criticism at the Jewish political and
economic elite, which sought to ally itself with non-Jewish regimes
and estranged itself from the masses among which the Jews dwelled.
Therefore her fury also targeted Ben-Gurion. She regarded the
Eichmann trial as a willful attempt, engineered chiefly by Ben-Gurion,
to shape Jewish awareness and unity by reinforcing consciousness of
the historical tension between Jews and gentiles. She rejected this
intent for two reasons. First she believed that, since Hitler, antisemitism was no longer accepted in Western civilization and thus
would no longer prompt tension and segregation between Jews and
gentiles. The second reason, the important one in our context, was her
opinion that the goal in establishing Jewish statehood was to eliminate
the abnormal historical situation that prevailed in Jewish–Gentile
relations:

> For a change of this mentality is actually one of the indispensable
> prerequisites for Israeli statehood, which by definition has made
> of the Jews a people among the peoples, a nation among nations,

a state among states, depending now on plurality which no longer permits the age-old and, unfortunately, religiously anchored dichotomy of Jews and Gentiles.[33]

Thus, paradoxically, according to Hannah Arendt, Ben-Gurion, arch-founder of the state and opponent of the Diaspora, actually fostered the Diaspora mentality. Arendt, in contrast, noted the historical importance of the Zionist revolution that had brought the Jewish state into being. In so doing, she also acknowledged that despite the disappearance of active antisemitism after the war, the formation of the State of Israel is the main factor in revising the historical relationship between Jews and non-Jews.

From this standpoint, Arendt distinguished herself from her intellectual comrades of Jewish-German origin, Bruno Bettelheim, Erich Fromm, and Oscar Handlin. In contrast to them, and beyond legalistic rationales, she was firmly convinced that Israel possessed the competence to prosecute Eichmann because it is the Jewish state. Eichmann's crime against the Jewish people was international in nature only because the Jewish people was dispersed across different territories, and as long as the Jewish cause did not find a political-national pleader, then the practice in international law that underlay the Nuremberg trials also applied to the crimes against the Jews. However, circumstances had changed since Nuremberg: 'Now that the Jews have their own territory, the State of Israel, they have the right and competence to adjudicate the crimes committed against them.'[34] After all, despite all the legalistic arguments against holding the trial in Jerusalem, it was unquestionably clear that the crimes had been committed against Jews *qua* Jews, irrespective of their civil and territorial affiliation. Although many of the murdered Jews would have preferred not to be enumerated among the Jews, justice could be done only if the murderers' intention were borne in mind, and their intention was to annihilate the Jewish people.

This was exactly the argument invoked by the Zionist Marie Syrkin to justify the abduction and the trial in Jerusalem. Parenthetically, Arendt held Syrkin's articles on this matter in great esteem: she even reinforced Syrkin's argument indirectly by adding a rationale from the philosophy of law. In Arendt's opinion, Israel should explain that its judicial competence stems from the meaning of 'territory' in international law: a legal and political concept, not only a geographical one. This legal perception pertains primarily not to a given piece of land but to people who maintain a special relationship as a group, even if the

group is dispersed among different political authorities. This relationship, in Arendt's opinion, is based on commonality of language,
religion, history, customs, and laws. This mirrors the Dubnowian
prescription for Diaspora Jewish nationhood and the pan-Jewish
Zionist perspective. Hence the key sentence follows:

> No State of Israel would ever have come into being if the Jewish
> people had not created and maintained its own specific in-
> between territory throughout the long centuries of dispersion,
> that is prior to the seizure of its old territory.[35]

This is undoubtedly one of the strongest and most profound arguments of principle concerning Israel's right to represent the Jewish
people in this case and, perhaps, generally. After all, if a supraterritor-
ial Jewish entity exists, Israel presumably represents it in other
matters, too, apart from punishing the perpetrators of crimes against it.
If this interpretation is correct, Arendt's views also approximate those
of Ben Halpern, discussed above. In fact, both affirmed the existence
of two-dimensional national entities, i.e., nation-states and national
diasporas. Therefore Arendt agreed unreservedly with the preliminary
ruling of the court in Jerusalem that Israel was founded as the state of
the Jews and was so recognized.

One may gauge the importance of this matter in terms of her worldview by reviewing the debate she conducted in this matter with her
friend, the philosopher Karl Jaspers. Jaspers rejected Israel's competence to try Eichmann on behalf of the Jewish people. In his opinion,
the essence of Jewish peoplehood transcends any national political
organization, and this supranational spiritual-religious property of the
Jews circumscribes Israel's competence with respect to Jews and with
respect to the world. In response, Arendt asserted that even if Israel
lacked the competence to represent all Jews worldwide 'Israel is the
only political entity we have'. Here she added, with characteristic cynicism, that she was displeased with this situation in which the extant
Israel, the one she is so wont to criticize, is the entity representing the
Jewish nation – including herself as a conscious partner therein.
However, this situation, she stressed, could no longer be changed, especially after Israel had taken in hundreds of thousands of Holocaust
survivors. Against Jaspers's argument that Israel had not yet existed
when the massacres were committed, Arendt replied that Palestine
'became' Israel on behalf of those victims.[36] Thus, Arendt's attitude, in
principle, was arguably no different from the famous assertion of

Eichmann's prosecutor, Gideon Hausner, in his opening remarks: that he stood before the judges of Israel as the spokesman of the six million Jews who had been murdered.

Finally, to reinforce the argument concerning Arendt's unconscious Zionist predisposition, I cite remarks she made in a 1964 panel discussion sponsored by the Israeli newspaper *Maariv*, moderated by Geula Cohen, on the role of the Jewish leadership in Palestine and the Diaspora during the Holocaust. Arendt said that, even if one accepts some of the arguments about this leadership's insufficient audacity, vigor, and imagination,

> I believed then and tend to think today that under the existing circumstances nothing could have helped other than the 'normalization' of the Jewish condition. In other words, a literal declaration of war, the formation of a Jewish army composed of Palestinian Jews and stateless Jews from all over the world, and a demand that the Jews be recognized as a belligerent.[37]

Then European Jewry might have been treated as were Jewish POWs from Allied forces other than the Red Army. (One doubts that this argument would have saved those millions of Jews who were POWs from the USSR, which was a belligerent.) What matters for our purposes, however, is Arendt's principled attitude toward Zionist activism. It prompts me to inquire about her attitude toward the Jewish state beyond the problems stemming from the Eichmann trial.

Hannah Arendt had an emotional attitude toward Israel, replete with concern and even dread for its well-being and, especially, its continuity. She voiced these sentiments in official letters and in correspondence with close friends. Her concern was constant: it transcended the country's military emergencies, such as the Six-Day War or the Yom Kippur War. This existential concern was, by complexion and by content, very Jewish, and it was not divorced from the feelings of most Diaspora Jews at that time.

In a letter in response to the leaders of the anti-Zionist American Council for Judaism, which had offered her its support in the public tempest surrounding her book *Eichmann in Jerusalem*, she wrote:

> You know that I was a Zionist and that my reason for breaking with the Zionist Organization was very different from the anti-Zionist stand of the Council: I am not against Israel on principle, I am against certain important Israeli policies. I know or believe,

that should catastrophe overtake this Jewish state for whatever reasons (even reasons of their own foolishness), this would be the perhaps final catastrophe for the whole Jewish people, no matter what opinions every one of us might hold at the moment.[38]

Thus, Arendt associated Jewish continuity with the Jewish state. In this sense, she had advanced beyond the national concept of Dubnow, who, perceiving national existence as a process of centers of disappearance and resurrection, could not link national existence to the existence of any particular center. Hence we may understand why Arendt, who had angrily withdrawn from general Jewish public affairs, made a donation in the emergency fundraising campaign during the Six-Day War.

Even in times of calm, without public tempests and national emergencies, Arendt continued to favor the existence of Israel. In 1969, her friend, the writer Nathalie Sarraute, a French Jew, visited Israel and wrote enthusiastic letters to Arendt about cooperation and equality in kibbutz life. Arendt described these impressions to her good friend, the author Mary McCarthy. In her conservative-liberal fashion, she expressed skepticism about cooperative life on the kibbutz, opining that this egalitarian society was a temporary phenomenon. She admitted that with respect to those who still believed in equality, like their mutual friend Nathalie Sarraute, Israel was an impressive place. What disturbed her peace of mind, however, was not the nature of Israeli society but the existence of the Jewish people. Thus she mentioned this concern even in the context of a discussion about the kibbutz. She noted the two-faceted trait that has typified the Jewish people since the destruction of the First Temple: indefatigable hunger for national survival on the one hand, and constant dread of disappearance, whether through physical annihilation or cultural assimilation, on the other hand. She wrote in amazement about this phenomenon, evinced by a collective that believes in its continued existence and is confident that, even if a further disaster befalls it, its memory and tradition will combine to sustain it, and about the cement of fate, in which peoples have climbed onto the stage of history and vanished while the Jewish people remains alive and active. Arendt herself, she attested, remained a liberal-radical Jewish intellectual who was sorely of two minds with respect to her people. She admitted that there was something both 'grand' and 'ignoble' in her compatriots' existential yearnings. Ultimately, however, she acknowledged, she had no portion in either, although 'I know that any real catastrophe in Israel would affect me more deeply than almost anything else'.[39]

The source of Arendt's concern for Israel's well-being and existence may not stem solely from her human and Jewish angst; it may well have been fostered by the doubt she had developed about the possibility of Jewish national existence in the Diaspora. As stated, she was a grass-roots activist – a conscious and unconscious 'Dubnowist'. For example, she explained her advocacy of the establishment of a Jewish people's army during World War II by arguing that it was important to show the world a different facet of Jewish identity, cleansed of what she called the 'schnorrer syndrome'.[40] From the same Diaspora national perspective, she took up with her friend Karl Jaspers an idea that even she considered impractical, but the very fact that she expressed it in writing attests to her ideational perspective and her intellectual and moral insensitivity. In 1946, she toyed with the idea of urging the government of the German republic to grant German citizenship to any Jew who desired it, irrespective of his or her country of origin, solely on the basis of Jewish nationality and without having to forfeit said nationality.[41] She bruited this not as an alternative to the wish of the Jewish inhabitants of the DP camps to settle in Palestine, but as a complement to this option for those who did not so choose. She considered this possibility important because of her awareness, as a secular Jew, that the only way to maintain the secularizing Jewish nation was by trying to create political conditions that would allow Jews to continue existing collectively, i.e., a Diaspora national organization. Only after these conditions come about, she said, will it be possible to contemplate future developments with equanimity. In the meantime, Arendt was troubled by the state of the people. In another letter to Jaspers a year later,[42] she rued the Jewish people's loss of desire to maintain national existence and the willingness of most Jews to forgo their people's traditional singularity and destiny. She also fiercely criticized Zionism for speeding up the assimilation process by striving relentlessly to normalize the Jewish condition. From this standpoint, normalization was more dangerous to Jewish existence than assimilation, which she had opposed since the early 1930s. However, Arendt also pointed to favorable developments, such as the evolution of a free and self-confident Jewish community in America and the growth of that in Palestine which, as Jaspers expressed it, was unifying the Jewish nation from afar.

Several years later, in the early 1950s, Arendt's outlook changed again: she shifted from fervent identification with the Zionism of the 1930s to opposition to political Zionism in the 1940s then to a certain rapprochement with Zionism in the 1950s. Whereas in 1947 she had spoken about Zionist encouragement of assimilation, she now changed her assessment. In 1950, she corresponded with Jaspers about the publication of her biography of Rachel Varenhagen, a Jewish woman in late eighteenth-century Germany who stood between two worlds, the Jewish and the German. She stressed, without remorse, that she had written the biography in a critical Zionist spirit with which she had identified and that she still upheld.[43] In this letter, Arendt also developed a theory of Jewish historiosophy. Under the influence of Gershom Scholem's writings, she had concluded that Jewish history as a distinct history had ended with the Sabbatean movement. The advent of Zionism, she believed, marked the beginning of a new chapter in this history; and she added to this the emigration to the United States. She derived from both historical phenomena hope for a Jewish national renaissance, although she was not confident that one would come about.

This, I believe, leads us to the greatest paradox in Hannah Arendt's confrontation with her Jewishness: that the schism between her and the Jewish political and intellectual elites developed precisely during and after the Eichmann trial. This period of time corresponded with the pinnacle, from her standpoint, of her identification with Jewish nationhood, including concern for Israel's existence and the status she accorded Israel as the representative of the Jewish collective interest. At issue here is the State of Israel – not the government of Israel, toward which she had been fiercely critical since the State of Israel was formed – not as a substitute for the Jewish people but as an expression of its national wish to apply political sovereignty in a specific territory, this also being the territory to which it is historically attached. Thus Arendt became one of the most prominent and vehement personalities who, for historical, moral, and legal reasons, created an unbreakable relationship between Israel and the Holocaust.

Summing up, one may say that there were two different (although not separate) Hannah Arendts: the overt and public Hannah who took the Jewish world by storm, and the covert Hannah who only in the past generation has begun to surface. The overt Arendt was a condescending intellectual who held in contempt anyone whom she considered inferior in personality or stature; the Arendt of extremist views, who tended to level sweeping charges against the Jewish leadership in the ghettos; the Arendt who did not conceal her venomous hostility toward the Zionist leadership and the prime minister of Israel; the dogmatic Arendt, who to no small extent aligned her conclusions from the Eichmann trial with her pre-trial views and prejudices;

the Arendt who, in her uncompromising extremism, adduced superficial conclusions about Jewish history at large and showed herself emotionally estranged from the behavior of people engulfed in distress and emergency. Although she changed her views regularly, she adhered to her typical extremism and vehemence in each change. All of the foregoing relate to the characteristic that I have called 'the banality of the radical intellect'.

The second and different Hannah was the one who pledged all of her intellectual strength to the idea of secular Jewish nationhood, in which the prime and most important fundamental is the existence of a worldwide Jewish nation. This Arendt was hostile toward assimilating Jews, especially those who stood out for their wealth or political status. This is the Arendt who sought at all times, since the accession of Hitler, the favorable aspects of Jewish nationalism in view of the advent of fascism; who did not want the Jewishness of pariahs but the Jewishness of identifiers; who always recognized Zionism as the dynamic national voice of Jewry, even though she criticized it and took public exception to it with her characteristic extremism. This is the Arendt who vigorously upheld the right of the Jewish state to prosecute Eichmann in the name of the millions who had been murdered outside the Jewish national territory.

The Hannah Arendt affair did not end with the ebbing of the public tumult surrounding her book, *Eichmann in Jerusalem.* The issue that had provoked the commotion declined in importance, thanks largely to systematic research on the leaders of the Judenrate, which showed how groundless and erroneous her extreme generalizations were.

In the 1960s, after her book appeared, most of Arendt's critics actually positioned her beyond the ambit of the Jewish people, as they did with extreme and proclaimed assimilationists and anti-national Communists. In the late 1970s and in the 1980s, however, there was ceaseless interest in Hannah Arendt as a Jew. This was because, in both her personality and her views, she personified the dilemma of the Jewish identity of intellectuals poised between two worlds: between the particularism determined by their origin and the universalism that expresses their aspirations; between fealty to the truth as people who attained truth through philosophy or research and the cultural and emotional context of the collective about which they intended to express their critical views.

Daniel Bell, a member of the 1960s New York radical intelligentsia who eventually became well-known in American academic life, was the first to put his finger on the Jewish identity problem in the Arendt controversy. Bell stressed that Arendt had written her book from a universalist point of view that ruled out a parochial identity. He agreed with her criticism of Israel – a country like any other – according to the principles of universalism, but he eschewed universalist criteria in considering her attitude toward the Jewish people. As Bell put it, Israelis are a nationality but the Jews are a people, and their historic experience contains the fundamentals that lend the identity of every Jew its contours. It is the special existential situation of the Holocaust, to which the Jew as a person was subjected directly and indirectly, that affects his or her identity. Notably Bell, who in the 1940s had a Marxist–Trotskyite outlook and in the 1950s believed that alienation in the name of universalism is the existential fate of the Jewish intellectual in an unreformed society, changed his mind in the early 1960s. In 1961, in an article entitled 'Reflections on Jewish Identity',[44] he drew the opposite conclusion, asserting that some of the intellectual's overall responsibility lies in identifying with his/her collective heritage, even if it is more a memory than a practical reality. In 1961, in the midst of the Eichmann trial, Daniel Bell identified publicly with the collective memory of the Jewish people and internalized it with mercy and kindness, in contrast to Hannah Arendt's intellectual chill.

A view contrary to Bell's was expressed about four years later by Norm Fruchter, the editor of a far-left journal. Fruchter's remarks, written in the midst of an uprising borne on the waves of youthful utopia, reflected the *zeitgeist* beautifully. Fruchter attacked those Jewish intellectuals who had once espoused a leftist and universal outlook for clinging to the Holocaust and turning it into a tragic myth, to which rational criticism does not apply, in order to preserve the remnant of their Jewish identity. This remnant, he said, is the myth of persecuted, suffering members of a people. Stressing the differentness of this myth, in his opinion, is an indication of its bearers' condescension toward the society in which they live. This differentness is manifested primarily in identification with Zionism and Israel's nationalist policies, which they turn into a counterweight of strength and security, so to speak, to the myth of suffering and victimhood of which the Holocaust is emblematic.[45]

Actually, both of these thinkers, Bell and Fruchter, on the basis of different and clashing outlooks and assessments, placed Hannah Arendt outside the Jewish national memory. Bell criticized Arendt for this relegation; Fruchter congratulated her. Fifteen years later, in the late 1970s and early 1980s, there began an intellectual effort to reinterpret Hannah Arendt and, in so doing, to return her to the bosom of her people.

In 1978, a young researcher named Ron Feldman edited Arendt's articles on Jewish themes.[46] The historian Henry Feingold concluded his critique of this collection with the assessment that Arendt, despite all her weaknesses, was a provocative Jewish philosopher, and therefore, for this reason only, the time had come to reclaim her for her people.[47]

Response, the radical journal of the Havurah movement, devoted an entire issue to the persona of Arendt. In this issue, David Biale, a Zionist Jewish student leader in the 1980s, noted Arendt's proximity to Dubnow on the national issue.[48] Her biography, published in the early 1980s by Elizabeth Young Brunel,[49] did much to re-evaluate Arendt's Jewish attachment.

In the 1990s, with the upsurge in universalist liberal tendencies among Jewish intellectuals, a perceptible schism has taken shape in assessing the validity of Hannah Arendt's Jewish doctrine. Professor Jeffrey Issac sees her as the standard-bearer of the liberal Jewish struggle against the radical Jewish anti-Zionist plutocracy (the 'die-hard Zionists'). In his opinion, she wished not to abandon her people but to reform Jewish society, in the Diaspora and in Israel, to make it freer, more critical, and more liberal.[50] In contrast, Professor Leon Boltstein states that her secular Jewish national perspective is progressively dying out as Jewish identity becomes increasingly religious while secular and radical Jews rapidly integrate into society at large. In other words, secular Jews in the Diaspora no longer need Dubnow-style Jewish nationhood, the Israelis have normal nationhood, and Orthodoxy does not need nationhood to maintain its Jewish identity.[51]

Thus, if we connect the two outlooks, from the Jewish perspective one Hannah Arendt disappears and another comes into being. The one who bore the utopia of secular Diaspora Jewish nationhood has vanished, and the radical moralist who rebels against the plutocratic Jewish establishment and her compatriots' injustice against other peoples has come to life. Her courage in standing up to Ben-Gurion in the 1960s became an example for Jewish liberals in criticizing the government of Israel for its treatment of the Palestinian problem. The process of revision in the approach toward Arendt and her views on the Jews – from an angry eruption to a gradual, posthumous reinstatement of her Jewishness and her stature as the symbol of Jewish radicalism – is an expression of the changes that have occurred in the self-identity of Jewish intellectuals. These intellectuals' attitude toward the Holocaust, which incorporates their posture on Arendt, aptly illuminates this change. When the Holocaust was perceived mainly as a reckoning between Jews and gentiles, the critical and offensive Hannah Arendt was banished from the Jewish realm. In the 1980s, when they began to perform a reckoning with the Jewish leadership – especially that in the United States and Palestine – for not having done enough to rescue its compatriots, they began to reassess Hannah Arendt. Finally, when the Holocaust was given a universalist message, she became a symbol of liberal radicalism.[52]

Thus, Hannah Arendt has again met a paradoxical fate.[53] Jewish liberals of various kinds, unable to dissociate themselves from their people's affairs, turn to Hannah Arendt as the bearer of the idealistic notions of Brit Shalom regarding the Jewish–Arab conflict. The idea of the democratic and liberal binational state, the state of its citizens, is associated with the name and teachings of Hannah Arendt. In this fashion Arendt is returned to her people, both as a critic of the Holocaust-era Jewish leadership and as an opponent of nationalistic, power-reliant Zionism on behalf of the Zionist moral ideal. This represents the closing of a circle with respect to Arendt. She came to Zionism and the Jewish people at a time of distress, aware of the Jews' helplessness, and has been returned to them by her followers, again at a time of distress that originates, they believe, in overreliance on Jewish power.

NOTES

1. Hannah Arendt, *Eichmann in Jerusalem: A Report on the Banality of Evil* (New York: Viking Press, 1963).
2. *The Eichmann Case in the American Press* (Institute of Human Relations, American Jewish Committee, 1962).
3. See also an Anti-Defamation League survey that encompassed many European and Asian countries in addition to the United States. The conclusions of the survey, which was conducted and finalized during the trial, express a sigh of relief by disproving fears that the abduction and prosecution of Eichmann would cause antisemitism to resurge. The survey also expresses ironic satisfaction that genocide was recognized as a crime in the laws of at least one nation in the civilized world – Israel. See *The Impact of the Eichmann Trial: Facts, Reports on Organized Antisemitism*, published by the Anti-Defamation League of B'nai B'rith, August–September 1961, Vol. 14, No. 4.
4. Ibid., American Jewish Committee, p. 45.
5. David Ben-Gurion to Joseph Proskauer, 7 June 1960, Ben-Gurion Heritage Center Archives. Since Proskauer's letter to Ben-Gurion is not in the archive, his views are quoted from Ben-Gurion's response.
6. Oscar Handlin, 'Ethics and Eichmann', *Commentary*, August 1960.
7. Oscar Handlin, 'The Ethics of the Eichmann Case', *Issues*, Winter 1961, American Council for Judaism.

8. See Chapter 1 of my book *The State of Israel in Jewish Public Thought: The Quest for Collective Identity* (London: Macmillan, 1994).
9. Elmer Berger, 'The Eichmann Case Judgement: Meaning for Americans of Jewish Faith', American Council for Judaism, New York, 28 March 1962.
10. Marie Syrkin, 'Eichmann and American Jewry (A Reply to Oscar Handlin)', *Jewish Frontier*, May 1961.
11. Ben Halpern, 'Reflections on the Eichmann Trial', *Jewish Frontier*, March 1961. See also Shlomo Katz, 'Notes on the Eichmann Case', *Midstream*, Summer 1960.
12. See Yosef Gorny, *The State of Israel in Jewish Public Thought: The Quest for Collective Identity*, p. 205.
13. Paul Jacobs, 'Eichmann and Jewish Identity', *Mainstream*, Summer 1961. The article was reprinted from the left-liberal journal *The New Leader*.
14. See David Ben-Gurion, *The Restored State of Israel*, Vol. 2 (Tel Aviv, 1969 [Hebrew]), p. 654.
15. *Davar*, 27 May 1960.
16. Ben-Gurion to Proskauer, 8 June 1960, Ben-Gurion Heritage Archives [Hebrew].
17. See Ronald W. Zweig, *German Reparations and the Jewish World: A History of the Claims Conference* (USA, 1987), Chapter 1, pp. 1–13.
18. See Devora Hacohen, *The One Million Plan: Ben-Gurion's Plan for Mass Emigration to Palestine in 1942–1945* (Tel Aviv, 1994).
19. See Dinah Porat, *Leadership in a Trap: The Yishuv in View of the Holocaust 1942–1945* (Tel Aviv: Am Oved, 1986 [Hebrew]); Tuvia Friling, *An Arrow in the Mist: David Ben-Gurion, The Yishuv Leadership and Rescue Attempts in the Holocaust*, manuscript.
20. To support my view, I quote his remarks immediately after the war broke out and after Nazi Germany and the Soviet Union partitioned Poland. In a meeting of the Jewish Agency Executive on 17 September 1939, Ben-Gurion remarked: 'The general turnabout of world affairs is a bad augury; it is our duty to focus specifically on our concern for the affairs of Palestine, because concern for the Jewish people and its Diaspora is *beyond human powers* today.' Quoted from Meir Avizohar (ed.), *Let Us Fight as a Nation: The Memoirs of Ben-Gurion (from the Estate) September 1939–April 1940* (Tel Aviv: Am Oved, in press), pp. 81–2.
21. Mapai Central Committee, 19 May 1960, Labor Party Archives at Beit Berl.
22. *Attorney General* v. *Adolf Eichmann: Verdict and Sentence* (Jerusalem, 1974), pp. 39–46 [Hebrew].
23. Gershom Scholem, 'Eichmann', *Amot* A, Summer 1962; also published in Gershom Scholem, *Reflections from Within*, pp. 118–20 [Hebrew].
24. See Yosef Gorny, *The State of Israel in Jewish Public Thought: The Quest for Collective Identity*, Chapter 3.
25. Mapai Central Committee, 2 June 1960, Labor Party Archives, Beit Berl.
26. Nahum Goldmann's proposal to invite representatives of other countries that had suffered from the Nazi regime as judges in the trial attracted an angry and even insulting response from Ben-Gurion. See exchange of letters between them, dated 2 June 1960, Ben-Gurion Heritage Archives. The press termed their dispute a Ben Gurion–Goldmann 'duel'. See *Haboker*, 5 June 1960; *Davar*, 3 June 1960, and 5 June 1960; *Lamerhav*, 3 June 1960; *Al Hamishmar*, 3 June 1960, and *She'arim*, 3 June 1960.
27. See Hannah Arendt, *Eichmann in Jerusalem: A Report on the Banality of Evil*, and Hannah Arendt, *The Origins of Totalitarianism* (New York, 1956).
28. *Hannah Arendt, Karl Jaspers – Correspondence 1926–1969*, Lotte Kohler and Hans

Saner (eds) (New York-London), pp. 435, 511.

29. Gershom Scholem and Hannah Arendt, 'Eichmann in Jerusalem – an Exchange of Letters', *Encounter*, January 1964.

30. Dan Diner, 'Hannah Arendt Reconsidered: The Evil and the Banal in Her Holocaust-Narration', unpublished.

31. *Hannah Arendt, Karl Jaspers*, p. 423.

32. Hannah Arendt, 'Zionism Reconsidered', in Michael Selzer (ed.), *Zionism Reconsidered* (London, 1970.)

33. *Eichmann in Jerusalem*, pp. 10–11.

34. Ibid., p. 259.

35. Ibid, p. 263.

36. *Hannah Arendt, Karl Jaspers*, p. 415.

37. 'How European Jewry Was Annihilated', *Maariv*, 17 July 1964.

38. Elizabeth Young-Brunel, *Hannah Arendt – For the Love of the World* (USA, 1982).

39. Carol Brightman (ed.), *Between Friends: The Correspondence of Hannah Arendt and Mary McCarthy, 1949–1975* (New York/London, 1995), p. 249.

40. Young-Brunel, *For the Love of the World*, pp. 174–5.

41. *Hannah Arendt, Karl Jaspers*, p. 53.

42. Ibid., pp. 98–9.

43. Ibid., pp. 197–9.

44. Daniel Bell, 'Reflections on Jewish Identity', *Commentary*, June 1961.

45. Norm Fruchter, 'Arendt's Eichmann and Jewish Identity', *Studies on the Left*, 1965.

46. Ron H. Feldman (ed.), *Hannah Arendt – The Jew as a Pariah: Jewish Identity and Politics in the Modern Age* (New York, 1978).

47. Henry Feingold, 'Arendt Revisited', *Judaism*, Winter 1980.

48. David Biale, 'Arendt in Jerusalem', *Response*, Summer 1980.

49. See Note 38 above.

50. Jeffrey C. Issac, 'At the Margins: Jewish Identity and Politics in the Thought of Hannah Arendt', *Tikkun*, January–February 1990.

51. Leon Boltstein, 'Liberating the Pariah: Politics, the Jews, and Hannah Arendt', in Reuben Garner (ed.), *Responses to the Writings of Hannah Arendt* (New York, 1990).

52. A recent article by Edna Brocke traces Arendt's ambivalent attitude toward Jewishness but shows that she nevertheless remained a member of her people to her last day. See Edna Brocke, 'Treue als zeichen der Wahrheit: Hannah Arendts Weg als Judin', in *Hannah Arendt – Lebensgeschichte einer deutschen Judin* (Alte Synagoge (Hg), 1995), pp. 43–66.

53. Those who reacted to Arendt's book may be divided into three sociocultural groups: (a) Zionist intellectuals, including philosophers, historians, and pundits; (b) radical intellectuals, most of whom are Jewish and a majority of whom reject her book fiercely; and (c) academics in American universities. Below is a selection of articles, arranged by these groups.

(a) *The first group:*

Joachim Printz, 'On the Banality of Hannah Arendt', *Congress Biweekly*, 24 June 1963.

Shlomo Katz, 'Notes in Midstream', *Midstream*, September 1963.

Marie Syrkin, 'Miss Arendt Surveys the Holocaust', *Jewish Frontier*, May 1963.

Ernst Simon, 'Revisionist History of the Jewish Catastrophe', *Judaism*, Fall 1963.

Ernst Akiva Simon, 'Hannah Arendt: An Attempt to Analyze', *Molad*, July–August

1963 [Hebrew].
Gershom Shalom and Hannah Arendt, 'Eichmann in Jerusalem – An Exchange of Letters', *Encounter,* January 1964.
Israel Gutman, 'Self-Hatred, Arendt-Style', *Yalkut Moreshet,* December 1966 [Hebrew].

(b) *The second group:*
Norman Podhoretz, 'Hannah Arendt on Eichmann', *Commentary,* September 1963; *Commentary,* February 1964.
Lionel Abel, 'The Aesthetics of Evil', *Partisan Review,* Summer 1963.
Daniel Bell, 'The Alphabet of Justice', *Partisan Review,* Fall 1963.
Arguments: Irving Howe, Dwight Macdonald, Lionel Abel, Mary McCarthy, William Phillips, Harold Weisberg, Marie Syrkin, *Partisan Review,* Spring 1964.

(c) *The third group:*
Michael A. Musmanno, 'Man with an Unspotted Conscience', *New York Times Review of Books,* 13 May 1963.
Bruno Bettelheim, 'Eichmann: The System; the Victims', *New Republic,* 29 June 1963.
Oscar Handlin, 'Hannah Arendt's Eichmann', *New Leader,* 5 August 1963.

2

The Theological Discourse

The public debate on Holocaust consciousness as a component of Jewish identity began with a theological discourse. After the State of Israel and the Jewish Holocaust were inseparably connected, practically and theoretically, in the Eichmann trial in the early 1960s, it was but natural that the question about the substance and contents of this nexus would follow. In this respect it was also natural that the debate would develop into a theological discourse since Jewish theological thinking has always been noted for its efforts to comprehend the Jews' very existence as an ongoing historical process of destruction and upbuilding, exile and yearnings for redemption. Therefore, the dialectic relationship between Auschwitz and Jerusalem, between physical disaster and physical redemption of a sort hitherto unwitnessed in Jewish history, was the supreme concern of this thought. Symbolically, public debate over the theological meaning of the Holocaust for Jewish faith began concurrently with the Six-Day War, which, as noted above, created the first fissure in the public rampart of repression of the Holocaust. Therefore, naturally again, borne on the surge of enthusiasm that followed the great military victory and led by the messianic climate occasioned by the sudden and swift transition from dread of annihilation to a sense of redemption, there began a discourse on the theological relationship between the Holocaust and the state.

It is important to stress that, much as the abduction of Eichmann and his prosecution in Israel enshrined Israel's historical right to represent the murdered Jewish people, so did the victory in the Six-Day War give rise to a 'civil religion' among the living Jewish people: the centrality of Israel, definable as a secular-traditional, ethnic-cultural, grass-roots trend of thought that is attached, although not identical, to a national worldview. The theological discourse, upon its inception after the Six-Day War, aimed to augment the religious contents of this civil religion, in which the nation's Holocaust and political resurrection converged. For this reason, and in view of the religious complexion of

American culture, this discourse came into being and continued almost exclusively in the United States. In contrast, in Israel – with governmental encouragement – it has taken on a national Zionist complexion. Finally, Orthodox circles have abstained in the theological debate on this question, for reasons that we explore below.

In the theological discourse itself, one may distinguish between two groups of thinkers with different approaches. One struggles with the question of God's role in history and, for this reason, with the extent of His responsibility for both the Holocaust and the rebirth. The second school seeks to separate Him, as it were, from historical events at various levels, especially with respect to the existence of Jewry after the Holocaust. Stationed between these two approaches is Elie Wiesel, who did more than anyone else to disseminate Holocaust consciousness in Jewish and general society, and whose attitude toward the matter includes a theological dimension peculiar to him alone, as we will see.

The doyen of the first group is Rabbi Eliezer Berkovits, whose Zionist outlook inspired him to move from the United States to Israel. In his view, the establishment of the Jewish state after Auschwitz is part of a secret divine plan that also manifests God's partnership with His people. Without the return to Zion, he argues, Judaism and Jewish history would be meaningless. This return is also a prerequisite for the establishment of the kingdom of Heaven on earth – for which the divine plan is associated with a process of fulfillment in historical reality. Responsibility for this process is divided, so to speak, between God the planner and man the fulfiller. Therefore, human actions bring the kingdom of Heaven closer or make it more remote. Auschwitz accomplishes the latter, the inauguration of Jewish statehood accomplishes the former. Thus, Berkovits absolves God of responsibility for the Holocaust without banishing Him from history. In this fashion, too, he attempts to explain the Jews' horrific sufferings at various times in history, including the climax of this suffering in the Holocaust. The Jewish people, in his view, are the carriers of the messianic idea or the grand Divine plan to establish a corporeal kingdom of Heaven. Therefore, God knew of Auschwitz and has been *en route* to Zion throughout history. This is surely a terrifying thought – one that may imply that Auschwitz is the price of the resurrection of Zion – unless we recall that Berkovits apportions responsibility between God and man-made history. This, however, does not resolve the moral quandary, because Berkovits does not disengage God from the historical act altogether. Thus, both the establishment of the state and the

Six-Day War are 'in conformity with the divine plan'. For this reason, the actions of human beings, and especially those of the Jews, for better or worse, cannot fall totally outside the domain of Divine providence. According to Berkovits, the collective actions of this people also represent the footsteps of the Messiah, because the people rebuilds itself after each bout of devastation. After the first, it founded synagogues; after the second, it authored the Talmud; and after the third, it established the Jewish state. Thus, for the first time after years of exile, after having to adapt to changing political situations and different cultures, the Jewish people created in Israel an all-embracing and complete Jewish reality. This indicates that God is readying a 'new thing' in Zion, the ultimate meaning of which is unknowable. However, it is already clear to Berkovits that all of Israel's daunting problems and challenges stem from one fact: a new inclusive reality has come about, in which the great hope of the Jews and the world is embedded.

To sum up, Berkovits has seated himself in an unbalanced posture in the matter of God's role in history and the connection between this issue and that of Holocaust and rebirth. He argues that God's presence in world history is fulfilled only by means of the Jewish people, His messianic agent. He does not explain, however, why this people is doomed to suffer so grievously. He considers the Jewish people a participant in God's plan to establish a heavenly kingdom on earth, but acknowledges that this plan with respect to humankind and the Jewish people is swathed in mystery.[1] Nevertheless, this is the essence of God's covenant with the Jews,[2] and it is this that lends the Jewish people its eternity. Therefore, the Holocaust and the rebirth belong to this covenant, and although human beings cannot fathom the covenant itself, they know its thrust by virtue of their faith.

Berkovits's imbalance recurs in his explication of God's role in the Holocaust and in the act of establishing the state. In the first case, as Eliezer Schweid explains, Berkovits speaks about the mystery of God's *refraining* from intervention in history.[3]

After Berkovits, Jewish public theology shows a gradual tendency to reduce and circumscribe God's involvement in history. The tendency begins with Emil Fackenheim, the philosopher whose outlook is closest to Berkovits's. Fackenheim also pioneered the theological discourse about the meaning of Jewish existence and faith after the Holocaust and the establishment of the state. Fackenheim, like Berkovits, is a Zionist who fulfilled his worldview and destiny by settling in Israel. However, unlike Berkovits, an Orthodox rabbi, Fackenheim moved not only from the Diaspora to Israel but from the Reform movement to Conservative Judaism.

For Fackenheim, Holocaust consciousness is a categorical imperative of sorts that orders Jews to continue maintaining their collective
identity. Two months after the Six-Day War, in a public symposium on
Jewish values in the post-Holocaust future,[4] Fackenheim tried to elab-
orate a doctrine of Jewish unity that bases post-Holocaust Jewish
existence on three contrasts. The first is between the universalistic
principle, in view of which Western Jewry was given an equality of
rights never before witnessed in Jewish history, and the particularistic
principle, which underlies the reinstatement of Jewish national independence in the Jews' historic homeland. The second is between
modern secularism, embraced by a majority of Jews in the Diaspora
and in Israel, and the collective acknowledgment that Jewish continuity cannot occur unless Jewish tradition is fostered. The third is the
contradiction between the freedom that Jews enjoy in Western society
and the awareness that the disaster of the Holocaust occurred in this of
all societies. In Fackenheim's opinion, these contradictions coexist in
harmony despite their internal contrasts and the various players who
wish to erode it – such as the Ultraorthodox, the 'Canaanite', and the
American Council for Judaism – because it is based not only on the
tribal reality but on faith. This, he believes, is a dialectic product of
negation, i.e., of a Holocaust remembrance that has become a categorical imperative instructing Jews in how to continue living. According
to this imperative, which Fackenheim terms 'the 614th commandment', the modern Jew must not hand Hitler his final victory, the
disappearance of the Jewish people, and must fight assimilation on
behalf of the people's continued existence.

Immediately after the Six-Day War, only three months after he
coined the phrase 'the 614th commandment', Fackenheim attributed
religious significance to Israel's military triumph and linked this significance to the Holocaust. In his view, this triumph was a beam of light
that pierced the darkness of Auschwitz, instilled hope in the heart of
every Jew who wished to continue being Jewish, and provides a rationale for Jews' identity as Jews. Hereinafter, Fackenheim ruled, Jewish
existence should be based not only on *negating* Hitler's malevolent
intent but also on affirming one's identification with the act of Divine
providence revealed in what he termed the miraculous victory in the
Six-Day War.[5]

From this point, Fackenheim began to develop a doctrine of total
unity of Holocaust and resurrection, between Auschwitz and
Jerusalem – the celestial, utopian one and the corporeal, political one.
The key to understanding this dialectical unity lies in the term *tikkun*

(mending). The theological meaning of *tikkun* is universal, in the sense of the expression *tikkun 'olam* (mending the world) in the traditional sense. This kind of *tikkun*, however, would be valueless in the absence of *tikkun* of the collective posture of the Jewish people in history, and this *tikkun* is found in the fulfillment process that ensued from the inauguration of Jewish statehood.

Fackenheim considers the state's very existence a *tikkun*, although he realizes that the ways of life practiced there are flawed in many senses and still require *tikkun*. They embody difficult social problems, but these are in part the result of a Diaspora heritage that resists disengagement. The primary *tikkun*, however, has occurred, because a nation deemed unfit for statecraft by reason of its historical fate has normalized itself in statehood; a country that, according to experts, could not absorb further immigrants has taken in mass immigration; unsettled lands have been made to blossom; the Hebrew language, considered dead even by its champions, has been revived; and the Jewish Jerusalem that humankind had meant to leave in the sanctity of its ruins has been rebuilt. These, in Fackenheim's opinion, add up to a special celebration of life after an episode of devastation and death hitherto unknown in human annals.

Fackenheim construes the transition from the terror of death to the celebration of life as a quasi-messianic phenomenon. However, the impetus for redemption, in his view, is the opposite, emanating from the ground up. 'The "impulse from below"', he explained, 'will call forth the "impulse from above".'[6] In other words, the human act will lead to the will of divine providence.

It was in 1989, when Fackenheim's English-language book appeared in its second printing, that a collection of his articles was published in Hebrew.[7] In his introduction to the Hebrew book, he alludes explicitly to the mystic relationship between the Holocaust and the rebirth. In his opinion, 'Zionism did not need the Holocaust to justify its path; however, the Holocaust was a revelation by way of negation', a revelation not of the divine will but of 'the unprecedented conjugation of the evildoers' unprecedented hate and their victims' unprecedented helplessness', a climactic revelation of the shame of life in exile. 'The shame of this conjugation gave the victims' successors the imperative: to rupture this conjugation by terminating their helplessness.' The Holocaust terminated Jewish passivity – both among the religious, who awaited divine intervention, and among the secular, who awaited the denouement of the historical process. As Fackenheim understood the matter, 'Out of the Holocaust grew the imperative to wait neither for God nor for man, but to establish the state at once; the Jews obeyed this imperative and rose up to fulfill it'. He regards this action by the Jews as a mystery of sorts. He is convinced that 'in vain will we seek historical parallels to this feat of drama, courage, and devotion. … The implications of this act, for the Jews and for Judaism, will yet come to light. It is the role of Jewish philosophers to fathom it.'

Fackenheim himself attempts to unravel the mystery of Jewish existence after the Holocaust and the formation of statehood by way of absurdity, arguing that it cannot be fathomed. This is because he believes that, although God is present in history and the course of history cannot be described without taking account of His providence, His actions cannot be fathomed. Therefore, just as the tragedy of the Holocaust defies perception, so does the miracle of the rebirth. Neither event has a historical explanation that 'seeks reasons' or a theological explanation that 'seeks meaning'. Thus, the Holocaust and the state are intertwined in a nexus of mystery that acknowledges the limited powers of the intellect to probe historical events fully. The reason for this limitation, beyond doubt, is that the meaning of these events is not only corporeal but also divine. Again, however, this meaning is beyond our grasp. Thus the human capacity to *comprehend* by means of historical causality on the one hand, and the capacity to *believe* by means of religious meaning on the other hand, are adjoined. Any other perspective leads to rational frustration or religious sacrilege. What remains, then, is to notice the relationship between the Holocaust and the rebirth and acknowledge the categorical imperative of acting to thwart the possibility that the tie will be severed.[8]

The main manifestations of this relationship between Auschwitz and Jerusalem are amazement and astonishment over the incomprehensible feats of divine providence and a staunch resolve to prevent Auschwitz from recurring. Fackenheim adduces two conclusions from these premises. First, life in Israel, even that of the secular, has a religious significance expressed in hope and courage amidst the horror of the Holocaust, fealty and adherence to a Jewish history that has proved that it has not yet ended, and the imperative of renewing Jewish national life in the historical Jewish homeland. The second conclusion is the need to change the nature of Jewish nationhood and base it on physical force so that Auschwitz cannot recur.[9] This force is the Jewish state's only response to that tragic confluence, revealed during the Holocaust, of the Jews' collective helplessness and their enemies' murderous stance.

Summing up, Fackenheim's worldview expresses a unique combination of religious faith, acknowledgment of the divine presence in history, and an existentialism manifested in Zionist activism. He proves this by citing the example of Nahshon son of Amminadav: comparing the Biblical era to modern times, Fackenheim stresses that a miracle occurred in the past and that only hope remains in the present. Therefore 'the modern Nahshon has no time to await miracles. He has only two choices: to die or to leap into the stormy waters without knowing whether the sea will part, or, if it does not part, whether he will have the strength to cross it by swimming and, if necessary, alone.'[10]

For Fackenheim, then, there are two situations: *aloneness*, manifested in the Holocaust era, and *being alone*, manifested during the struggle for statehood. The linguistic difference between them is minute, the difference in substance vast. Nahshon's being alone as he waded into the Red Sea reflected his audacity and resolve, whereas in the Holocaust, the Jewish people was alone by reason of its helplessness.

Thus, the establishment of the state transformed not only the historical condition of the Jewish people but also its collective identity. From a dependent entity it became an entity in charge of its fate. This begs the question: What would have come of Fackenheim's faith had the Jewish state not come into being after the Holocaust? This question, however, is not ours to answer.

The difference in the outlooks of Berkovits and Fackenheim concerning God's presence in history, and the implications of this difference for the Holocaust–rebirth nexus, are rooted in two matters. Berkovits, as a messianic believer, argues that the establishment of the state is part of a general divine plan to create a kingdom of heaven on earth. For him, statehood or national redemption is a precondition and a cornerstone for universal redemption, even if he cannot fathom its meaning. Fackenheim differs in that he is an existentialist believer. He, too, believes in God's presence in history, but the essence and thrust of this presence are concealed from him. Therefore he stresses the bold actions of human beings. Thus the condition for *tikkun* – the focal concept of his worldview – is the parable of Nahshon's wade into the Red Sea. Although Nahshon is beset by doubt and uncertainty as he makes his leap, only by virtue of it does the divine miracle occur and the waters part. The object of the parable, of course, is the Jews' action in reestablishing their state and sustaining it under turbulent historical conditions. To put it differently, Berkovits integrates the Jews' actions into God's plan while Fackenheim treats them as prerequisites for His involvement in corporeal affairs. In terms of the collective Jewish identity, Berkovits views it as mission and Fackenheim as activism. For this reason, Fackenheim bases contemporary Zionism on four imperatives: the Land of Israel, the State of Israel, the Law of Return, and Jerusalem – a quartet that pulls him very close to the activist right in Israel.[11]

Irving Greenberg followed this trend of valuing the actions of human beings over those of God by attempting to establish a new practical equilibrium between God and the People Israel. Greenberg, who occupies a special station in American modern orthodoxy, is a philosopher, educator, and public figure who, as the head of a public project for education in Jewish leadership – CLAL[12] – provides an example of the transformation of an intellectual's academic cerebration into public thought.

He begins his discussion of the Holocaust-rebirth nexus by developing an inclusive historiosophic view of Jewish history. He divides Jewish history into three main periods: In the biblical era, the covenant between the people and its God was formed and the Jews' collective image as a chosen nation was stipulated. In the rabbinical era, from the destruction of the Second Temple to the late eighteenth century, the people's identity coalesced as a community of believers that lived in accordance with the rabbinical rules of *halakha*. The defining indicator of this time is political powerlessness in relations between the Jews as a national entity and other peoples.

The third period is that of political strength. It began with the Jews' encounter with modernity in the late eighteenth and early nineteenth centuries, continued with the struggle against antisemitism and the cataclysm of the Holocaust, and climaxed with the establishment of the Jewish state. Four basic changes in Jewish existence occurred during this time. The first was political: the transition from national statelessness to national statehood. The second, the theological, marks a change in Jewish self-perception, primarily in challenging Jewry's covenant with its God during the Holocaust and in renewing it afterwards. The third, the community change, represents the emergence of a new Jewish leadership that validates itself by responding to the needs of the State of Israel – the national need for political strength and the aspiration to revive Jewish life. The fourth change is structural: the formation of new institutions and organizations to serve the needs of Jewish communities. These substantive changes did not occur evenly across this period; they congregated at its end, after the Holocaust and the establishment of statehood. These four transformations are the four pillars of the post-Holocaust era. Thus the Jews succumbed to others' political power during the third period but they acquired political power of their own at its end. Greenberg's outlook is well expressed in his paraphrase, meant in a manner opposite to the original, of Lord Acton's famous aphorism: after the Holocaust, the Jews should realize that, 'power corrupts, absolute power corrupts absolutely, but absolute powerlessness corrupts even more'.[13] For Greenberg, the essence of political power is not an instrument of governance but a moral state, since powerlessness is a state of humiliation, as the Holocaust that befell the helpless Jews proves. Thus Greenberg adopts the principle of redistribution of power as a universal moral–political imperative of sorts: after the Holocaust no one should depend on others for his or her security and right to exist; all are entitled to power that will safeguard their dignity. Greenberg understood that the issue of the right to and use of political power brings many political and moral questions to the fore; for this reason, he refrains from discussing them. It is clear to him, however, that the Holocaust elevated the problem of political and military power from the political level to the moral, religious, and educational plane[14] that finds expression in the Jews' self-assumed responsibility for their fate. This responsibility, based on political strength, is one of the fundamental clauses in the covenant that the Jewish people renewed with its God after the Holocaust.[15] This premise, according to Greenberg, implies that the Jewish state has profound religious significance. Indeed, despite its being an essentially secular institution, the state is the most important religious statement that the Jews have made since their disaster. Israel also proves, in a sense, that God's assurances are themselves of value. Buried in this argument is Greenberg's difficult uncertainty about the moral probity of God in view of the death of the Jewish children. He argues that the establishment of statehood returns God's actions to moral equilibrium. This notion leads Greenberg to adjoin, inseparably, the sanctification of the victims of the Holocaust and of life in the Jewish state, because from then on, 'In death as in life, the religious–secular dichotomy is essentially ended'.

Greenberg is not at all confident that statehood has solved the Jewish problem in every respect. On the one hand, he regards the state as evidence of Jewish vitality and the restoration of faith, but he is also aware of the menace of annihilation that threatens it. Therefore, all he can do is hope.

This hope, in Greenberg's opinion, resides in reviving the covenant that the Holocaust had undermined, that between the Jewish people and its God. This revival, however, is primarily not an act of God but the result of the Jews' will. Since the Holocaust, God can no longer command His people. From now on He does not choose them; instead, they choose Him. 'God was no longer in a position to command, but the Jewish people was so in love with the dream of redemption that it stepped forward to carry on its mission.' Once the Jews chose to carry on the Divine mission, i.e., the striving for redemption, the state became an instrument for its fulfillment. The establishment of state-hood shifted responsibility for Jewish life entirely to the Jews' domain, thus totally transforming the essence of the covenant between the people and its God. Henceforth, the covenant cannot be fulfilled merely through observance of the commandments and devotional study; actions in the realm of state are also needed. Now that God's validity and responsibility for His people are diminished, the acquisi-tion of power, manifested above all in support of Israel, has become a central feature in Jewish life worldwide.[16]

The political responsibility that Diaspora Jewry assumed for Israel's continued existence and well-being has terminated the exilic condition of the Jewish people. After all, if Diaspora means depend-ency on others, then under the new circumstances the Jewish people in its state and in the Diaspora relies principally on its own force. Thus, in a positive paradox, 'Galut Judaism is coming to an end – even in Galut'.[17] This paradoxical assertion sheds interesting light on Greenberg's personality and worldview. As a believer, he knows that Jewish dispersion means Jewish exile. As a public figure close to the center of American Jewish political action, however, he is convinced that from this point on the state of exile is approaching its end in the Diaspora. Therefore, Greenberg proposes to do away with the tradi-tional collective Jewish identity as an exilic people in favor of a new identity: that of a political people. This deepens the paradoxicality of his thinking, since the event that liberated the Jews from exile is the greatest disaster that ever befell them. This view verges on the claim that, by rendering antisemitism morally illegitimate, the Holocaust elevated the Jews at long last to full emancipation in the West. However, Greenberg's reasoning differs from that of the champions of this view. They usually take a reserved attitude toward the Jewish state; for Greenberg, the transformation of the Jewish identity is mean-ingless without the State of Israel.

Comparing Greenberg with Fackenheim shows that both consid-ered the reborn Jewish political identity a *tikkun* of the people's existential condition. However, while Fackenheim stressed the spiritual *tikkun* and endowed it with political significance, Greenberg under-scored the political *tikkun*, which he endowed with spiritual significance.

The last member of this group of theologians who wrestled and struggled with the tripartite nexus of God, Holocaust, and the state was Richard Rubenstein. However, while the others fluctuated between acknowledging the mystery of God's plans and intentions and shifting some of the responsibility from Him to the Jews, Rubenstein banished God from history and was the first to place this issue on the public agenda.[18] Affected by Auschwitz and influenced by a certain school in Christian thinking, Rubenstein embraced the view that 'God is dead'. Instead of nullifying God's existence altogether, however, he argues that, in view of what happened, there is no further divine providence in history. Dialectically, the departure of God from history does not lead to the nullification of religious faith. On the contrary: without God as a guiding force for man, as an active participant in reality, human beings are urged to attain even stronger faith and can find it within a religious framework but not necessarily in adherence to God. He elaborated this outlook before the Six-Day War and, immediately after it, remade his denial of supreme providence in history and adherence to religious faith into a theory of Jewish existence.[19]

In this theory, Jewish power and interests are what count. In his estimation, the victory that placed the land of Israel under Jewish control would prompt the evolution of a new Jewish faith in Israel, unlike the formulation accepted by most Diaspora Jews. In the future, he maintained, there would be two sociologically, culturally, and devotionally distinct Jewish entities. That in the Diaspora would comprise middle-class people, mainly people with college education and business people, who would adhere to the traditional modalities of faith. In Israel, however, a new Jewish entity would form a Sparta of the Middle East, a society of warriors rooted in the soil. Its inhabitants, he believed, are the *real* Jews, because they personally brought about the requisite change in the post-Auschwitz modalities of Jewish existence. This outlook brought Rubenstein's political perspectives close to those of the American neo-Conservatives and Gush Emunim in Israel.[20] In certain senses, his ideas even preceded theirs, although he certainly had no influence on them.

During the ensuing generation and more, as the times and the public climate changed, Rubenstein moderated his political views but did not reconsider the supreme importance of the Jewish state for post-Auschwitz Jewish existence. Furthermore, although in Rubenstein's view Israel's status as a mainstay in the existence of the Jews and Judaism diminished, he became even more firmly convinced of Israel's revolutionary historical value for the Jewish people.

In his debate in the 1980s with the theologian Arthur Cohen, who belittled the value of political organization, Rubenstein argued that this view disregarded the lesson of the Holocaust, which is that there is no limit to the malevolent intentions of a power-flushed aggressor toward a politically unorganized collective. Indeed, pursuant to the Holocaust the survivors chose the political path and built themselves a state. Although this state is liable to be destroyed, as long as it exists it assures them a status of human dignity. In the world that we inhabit, Rubenstein stressed, 'there are few, if any, human conditions worse than statelessness'.[21]

Thus Rubenstein rejects the view, advanced by theologians such as Arthur Cohen and the Jewish radical liberals, that there is a universal doctrine of ethics to which all of humankind is bound. The war, he asserted, proved that only Jews shared this belief – to their disastrous disadvantage. Therefore, he adduces, only a particularistic political organization can assume the universalistic undertaking immanently: 'It is only possible to have an effective universe of moral obligations in a shared political community.'

Rubenstein made these remarks at a symposium on the role of the Judenrat during the Holocaust. Rubenstein regarded the Judenrat as a pronouncedly exilic phenomenon, an organizational institution of a stateless people, which, he believed, might recur in the United States if conditions similar to those in Europe take shape.[22]

For Rubenstein, the Judenrat embodied the Jews' exilic condition of permanent, constant, and unchanging stateless dependency. Because of their dependency on others, they were treated as non-persons during the Holocaust. The purpose of the Jewish state is to terminate this situation. Even though only some of the Jews live in this state, statehood is a revolutionary apparition in Jewish history.

Thus, following Rubenstein, one may say that even if Auschwitz, which marks a watershed in the Gentiles' attitude toward the Jews, does not recur, the exilic situation embodied in the Judenrat will continue to exist for those Jews, including Rubenstein himself, who choose not to dwell in their own state. Rubenstein's extreme diagnosis of the 'Judenratic' Jewish situation in exile is exceptional in American Jewish thinking, as is his assertion of the 'death of God' in history. Even if one should take exception to it with respect to the current situation, one should not dismiss it altogether, because even if Jews as individuals are free and independent citizens, in the Diaspora the general Jewish interest is still dependent. However, Rubenstein admits that since Jewry in Israel faces constant physical danger, the Israel–

Holocaust nexus is not only metaphysical or historical but *political*, linked to the present. In 1991, during the Gulf War and following the missile attacks on Israel, he wrote: 'The Holocaust and Israel remain inextricably bound to each other.'[23]

This inextricable tie between Israel and the Holocaust, enunciated by Rubenstein in view of the existential dangers facing Israel, resurfaces in the political approach of those theologians who vacillated on the question of God's role in history. The factor they share in common is the moral justification of the use of military force and coercive state power in defense of national existence. However, their justification for this use of force, and the immoral actions connected with it, is graduated: the less God intervenes in history, the greater the permissible use of force.

Thus, Eliezer Berkovits, who believes in the existence of a divine meta-plan for human redemption, justifies the use of force against the Arabs during the intifada by arguing that this assault on the isolated State of Israel exposed it to existential danger. In this sense, he says, its condition was no different from that of Diaspora Jews during *and* before the Holocaust. This justification contains an audible undertone of self-righteousness, emanating from Berkovits's belief that the Jewish people in its state has a divine mission to perform, imposed on it as part of the grand scheme of redemption of humankind.

To Emil Fackenheim, it was clear that the Jewish *tikkun*, which began with the Jewish people's Nahshonic leap into the sea of historical action, affirms the use of means that had not been acceptable among Jews during their history in exile for the self-defense and fulfillment of the *tikkun*. Thus Fackenheim, unlike Berkovits, believes that the revolutionary change in the Jews' status and identity affirms *in itself* the use of military force. In his view, then, the undertone of self-righteousness gives way to an undertone of acquiescence in the prevailing world order, in which collective existence without force is untenable. For Irving Greenberg, who shifted some of the responsibility for Jewish survival from God to the people, Fackenheim's acquiescence becomes a realization of principle. Since Jewish powerlessness is inconsistent with Jewish existence and the Jews' responsibilities under their current covenant with their God, one must acknowledge that 'Jewish power is incompatible with absolute Jewish moral purity'. It is true that, for Greenberg, reliance on force does not obviate hope for a future peace settlement – a humanistic utopia of sorts with Jerusalem, capital of the three faiths, at its forefront. What counts, however, is the use of force, even though such a doctrine is ostensibly incompatible with the Jewish moral code. On this basis, Greenberg develops a doctrine of moral realism of sorts, endowed with universal significance. In his opinion, in the test of the use of force, the Jewish people resurrected God's earthly avatar. After all, the Jews and their history reflect the problems with which all of humankind wrestles. Thus, Israel knows neither political nor moral security, and the Jews are not immune to the errors and corruptions of human existence. Nevertheless, Greenberg would bet his life that in the long run, in its overall behavior, Israel will serve as an example to the peoples and a light unto the nations.[24]

Richard Rubenstein, in contrast to Greenberg, asserts no utopian moral echelon in relations among peoples. After he stopped believing that Israel's safety is embedded in divine mercy, he replaced this source of security with reliance on the destructive power of the nuclear bomb. Even after he modified and moderated his political outlook, realizing that extreme messianic zealotry might lead Israel to great misfortune, he continued to assert that Israel's existence depends on its enemies' fear of the price they would have to pay for its annihilation, because 'that is what a morality between enemy nations has been reduced to'.[25] Thus, as long as the Jewish state is capable of responding to the risk of its annihilation with a nuclear strike, he does not despair of the prospects of its continued existence. Hence, Rubenstein has exchanged the divine promise for the promise of the nuclear bomb. This extreme stand is consistent with his general attitude toward modern technological society, which develops means of mass annihilation such as those used against European Jewry. In Israel's case, however, this technology also has an affirmative meaning: it assures Israel's existence.

Having noted that Greenberg and Rubenstein think similarly, we should compare their views. Both thinkers base post-Holocaust Jewish existence on force. However, Rubenstein, who has banished God from history, is left with the military force of the state only, while Greenberg, by continuing to believe in divine providence and merely downscaling God's absolute and all-inclusive responsibility, also looks forward to the eventual fulfillment of a realistic utopia in relations among peoples.

Using the tension between force and morals, the four theologians in this group fashioned a dialectical doctrine of sorts that unifies the contradictions. True, force is contrary to utopian morality, but ultimately it is the only staff on which to rely in fulfilling this morality in historical reality. In this sense, the nexus of destruction and rebirth oversteps its particularistic Jewish meaning and becomes a universalistic phenomenon of moral praxis.

Elie Wiesel rejected this formulation, as did a series of theological thinkers from Orthodoxy to Reform. Wiesel is a key figure in the public thought that made Holocaust consciousness a component of the Jewish national identity. An author who carries the night of Auschwitz in broad daylight, a folk philosopher, a hasidic preacher, and a courageous public figure, Wiesel is a Jew who commutes between Auschwitz, New York, and Jerusalem, the three permanent way-stations in his life: Auschwitz as an existential human experience that he underwent in childhood; New York as a Diaspora Jewish reality to which he belongs with his every fiber; and Jerusalem representing hope and a nearly messianic promise. He maintains each of these way-stations – the Holocaust, the Jewish people, and Israel – independently of the others, each in its special mysterious sense, with no causal relationship among them.

If we take a more penetrating look, however, we may, I think, discern a watershed in Wiesel's thinking on the hidden relationship between Holocaust and rebirth after the dramatic events of 1967.

Before the Six-Day War, Wiesel publicly criticized the argument, voiced by Israeli political leaders, that the state is a response to the Holocaust. In his opinion, Israel is no such thing and has no right to claim such a status. The attempt to link these two events, which he considers historically and messianically mysterious, diminishes their value and significance. In his view, the claim that the state came into being because of the Holocaust foists a heavy burden of responsibility on future generations, which may feel that they owe their lives as free people, in their Jewish state, to the disaster that befell the previous generation. No one is entitled to do this, because the actions of God transcend the human intellect. Thus, no one can understand how human beings committed such brutalities, why God allowed them to do so, why the Jews were silent, and how one can speak of, and seek meaning in, this terrible experience. Thus Wiesel also criticized Fackenheim, who coined the term 'the 614th commandment' in this very debate.

The unfathomability of God's actions does not prompt Wiesel to deny His existence. After all, one cannot ask why and wherefore of a nonexistent entity. However, Wiesel's acknowledgment of the existence of God as part of reality and human experience also leads him into a confrontation with Him. In his view, the God who remains silent as the victims are led to the gallows has subjected the Jewish people to a test of allegiance to itself, and the people have rebelled against Him by adhering to their Jewishness. In his hasidic style, in English, he expressed it thus: 'You, God, do not want us to be Jewish; well, Jewish we shall be nevertheless despite Your will.'[26]

By implication, the basic existential experience of the Jew is the Holocaust, because by its means the Jew re-chooses his people, perhaps even against God's will. In other words, responsibility for the singular Jewish existence belongs primarily to the people itself, and not to its God. In this sense, Wiesel preceded Greenberg's 'new covenant' between the two.

One may understand from these remarks that, for Wiesel, the Holocaust created a more intensive shock than the excitement surrounding the establishment of the Jewish state as the experiences that shaped the people's image. For Fackenheim and Greenberg, the prime experience is related to statehood: the Jews' Nahshonic leap for Fackenheim, the perception of strength for Greenberg. For Wiesel, however, the Holocaust experience stands alone in shaping the Jewish image. He enunciated this at a conference of Conservative rabbis before the Six-Day War, expressing the fear that the Jews had 'sold [the Holocaust] too cheaply' at all levels: from the lowly level of the reparations agreement up to the loftiest level, the establishment of the State of Israel. Often, he told his audience, he has the terrible sneaking suspicion that the establishment of Israel, a mystery in itself, was more corrective or remedial for the Gentiles than for the Jews. For example, the despairing young Jews who had emerged from the extermination camps could have embarked on a campaign of revenge against their murderers had the struggle for statehood not diverted their furious energies. However, now that matters have turned out as they have,

> My terrible thought is this: perhaps because of the state of Israel we have missed an opportunity. Perhaps we could have imposed a different destiny upon mankind then. Because then they were positive, we had something to give, or to demand, or to destroy, or to propose.[27]

Thus, the establishment of statehood was a way of compensating the Jews in normal coin for their sufferings. Wiesel, however, does not settle for this compensation; he is beset by the thought that this normal compensation has deprived the Jews of their universal mission. After their catastrophe, the Jews could have given something to the world precisely because of the abnormality of their existence. It seems that in these surrealistic reflections, utterly divorced from historical reality, lie two basic concepts that are important in understanding Wiesel's worldview: the Jewish people and its universal singularity.

From Wiesel's standpoint, the Jewish people and the Jewish state are not one and the same; the existence of the former does not depend solely on the latter. In the mid-1970s, a decade after he expressed these reflections and after the Six-Day War, he argued, in a series of conversations with the author Harry Cargas, that, true, the Jews cannot exist as a people without Israel, but this applies to any other Jewish community to the same extent. Thus, in terms of the people's future, Israel has no advantage over the Diaspora. Furthermore,

> If in 1948 there would have been no Israel, we could have gone on living for centuries and centuries. Since Israel is here, and it came – I hate to admit it – as a result of the Holocaust if not as a response to it, the disappearance of Israel would mean another Holocaust, and our generation is too weak.[28]

These remarks, made under the influence of the severe shock of the Yom Kippur War, imply that not only do the Jews not need Israel for their continuity, but had Israel not been established and threatened constantly with annihilation, the Jews would have avoided the threat of a further Holocaust. Wiesel probably did not think this idea through to its end – it may have terrified him – and I have found no evidence that he repeated it. However, it underscores the supreme importance that he attributes to the Jewish people, an importance further stressed by the very separation of the state and the Holocaust – a separation of general *and* personal significance.

In an interview with Israel radio, Wiesel was asked why he did not settle in Israel, which had been formed in response to the Holocaust. He replied that, from his standpoint, Israel and the Holocaust negate one another, and he is psychologically unwilling to live in a reality that negates his prior world.[29]

Thus, his outlook is one of 'negation of exile'. This idea cannot be contested but rather met with an objective statement: Israel, by its very creation in the political and cultural senses, represents so complete a transformation as to negate Jewish reality. True, one may respond by arguing that the reality of Jews in New York, too, does not resemble that of Jews in the *shtetlakh* of Eastern Europe, but in New York, Wiesel feels that he is living in the Diaspora, with all the uncertainties and even the guilt feelings that this engenders, as he admits. He needs the Diaspora because it represents the essence of most of Jewry. In this sense, his Jewishness, as he remarked in the interview, is not at all problematic. Because Jewishness resides in a living, freely standing existential culture, it does not require a state to solve its problem – because there is no problem.

This question, which was put to him not for the first time, came with a provocative undertone that – in view of the messianic fervor that Wiesel had expressed poetically after the Six-Day War – he practically begged. At that time, he spoke of the people, the return to Mount Sinai, and the dream two millennia old of returning to Jerusalem – the city with which every Jewish child in the Diaspora, especially in Eastern Europe, grew up; the city that resided in every shtetl; the city to which the Jews were now returning.[30] Then he had deviated from his policy of separating the Holocaust from the state. At that time, Wiesel wrote, in those days of waiting, he felt that 'suddenly all Jews had again become children of the Holocaust'. He felt so because it was clear to everyone that the loss of Israel would mark the end of affirmation, the end of hope, the end of the Jews' shared history with other peoples.[31] The shock that swept the Jewish people on this account is incomprehensible unless one bears in mind the Holocaust and the anxiety about the possibility of its recurrence. Wiesel, however, stresses that the Jews' rebirth, like many events in their history, entails an exogenous existential risk. Consequently, even if the Holocaust is in some way meaningful from the Jewish perspective, this meaning is indirect, prompted by exogenous factors and not by an internal awakening. The meaning of this awakening is negative, because it flows from the threat to Jewish existence. Wiesel does not criticize this nexus of Jewish rebirth and national danger. On the basis of this view, however, he rules out any meaningful relationship – substantive, religious, or mystical – between the Holocaust and the state. Furthermore, he accuses anyone who links Israel to the Holocaust of blasphemy. But since Wiesel cannot disregard the existence of this nexus in history, if only through the argument by negation that he adopts, he transfers the nexus from the substantial to the personal, from the transcendental to the existential. Accordingly, the nexus is comprised of the survivors: 'We are both survivors and witnesses, even those born after the events took place.'[32] Wiesel considers it a great privilege to be both a Holocaust survivor and a witness to the establishment of the state. At the personal level, he attested that 'I would choose whatever I went through again, because I see it as a privilege to have witnessed the Holocaust and rebirth of the dream.'[33] This statement walks a very fine line between exalted asceticism and forbidden moralizing, for it makes one ask about the price of redemption! However, one must of course keep in mind the historical context of his remarks, a context that explains both their spirit and their substance.

Notwithstanding the pathos in Wiesel's locution and in the remarks themselves, which are bound to a specific point in time, the existential personal connection Wiesel creates between the Holocaust and the Jewish rebirth points to the second basic concept in his worldview, noted above – the singularity of Jewish existence as a universal moral phenomenon that includes a political connection. Wiesel sees no point in establishing a State of Israel such as that which exists. There was no need to inflict such great suffering on the masses of Arabs who became perpetual refugees in the 1948 war, be it through flight or through expulsion. Zionism as the return to history fails to satisfy Wiesel. In the mid-1970s, more than a generation after statehood was proclaimed, he reached the conclusion that the aspiration of secular Jews to normalization in Israel is fundamentally mistaken: 'They are wrong because Israel cannot be a nation like all others. It is impossible. It's a counter-sense, it's a nonsense, really a contradiction its term.'[34]

Wiesel does not spell out the special Jewishness that he wants the modern Jewish state to exhibit. Nor does he define the non-secular Judaism to which he refers. Is it an Orthodox-style Judaism, rooted in the Eastern European shtetl that he carries with him, or is it the Conservative or Reform Judaism that he came to know as a modern Jew in the United States? In the field of political ethics, his answer is less vague: he expects Israel to be more considerate of the Arabs' suffering.

Wiesel, unlike his predecessors – Berkovits, Fackenheim, Greenberg, and, *a fortiori*, Rubenstein – is a moderate critic of Israeli policies. He admits that Israel has made political errors, but its actions should be judged only on the basis of a broad historical overview. In historical terms, 'Israel represents a triumph of mind and soul'.[35] From the standpoint of triumph, logic, and soul, Israel, he believes, embodies the great hope of universal morality. The very collective that suffered most is the one that will bring deliverance to the world, so it may never again experience the suffering that the Jews underwent. Thus, the universal and the particular merge in the Holocaust *and* in the State of Israel. With respect to the Holocaust, Wiesel argues that '[its] universality lies in its uniqueness'.[36] By implication, since the Holocaust and the state interrelate at the existential level, the state, too – despite its being a particularistic national entity – has universal meaning. Hence, precisely because of this state–Holocaust nexus,

Wiesel assigns the State of Israel a moral destiny and a mission vis-à-vis all of humankind. From this standpoint, Wiesel's remarks are closer in spirit to Reform and Conservative Judaism than to Orthodoxy, whence he came and to which he still feels an affinity. Wiesel's reference is to the moral political action that he preached in relations between Jews and other peoples, especially the Arabs. This sets him apart from the theological thinkers affiliated with Orthodox culture – Berkovits, Fackenheim, and Greenberg – who establish a connection between the state and the Holocaust and recognize, with different degrees of intensity, God's involvement in history. Wiesel, in contrast, separates the two totally. Where they see an unfathomable unity of Holocaust and rebirth, Wiesel observes an unfathomability in each but denies any substantive or divine relationship between them. Where the three aforementioned thinkers emphasize political force at the level of principle, Wiesel attempts to soft-pedal and, to the extent possible, circumscribe this aspect. Although one doubts that Wiesel would be willing to forfeit undivided Jerusalem as the capital of Israel for the fulfillment of the universal moral vision that he assigns to the Jewish people, Wiesel personally attests to the difficulty and the built-in contradictions of such a mission. Wiesel, who carries the universal lesson of the Holocaust to its limits with the confidence of one who understands its particularistic significance, understands that universalism has achieved too great a victory in the past decade. Thus, in an interview with a German newspaper in 1995, he stated that he no longer uses the term Holocaust and is seeking a surrogate term more strongly connected with Jewish history, such as *Churban*.[37]

In this in-between posture – between the State of Israel and the people of Israel, between Holocaust and redemption, between particularism and universalism – Wiesel does not identify totally with the Zionist-theological approach but keeps his distance from the Jewish-theological alternative. The concepts used to distinguish between the two – Zionist theology and Jewish theology – are not mutually exclusive for the thinkers in this discourse, except in extraordinary cases. Since the Jewish group also contains theologians with Zionist worldviews, the distinction is more a matter of emphasis than of substance. Two concepts, modern and post-modern, may typify it to some extent. Thus, the Zionist theology takes a post-modern attitude in that it reflects a protest against the modernity within which, and by means of which, the Jewish catastrophe occurred; whereas Jewish theology represents a national and even Zionist continuation of neo-Orthodox theory, along with the ideas of classical Reform.

The factor that typified the public thought of the second group, with its diverse personalities, outlooks on faith, and attitudes toward Zionism and Israel, was staunch opposition to what may be called the national theology of the Holocaust that their predecesors had developed and nurtured. This group includes the luminaries of Zionist modern Orthodoxy: Immanuel Jakobovits, the former chief rabbi of Britain, and Jonathan Sacks, the incumbent chief rabbi of Britain; Professors Eugene Borowitz and Jacob Petuchowski, two central figures in the American Reform Movement, both of whom may be defined as non-Zionists; and the most recent and youngest of them, the anti-Zionist Marc Ellis.

The factor that these personalities share, notwithstanding their profound differences in *Weltanschauung*, is that all see nothing unique about the Holocaust in either sense: the Jewish or the general-universal. It is this that sets them apart from the first group, including Elie Wiesel. Although all of these blur the uniqueness line, it is worth distinguishing between those who trace the uniqueness of the Holocaust to the history of Jewish martyrology and those who regard it as a universal phenomenon. Both approaches, however, make it possible to phrase a rule: the less unique one regards the Jewish Holocaust, the less important one considers the Jewish state.

Both Immanuel Jakobovits and Jonathan Sacks, the former and present chief rabbis of British Jewry, are Modern Orthodox thinkers of the Zionist persuasion.[38] Both treat the State of Israel as the basis on which the spiritual-religious structure of world Jewry will be erected, and both endow national and religious significance to the connection between the disaster of the Holocaust and the deliverance of the rebirth. To this point, they concur with their predecessors, the theologians of the Holocaust. From here on, however, the difference between them comes into sight.

Jakobovits rejects the intent to make Holocaust theology into a categorical imperative for the preservation of Judaism, as enunciated by Fackenheim, or a historical and philosophical adduction concerning the importance of power in modern Jewish history, as Greenberg asserts. In Jakobovits's opinion, the emphasis on the existence of Jewry during this time should be transferred to the existence of Judaism, for 'without Judaism, Jewish survival is both questionable and meaningless'. Jakobovits views with great concern the excessive fixation on Holocaust studies among young Jews. He fears that the stronger this tendency becomes, so will the desire to study the sources of traditional Judaism – the one irreplaceability – wither.

In Jakobovits's opinion, the catastrophe of the Holocaust does not merit special significance relative to the other catastrophes that have visited the Jewish people. After all, the sages of Yavne did not build the destruction of the Temple into a major element of their Jewish world-view and scholastic doctrine, which spared Jewry from extirpation. He adds: 'Nor would they have regarded an emotional identification with the *Churban* as an essential ingredient in Jewish consciousness or as an independent factor in Jewish survival.'[39]

Jakobovits's linear connection and equation between *Churban* and *Churban* prompt a historical question. The destructions of the First and Second Temples were not followed by an abrupt and revolutionary transition from disaster to rebirth. The transition at the present time, in contrast, created a nexus and a belief in a mysterious, God-guided relationship between these two events. This is apart from the difference between the destruction of the temple and succeeding events – exile in the first case and political repression in the second – and a systematic scheme to annihilate the entire people. Therefore, since the previous generations had experienced neither a disaster of Holocaustic magnitude nor the sharp transition from devastation to rebirth, one cannot know what their response would have been. Thus one cannot dismiss the slogan 'Never again' – although Jakobovits criticizes it – just as one should not dispute his basic contention that without fostering Judaism Jews will probably be unable to survive as a collective.

Jonathan Sacks asserts the state–Holocaust nexus more explicitly and with greater emphasis than Jakobovits. He also invests it with permanent existential significance: 'The Holocaust has taught us that Jews share a collective fate. The State of Israel has taught us that Jews share a collective responsibility.'[40]

However, Sacks is aware that the state–Holocaust nexus fashioned by the new theology evokes both religious and moral controversy among Jews, in matters such as the relationship between the Jews and their God and the need for a renewed covenant, and in the relationship between religion and the Israeli government's policies toward the Arabs under its control.[41]

This ambivalent result of the state–Holocaust nexus – creation of unity on the one hand and exacerbation of fractiousness on the other – led Sacks to Jakobovits's conclusion: that without full-force Jewish education, the continued unified existence of the Jewish people does not stand a chance.[42]

Consequently, Jakobovits and Sacks did not dismiss the state–Holocaust nexus but downscaled it and defined it in terms of its imme-

diate historical significance: the salvation of Jewish unity and responsibility. Beyond this, they were not willing to march with their
predecessors. Importantly, these predecessors – the leading Modern
Orthodox theologians – also ascribed importance to the return to
Judaism by means of study of its sources, as evidenced in Greenberg's
grass-roots educational enterprise, CLAL. For them, however, the
emphasis focused on the religious and messianic connection and the
state-power relationship between destruction and rebirth as the two
determining indicators of post-Holocaust Judaism.

A different and much less ambiguous message in reducing the
importance of Israel consciousness and Holocaust remembrance for
Jewish continuity is expressed by several Reform theologians, especially in the United States. The first and most moderate of them is
Professor Eugene Borowitz, whose general Jewish *Weltanschauung* may
be defined as non-Zionist. He belongs to the trend of thought in the
Reform movement that accepts the Jewish state, including its relationship with the Diaspora, but rejects the national ideology that it
represents. Accordingly, Borowitz resists the tendency to link the
collective existence of Diaspora Jewry to that of the State of Israel. He
agrees that the existence of Israel is vital for the Jews but stresses that
it is not indispensable.[43] His opposition to Zionism and his personal
principled indecision about the Jewish state provide both a background
and a basis for his view of the role of the Holocaust in shaping Jewish
identity. Borowitz does not deal with this issue at great length –
thereby attesting to the scant importance he attributes to it. However,
in the early 1990s, prompted by the public debate concerning the
establishment and nature of the United States Holocaust Memorial
Museum in Washington, he published an article called 'Rethinking
Our Holocaust Consciousness'.[44] The most important aspect of this
article is not its theological outlook on the essence of the Holocaust but
the trinity – worrisome from his standpoint – between the centrality of
the state, Holocaust consciousness, and the revival of Orthodox
Judaism. In his opinion, this triumvirate first became influential in the
1980s, and he has no doubt about the factors that invigorated it: the
war in Lebanon, the intifada, and the Likud government. This development, which created a profound political controversy between
liberal and conservative American Jews, signifies from his standpoint a
resurgence of particularistic and egocentric Jewish ethnic feelings in
the Diaspora and nationalist sentiments in Israel.

The origins of this process trace back to the Six-Day War. Before
that conflict, in Borowitz's opinion, Israel figured marginally in the

public consciousness of American Jewry. However, the threat to its existence, against the backdrop of the Holocaust, triggered a Diaspora Jewish awakening that elevated Israel to a position of centrality in its collective ethnic consciousness. To put it differently, the centrality of the Holocaust cannot be understood in the absence of national consensus about the centrality of Israel. The two centralities feed each other, and the former gains strength and momentum through the revival of Orthodoxy, which, in greater part, has assimilated religious nationalism.

Borowitz attributes this development to contemporary post-modern culture, which has relativized and particularized every absolute universal value. Consequently, the notion that what's good is what's good for the Jews has gained legitimacy. Therefore, the pairing of the Holocaust – what is bad for the Jews – with the State – what is good for the Jews – actually represents two sides of the same particularistic, anti-universalistic coin.

Borowitz came out against this phenomenon in the name of universal ethics in the spirit of liberal Reform Judaism, which he considers the true message of Judaism in the post-modern era. He believes that notwithstanding the strong ethnic perceptions that have gripped American Jews – in which he acquiesces, although with reservations – an outcome different from that described above is also conceivable. After all, the Jewish commitment to modern moral values is so strong that it can 'occasionally take precedence over the unique focus of our ethnic pride – the State of Israel'.

Consequently, Borowitz's commitment to modern ethical principles, which are essentially universal, transcends his commitment to the ethnic and political cause of the Jews. He enunciated these matters because the Holocaust consciousness had given the Jewish state's use of force a moral justification on top of the religious and political motives that powered it.

Borowitz avoids acute and extreme rhetoric, not only as a matter of style but also because he acknowledges the changes that have swept Jewish society, which has taken a turn for the conservative, and does not reject them all. The other thinkers went much farther than he did.

Indeed, Borowitz's colleague in the Reform movement, Jacob Petuchowski, surpassed him in objecting to the theologization of the Holocaust. Petuchowski was a proclaimed anti-Zionist who rejected the notion of Israel's centrality in the world Jewish reality and, in the old Reform style that survives only among a minority in this movement, ruled out Jewish nationhood altogether. To his mind, Judaism is singular in its religious faith and nothing more. These two premises led him to conclude that Diaspora Jewry, essentially a religious collective, should disengage totally from Israeli Jewry, which constitutes an Israeli nation. However, Petuchowski cannot deny that in historical reality, especially that of the modern era, Jewishness is more than religion alone. Therefore, he reasserts previous arguments to the effect that the Jews are a world family of sorts, endowed with various kinds of kinship, but not, as stated, with nationhood.[45]

Petuchowski began to coalesce his anti-Zionist philosophy after the Six-Day War in view of the national awakening that gripped the Jews. This made him one of an exceptional few in Diaspora Jewish affairs at that time. Thus it is not by chance that he presaged the opposition to the theology of the Holocaust, and it is this seminality that makes him novel. In 1981 – an early date in this sense – he came out against the assertions of Emil Fackenheim and those of like mind that the Holocaust is a unique event in Jewish history. He did not consider it exceptional among the depredations that have befallen the Jews in their history. Therefore, although the Holocaust is related to the formation of the State of Israel, neither event should be treated with such significance as to allude to a divine intent.

In his opinion, the establishment of the State of Israel is an act of political compensation that the Gentile nations gave the Jews for their suffering. This compensation, however, has moral significance and does not justify the policies of the government of Israel – especially the use of the Holocaust for its political needs – with respect to its territorial claims in Arab-populated areas.

By inserting political criticism into the historiosophic debate over the meaning of the Holocaust, Petuchowski laid the foundations for what may be called the politicization of the Holocaust, a counterweight to the theologization of the Holocaust. Thus both conservatives and liberals used the Holocaust as a moral yardstick for assessing the policies of the government of Israel and as a political litmus test in justifying or condemning its actions.

Ten years later, the politicization of the Holocaust reached a climax in the thinking of the young theologian Marc Ellis, whose views commanded space in publications of liberal Reform Judaism and whose books evoked no small interest in certain Christian church circles. Ellis was influenced by a current in church thinking that calls itself the Christian theology of liberation, in the wake of which he attempted to develop a Jewish theology of liberation. This theology addresses itself wholly to the social and political misfortunes of people in changing modern society, with special reference to the plight of Third-World peoples formerly repressed by Western society and now exploited by it. In this fashion, religion, as a social organization that touches upon politics, is involved in politics directly and in principle and uses politics to attain its religious and moral goals. By blurring the boundary between religion and politics, the struggle for liberation of humankind and improvement of its economic condition moves from the political level to the religious. This means that the separation of religion and state, so firmly anchored in Western culture and so funda-mental in Western democracy, becomes less clear. From this point, it is a short distance to the logical premise that society should be run by the clerics who bear these moral ideas.

Among all the personalities we have discussed thus far, Ellis is the least involved in Jewish society. His distance from it is even greater than that of his teacher, Richard Rubenstein, whom Jewish society once boycotted for his views. Because Ellis's radicalism is different from Rubenstein's, resting at the opposite pole, it has had almost no influence on Jewish society. However, for the very reason that it is radical and has attracted attention in non-Jewish society, it expresses a trend of thought that typifies the era and may even point to future developments. As evidence of this, one may cite the proximity of this approach to the views of several radical liberals in Israel, whom we discuss below.

Ellis, as a champion of liberation theology, made it his goal – a mission of sorts – to liberate the Jews from the yoke of Auschwitz and the hegemony of the State of Israel ('deabsolutation'). Auschwitz, he argued, has ostensibly given Israel's aggressive policy toward the Arabs a moral justification, and recognition of the state's hegemony creates a warped relationship of inequality between itself and the Diaspora. In Ellis's opinion, the two phenomena are interrelated, and therefore, 'deabsolutizing the state of Israel means at the same time deabsolutizing the Holocaust'.[46] To deabsolutize the Holocaust, this event must be placed in its correct context: as part of the tragic Jewish past, not as an expectation for the future. This would also liberate Israel from the throes of a redemption that it cannot deliver. Only then, when the historical meaning of the Holocaust is restored, will the Holocaust serve its correct purpose: an urging to stamp out the suffer-ing of human beings, including the Jews and, especially, the Palestinians.

About two years later, Ellis developed this premise by asserting that the liberation of the Jews from the absolution of the Holocaust and the absolute centrality of the state means 'the redefinition of Jewish identity'.[47] The State of Israel, he maintains, cannot stand at the forefront of this collective identity. After all, that the Jews need Israel at the present time does not mean that they will forever. Furthermore, should Israel be destroyed in its wars with the Arabs, the result would indeed be tragic but the Jewish people would continue to exist in far-flung communities. By so arguing, Ellis hopes to liberate Diaspora Jewry from its dread of collective extinction should the State of Israel vanish from the historical scene.

Therefore, the main determining factor in the new Jewish identity is a threefold liberation: from sanctification of the Holocaust, from recognition of the primacy of the State of Israel, and from the Diaspora's dread of extinction. The new Jewish identity, however, should be determined not only by liberation from something but by aspiration toward something: resumption of Jewish moral solidarity among Jews and between Jews and others, primarily the Palestinians. For Jews and Christians, the Palestinian question is fundamentally a theological problem that will be solved by political means, and any political solution that fails to take the Palestinian problem into account will be superficial and short-lived. At the crux of the political content of this theological–political solution is a federative binational state, in the tradition of Judah Magnes and Hannah Arendt in the past and of Noam Chomsky in the present.

Terminating the Jewish–Palestinian conflict is a matter of universal significance. This action will represent one of the last 'stops' in the historical process of oppression of peoples perpetrated by European and North American society. The process began with Columbus's discovery of America in 1492 and continued with the annihilation of Native Americans, the enslavement of African blacks, colonial exploitation, the extermination camps – of which Auschwitz is symbolic – and Israel's oppression of the Palestinians.[48] In Ellis's opinion, it is a matter of therapeutic significance for the Jewish people to merge into the process of liberation from the iniquities of the West. The Jews' convalescence depends on two things: first, they must acknowledge that their rebirth has cost the Jewish people its innocence; from now on, this people, formerly weak if not helpless, has returned to history as a warrior-nation that survives to no small extent through the enslavement of another people. Therefore, it must re-identify with the imperative that emanated from Sinai and Auschwitz and adopt the return to Jewish ethics that these two symbols embody. The second matter, stemming from the first, is the acknowledgment that 'the healing of the Jewish people – that is, the possibility of a Jewish future – is bound up with Palestine and Palestinians precisely because of Auschwitz and the history which preceded it in Europe'.[49]

Therefore, according to Ellis, the therapeutic process pertains to the entire Jewish people, in Israel and in the Diaspora, because of Israel's centrality in the pan-Jewish ethos. In this sense, the Palestinian problem has become the concern of all Jews, an overwhelming majority of whom support the State of Israel. This argumentation leads Ellis into an internal contradiction. By seeking to drive a wedge between the autonomous Diaspora and the Israeli nation-state, Ellis binds them together in fetters of political ethics. Consequently, in effect he reinforces the centrality of Israel in the pan-Jewish reality. The dialectic in his moral–political theology may be likened to the action of a modern Balaam, who steps forth to curse the Israel-Diaspora nexus and finds himself blessing it.

Consequently, by the very virtue of his ultramoralistic outlook, Ellis binds the state and the Holocaust strongly together. For him of all people the exalted object, Jerusalem, depends on the object taken lightly, Auschwitz. This dependency, however, is not theological but political. Dialectically, one may say that for Ellis the political solution is the precondition for a Jewish quasi-theology of liberation.

Summing up, the search for the theological meaning of Jewish existence after the Holocaust and the formation of the Jewish state did not avoid a linkage between the two events. This discourse brought diverse if not clashing types of connectivity to the surface. Berkovits regarded the connection as a covert one; Fackenheim construed it as a mystery that transcends rational perception; Greenberg sought to amend the covenant between God and His people; and Jakobovits and Sacks considered it a historical reality prompted by divine providence.

These thinkers – like Wiesel, who refused to discuss the nexus because of his utter inability to comprehend the actions of God, Rubenstein, who banished God from history, and Ellis, who sought to separate them from the ethical standpoint – could not disregard the connection between the Holocaust and Israel.

This nexus has a positive connotation for all of them, even if they attain it by tortuous paths. This is so whether they regard it as a covert divine plan to mend the world, a policy of force proclaimed to assure the Jewish people's existence, or a symbolic relationship between Auschwitz and Mount Sinai, occasioned either by a messianic revival after the Six-Day War or by a therapeutic process of liberation from the Auschwitz syndrome.

Furthermore, the characteristic feature of this discourse is a confrontation with Jewish identity in the new era of Jewish history occasioned by the aftermath of the Holocaust and the proclamation of statehood. All of these thinkers accept the element of state power as part of this identity. The difference among them resides between two symbolic poles: that of Richard Rubenstein, the teacher, and Marc Ellis, his former pupil. It is true that the former places his trust in the atomic bomb and the latter in ethics, but both agree that without political force and a political settlement a just, humane and Jewish existence is unlikely to occur.

It is these commonalities in the theological discourse, despite profound disagreements in faith and politics among its participants, that distinguish this discourse from the pronouncedly halakhic discussion of this question among *haredi* Jewry. The *haredi* community, even when it began to discuss the meaning of the Holocaust after severe internal vacillation that touched upon the tenets of the faith – as demonstrated in the studies of Eliezer Schweid and Dan Michman – totally disregards the *problematique* arising from the possible nexus, in its historical, political, and theological senses, of the state and the Holocaust.[50] This is apart from the crescendo of attacks on the Zionist leadership, which *haredi* thinkers accuse of malevolent intent to allow the Nazis to obliterate Diaspora Jewry as leverage for forming the Zionist State on the victims' graves.[51]

Thus, in terms of discussing the lesson of the Holocaust, Jewish theologians fall into two groups: those who vacillate about the Holocaust–statehood nexus and those who disregard it. The former group is enumerated among theologians who ponder developments in modern society, are affected by historical events and seek meaning for them, and confront the normalization processes that are sweeping the Jewish people in political and cultural terms. The latter, by disengaging from remembrance of historical time and disregarding normalization as an objective phenomenon, falls outside the parameters of our discussion.

NOTES

1. Eliezer Berkovits, *Faith After the Holocaust* (New York, 1973), pp. 153–8.
2. See Eliezer Berkovits, 'Understanding the Present – to Save the Future', in Yehuda Bauer (ed.), *Remembering for the Future: Working Papers and Addenda*, Vol. 3 (Oxford, 1989), pp. 2347–8.
3. Eliezer Schweid, 'Theological Confrontation with the Holocaust As It Occurred',

Mahanayim (Jerusalem, December 1995), pp. 18–21 [Hebrew].

4. 'Symposium: Jewish Values in the Post-Holocaust Future', *Judaism*, Summer 1967.
5. Emil Fackenheim, 'Jewish Faith and the Holocaust: A Fragment', *Commentary*, August 1967.
6. Emil L. Fackenheim, *To Mend the World*, 2nd edn (New York, 1989), pp. 311–13.
7. Emil Fackenheim, *On Faith and History: An Introduction* (Jerusalem, 1989), p. 23 [Hebrew].
8. Emil Fackenheim, 'The Holocaust and the State of Israel', in *On Faith and History: Essays on Contemporary Judaism* (Jerusalem, 1989), pp. 108–9 [Hebrew].
9. Emil Fackenheim, 'The Jewish Return into History', in *Reflections in the Age of Auschwitz and a New Jerusalem* (New York, 1978), p. 139.
10. Emil Fackenheim, 'Concerning Authentic and Unauthentic Responses to the Holocaust', *Holocaust and Genocide Studies*, Vol. 1, 1986.
11. See Emil Fackenheim, 'The Contemporary Zionist Imperative', *Nativ*, April 1994 [Hebrew].
12. CLAL – The National Jewish Center for Learning and Leadership.
13. Irving Greenberg, *The Third Era of Jewish History: Power and Politics Perspective, A CLAL Thesis* (New York, 1980), pp. 45–6.
14. Irving Greenberg, 'Cloud of Smoke, Pillar of Fire', in Eva Fleishman (ed.), *Auschwitz – Beginning of a New Era?* (New York, 1977), pp. 50–4.
15. Irving Greenberg, 'History, Holocaust and Covenant', in Yehuda Bauer (ed.), *Remembering for the Future*, Vol. 3 (Oxford, 1989), p. 2929.
16. Irving Greenberg, 'History, Holocaust and Covenant', *Holocaust and Genocide Studies*, 1990, No. 1, pp. 8–9.
17. Irving Greenberg, *The Jewish Way* (New York, 1988), pp. 385–6.
18. See his remarks in 'The State of Jewish Belief – A Symposium', *Commentary*, August 1966; and in 'Dilemmas of Jewish Power – Symposium', *Jewish Frontier*, May 1980.
19. Richard Rubenstein, *After Auschwitz: History, Theology, and Contemporary Judaism* (USA, 1966, 1991).
20. See my book, *The State of Israel in Jewish Public Thought: The Quest for Collective Identity*, Chapter 7, 'Neoconservative Radicalism'.
21. Richard L. Rubenstein, 'Naming the Unnameable', *Journal of Reform Judaism*, Spring 1984.
22. Yehuda Bauer and Nathan Rotenstreich, eds, *The Holocaust as Historical Experience: Essays and Discussions* (New York, 1981), pp. 244–5.
23. Richard L. Rubenstein, *After Auschwitz – History, Theology, and Contemporary Judaism* (USA, 1991), pp. xii–xiii.
24. Greenberg, *Remembering for the Future*, p. 2929.
25. Richard Rubenstein, 'Muslims, Jews, and the Western World', in *After Auschwitz*, pp. 288–9.
26. 'Jewish Values in the Post-Holocaust Future', *Judaism*, Summer 1967.
27. Elie Wiesel, 'Words from a Witness', *Conservative Judaism*, Spring 1967.
28. Harry James Cargas, *In Conversation with Elie Wiesel* (USA, 1976), p. 16.
29. Elie Wiesel, 'A Writer's Fears', *Against Silence* (April 1970), Vol. 3, p. 201.
30. Elie Wiesel, 'Are We Worthy of the History?', *Against Silence* (April 1973), p. 282.
31. 'Israel Twenty Years Later', *Against Silence* (April 1968), Vol. 2, p. 190.
32. 'From Holocaust to Rebirth', *Against Silence* (November 1970), Vol. 2, pp. 239–40.

33. 'The Three Times I Saw Jerusalem', *Against Silence* (November 1970), p. 7.
34. Cargas, *In Conversation with Elie Wiesel*.
35. 'Some Reasons for Hope', *Against Silence* (September 1980), Vol. 3, p. 210.
36. 'Elie Wiesel, An Interview', August 1989, in Carol Rittner and John Roth (eds), *Memory Offended: The Auschwitz Convent Controversy* (New York, 1991), p. 113.
37. 'Für die Toten und die Lebenden', *Frankfurter Rundschau*, 7 January 1995.
38. Immanuel Jakobovits, *If Only My People – Zionism in My Life* (London, 1984), pp. xi–xii.
39. I. Jakobovits, 'How the Chief Rabbi Sees the Holocaust', *Jewish Chronicle*, 12 August 1988. This is part of I. Jakobovits, 'Some Personal, Theological, and Religious Responses to the Holocaust', in Yehuda Bauer (ed.), *Remembering for the Future*, Vol. 3.
40. Jonathan Sacks, 'The Way Forward', *Jewish Chronicle*, 29 September 1989.
41. Jonathan Sacks, *Crisis and Covenant: Jewish Thought after the Holocaust* (Manchester/New York, 1992), pp. 50–1, 80–2.
42. Jonathan Sacks, *One People? Tradition, Modernity, and Jewish Unity* (London, 1993), p. 254; Jonathan Sacks, 'Restoring Mystery and Romance', *Jewish Chronicle*, 30 July 1993.
43. Borowitz's liberal-Reform Jewish outlook and attitude toward the State of Israel is discussed in my book, *The State of Israel in Jewish Public Thought: The Quest for Collective Identity*, pp. 240–7.
44. Eugene B. Borowitz, 'Rethinking Our Holocaust Consciousness', *Judaism*, Fall 1991.
45. Jacob J. Petuchowski, 'Dissenting Thoughts about the Holocaust', *Journal of Reform Judaism*, Fall 1981.
46. Marc H. Ellis, *Beyond Innocence and Redemption: Confronting the Holocaust and Israeli Power* (USA, 1990), p. 187.
47. Marc H. Ellis, *Toward a Jewish Theology of Liberation: The Uprising and the Future*, 2nd edn (New York, 1992), p. 131.
48. M. H. Ellis, 'Ending Auschwitz and 1492: Reflections on the Future of Jewish and Christian Life', *European Judaism*, Spring 1994.
49. Marc H. Ellis, 'Jewish Religious Thought and the Challenge of Solidarity', *European Judaism*, Spring 1990.
50. See Eliezer Schweid, *Until Dawn*, Part 2 (Tel Aviv, 1990), pp. 143–239 [Hebrew]; Eliezer Schweid, 'Theological Confrontation with the Holocaust As It Occurred', *Mahanayim*, (Jerusalem, December 1995), pp. 10–35 [Hebrew]; Dan Michman, *The Impact of the Holocaust on Religious Jewry: Basic Changes in the Jewish People Pursuant to the Holocaust* (Jerusalem, 1996), pp. 613–56.
51. See Dinah Porat, 'Amelek's Accomplices: Accusations of the Ultraorthodox in 1980s Israel Against Holocaust-Era Zionism', *Zionism*, 19 (Tel Aviv, 1995), pp. 295–324 [Hebrew]. See also Dina Porat, 'Manipulation of the Rebbes', *Ha'aretz*, 12 April 1991.

3

The Academic Discourse

In all cases of genocide, however brutal they may be, one can discern pragmatic motives – political, economic – that are translated into ideology. Whereas in the Holocaust, pure ideological falsehood is the prime motive.

Yehuda Bauer and Yisrael Gutman,
'The Archimedean Point is Ideology', *Ha'aretz*, 16 April 1998.

The academic discourse, unlike the theological discourse, concerns not the mysteries of God but historical reality – not a quest for the metaphysical meaning of the events but an attempt to understand them in corporeal terms. Therefore, it lacks the salient intermingling of ethics and politics that typified the previous discourse. The complexion here is determined, to a decisive extent, by its academic setting, in which methodology takes the place of theology. However, the academic discourse, like the theological discourse, is not free of ideological influence. Accordingly, as this chapter will show, it usually exhibits a correlation between methodology and ideology.

The main protagonists in this discourse are historians, sociologists, and philosophers. Notably, the historians stand apart from the others. Their sole concern is study of the Jewish Holocaust; the others deal mainly with the study of society at large. For this reason, the intellectual conclusions are affected not only by the methodology but by the *a priori* definition of the discipline.

However, notwithstanding its ideological nature, this discourse is free of political debate. Accordingly, it avoids direct discussion of the Holocaust–state nexus; instead, it deals with the nexus indirectly – more at the implicit than at the explicit level. This, of course, distinguishes it from its precursor, the theological discourse.

The academic discourse revolves around an attempt to determine where the Holocaust fits into world historical and social developments, especially in the modern era. The major question is whether the Holocaust is a particularistic Jewish phenomenon or a universalistic one. Therefore, one may consistently find a comparative dimension in this discourse between the singular and the general. This partly lifts the subject out of the Jewish framework, in which most of the theologians placed it, and sets it on a general plane. Thus, whereas the theologians asked themselves whether the Holocaust was exceptional relative to the Jews' previous catastrophes, the historians and sociologists attempted – to varying degrees – to compare it with massacres and annihilations that befell other peoples both during and before World War II.[1]

Notably, precisely because of the comparison method which by nature often blurs differences among historical or social phenomena, the relationship between ideology and methodology is complex and seldom lends itself to predetermined outcomes. To put it differently, the particularistic and universalistic approaches in the research are driven by worldviews, especially with respect to the national question as a general and, particularly, a Jewish problem. Paradoxically and tragically, the disaster that befell the Jews – which none of the discussants denies or belittles – has become a tool in the controversy over the existence or nonexistence of a Jewish nation with its own historical singularity. This controversy was, of course, stoked by the various researchers' Zionist, non-Zionist, and anti-Zionist attitudes, and it is linked to the tension – and at times the clash – between two views of Jewish existence: as a nationality, as in Zionism, and as an ethnicity, as in the Diaspora. In this sense, the distinction between universalists and particularists becomes very complex, because their attitudes are not stationed at opposite poles. Universalists do not disregard the uniquenesses of the Jewish ethnic collectivity, even when dealing with the context of the Holocaust, and particularists treat the Holocaust as a special case in the general historical process, admittedly different from similar instances of mass murder but not totally distinct from them. Even the earliest particularists, who launched the debate while the war still raged and pursued it afterwards, and who were susceptible to the shock surrounding the extent of the Holocaust, did not overlook the general context. The first to phrase this particularistic point of view was the patriarch of Zionist historiography, Benzion Dinur. Dinur laid the foundations of an integrated perspective that regards the Holocaust as the outcome of three factors: the Jews' state of exile, the rise of the modern totalitarian state, and the Nazi regime's exceptional murderous intent toward the Jews.

Dinur was the first to treat the Holocaust as an event that altered the progression of Jewish history and the first to link it with the national revival. In 1943, even before the results of the Holocaust were fully known and before anyone could grasp the full intent of the engineers of the Nazi genocide machine, Dinur asserted that 'the historical campaign, highly illuminated during these days of horror, is one of "exiles and their destruction"'. Thus in his famous essay of that name, he actually links the Jews' state of exile to destruction as a decree of historical fate, from which only one path of escape is known: a special exertion to return to the Jews' historical homeland. After all, he says, this ordeal, foisted upon the Jewish people, is 'a special engagement, unique to our history, and it is this that makes [this history] singular, to our disaster and our evolution'.

Here, in diametrical contrast to the views of his mentor, Simon Dubnow, Dinur elaborates a historical dictum, for which the reports of the mass annihilation of European Jewry served as the ultimate tragic support. Figuratively, he states: 'In fact, what is the real substance of that phenomenon that our historiography regularly terms a "transfer of centers", if not the annihilation of these Diaspora communities and the formation of other ones? Are these new communities not also on the verge of annihilation? Have they not been consigned to this fate from the time they were first formed?' This, however, does not suffice from his point of view. After all, 'If we give some slight thought to the size of these Diaspora communities and the extent of their annihilation, we will find that the word "annihilation" utterly fails to encapsulate their decline, with hardly a memory or a trace.' Therefore, he concludes that the current annihilation is 'not new in our history. Its novelty lies in its form and magnitude, in the calculated way in which it was organized, and in its horrifying magnitude.'[12]

Paradoxically, the Holocaust outlooks of the Zionist Dinur and of *haredi* and modern Orthodoxy are similar in one respect. For all of them, the Holocaust has no substantive singularity of its own; it is but one link in a chain of mayhems that has buffeted the Jewish people in its history. Each, of course, understands the reasons and draws the conclusions in different ways, but in the very assumption of a special continuity of annihilations, they are one and the same.

However, Dinur as a historian, not a theologian or a mystic, is not at liberty to disregard the novelty of this phenomenon. Its origins lie in the transformation of the Jews' status in the modern state, the nature of which is determined by developments utterly unrelated to the Jews. Back in 1943, in a lecture to teachers and educators, Dinur attempted to explain the fate of European Jewry in view of the nature of the modern state. About twelve years before Hannah Arendt published her famous book *The Origins of Totalitarianism*, Dinur spoke of a state that is 'total' irrespective of the nature of its ruling regime – communist, fascist, or even liberal – in contrast to liberal or democratic states, in which the government sets itself limits and demarcates certain areas for individual liberties. He also spoke about the Jews' special status in such a state. The total state, in his opinion, creates one life system that holds a dominant position in political power and political struggle. Such a state leads Jews into an objective existential contradiction. On the one hand, they are inseparably integrated into the culture of the modern state. They are active in general domains and struggle on behalf of general national interests. On the other hand, the very fact of this participation in life in the modern state elevates the traditional resistance, embedded in the culture of the European peoples, to a greater intensity. The result is a new rendering of antisemitism. The medieval Jews, cloistered in ghettos, were despised by the surrounding society, from which they were segregated, and the Jews in the modern state, who emerged from their ghettos spiritually, economically, and even psychologically, are similarly loathed. The Jewish tragedy is unique in that 'the Jew cannot gather himself into the ghetto as fully as our enemies wish. He cannot abstract himself from his reality, his essence. This is the origin of the antisemitic venom. In its every fiber and desire, antisemitism wishes to destroy us. Nor has it ever concealed this wish.'[3]

Two years later, at the end of the war, Dinur developed this view and focused it on the period beginning in the late nineteenth century and ending in the 1940s. In his opinion, 'The Jews' war for existence, in which we find ourselves in the midst of one of the most terrible campaigns, has already been waged in this form for sixty years or more. During these years, we have reached a grave watershed in our historical fate. Warning after warning, outcry after outcry have been enunciated throughout this period, each graver than its precursor.'[4] If we attempt to interpret Dinur in view of the principle that quantity determines quality, then the difference between the hatred of Jews in the ancient and medieval world and modern antisemitism and the Nazis' murderous racism, in terms of the intensity of their enmity toward the Jews, is not only quantitative but qualitative. Hence, the historical continuum of Jewish annihilations, at least in terms of their assailants' intent, is not so clear. Indeed, Dinur himself recognized the Holocaust as an anomaly both in the Jews' experiences in exile and in their relations with the surrounding Gentile peoples. In 1955, twelve years after he made these remarks, Dinur stated that the historiography of the Holocaust can never ignore the singularity of the event. In Dinur's view, the Holocaust, relative to the mayhem and persecution that the Jews have experienced since the late nineteenth century, is unique in that 'destruction of the Jews was proclaimed as a goal and a program. For the first time, we observe in history the systematic fulfillment of Haman's scheme – an "Operation Haman" – not as the decree of a king's minister, a command, but as a war of annihilation. A state, a great power, made available its entire political, administrative, and military apparatus for the purpose of annihilating the Jews, and it pledged its entire scientific might to this goal. Why? – they are enemies, they proclaimed overtly for all the world to hear. The Jews are such enemies that one does not argue with them but instead destroys them.'[5] This is a well-formed and current locution, based on research and study performed during the ten years that had lapsed since the war – an endeavor that he had initiated and whose contours he had elaborated at the end of the war. As early as 1943 he had observed the difference between the Holocaust and the destruction of Jewish communities in German towns in the Middle Ages. In the past, he says, the antipathy was harbored mainly by the illiterate masses; various rulers, princes, and bishops protected the Jews. Now, in contrast, the entire modern totalitarian state is mobilized for a sweeping campaign of utter, all-inclusive annihilation, and half of the Jewish people faced this menace.[6]

Dinur's views on the relative singularity of the Holocaust in the continuum of Jewish history were accepted by most Jewish historians who debated the matter; they were also invoked when they debated the universalistic as against the particularistic perspectives on the Holocaust. Thus, the doyen of Jewish historians, the great Salo Baron – who dealt little with the Holocaust – considered the Holocaust unique in that Nazism left the Jews no path of escape, not even conversion, as had been acceptable in the Middle Ages.[7] Baron clearly refrained from identifying with Dinur's inclusive historiographic *Weltanschauung*. Instead, his perceptions were close to those of his mentor, Dubnow. Because he observed everything that was favorable and vital in the lives of Diaspora Jews, he argued vehemently against the lachrymose perception of Jewish history, which stems directly and indirectly from the 'exile-and-destruction' teachings of Dinur. However, they concurred about the meaning of the devastation that the Holocaust had caused. This may reflect more than a rational analysis of the phenomenon, since after the Holocaust Baron partly accepted the teachings of Ahad Ha'am and concluded that the Zionist 'negation of the Diaspora' doctrine had positive value in Jewish life in Ahad Ha'am's time, because it motivated them to sustain their national culture and be creative within it. Before and during the war, Baron had viewed matters differently. In 1944, he believed that Jewish life in Europe could be fully restored with the help of American Jewry. At that time, he defined the Jews not as a nation but as a coreligionist community. Two years later, realizing what the Holocaust had done to the Jewish people generally and its European center specifically, he changed his mind. From then on, he spoke of an existential reciprocity between Jewry in the free countries and in the national center in Palestine/Israel.[8] In other words, after contemplating the harshest 'lachrymose chapter' in Jewish history, Baron recognized Zionism as essential for Jewish existence. Consequently, just as the destruction of European Jewry shed no light on the preceding devastations, as Dinur mistakenly believed – after all, he had noticed the singularity of the Holocaust – so Jewish history cannot be understood without the 'tears', because the crucial turning points in the progression of this history took place as a result of destructions: obliteration of the Jewish center in Palestine, the expulsion from Spain, and the Holocaust.

Jacob Talmon, another member of the group of historians who mentored a generation of successors who discussed and probed the Holocaust, followed Dinur's line but adopted a different emphasis and a different rationale. As a historian of the modern era who discovered the baggage of destruction that political messianism carries, he compared the annihilations of the past with the Holocaust and, from the general perspective, reached the same conclusion that Dinur and Baron had adduced from Jewish history. After enumerating most of the mass killings from antiquity up to World War I, he concluded that the Nazis' annihilation of European Jewry was different – in its conscious detail, its painstaking planning, its methodical fulfillment, its lack of a factor of emotional fervor, and its stringently implemented decision to wipe out everything[9] and thwart any possibility of rescue, as, for example, by the public denial of Jewish origin.

However, Talmon does not fully accept Dinur's main contention that the roots of the Holocaust lie in a unique antisemitism dating uninterruptedly to the Hellenistic period. Even if one admits that 'antisemitism is an autonomous spectacle or a primeval and uninterrupted phenomenon', he argues, 'it is, in whatever form, a function of factors exogenous to it; it is set within a web that provides more comprehensive support'.[10]

To put it differently, the advent of antisemitism during the era that began with the French Revolution and lasted until the Bolshevik revolution, the Fascist coup, and the two world wars; a time in which the political messianism that promised to redeem humankind lured the masses; a time of which mass killing became emblematic; this is the time that Talmon defined as 'the age of violence'.

Dinur and Talmon disagree in that the former ascribes the greatest importance to antisemitism as a singular phenomenon and treats general factors such as the totalitarian state as of secondary significance. The latter, in contrast, does not belittle the importance of the singular element but tends to emphasize the general element more strongly. In one respect, however, the two scholars are indistinguishable: both Dinur and Talmon – although they demanded that Holocaust research and discussion be liberated from various kinds of mystification and treated from a balanced, empirical, rational, historical perspective devoid of metaphysical and theological questions – exhibit such sentiments in assessing the birth of the State of Israel after the Holocaust. This spirit emanates from Dinur's remarks about the Yad Vashem bill[11] (the Remembrance of Holocaust and Heroism – Yad Vashem Law), which Jacob Talmon expressed in his poetic rhetoric. In Talmon's view, 'There isn't a person whose heart will not pound and whose imagination will not sing at the sight of our amazing recovery, [our] eruption of tremendous energy, [our] stunning power of resourcefulness on the morrow of the greatest disaster and humiliation in our history.'[12] Even when he criticized Israeli government policies after the Six-Day War, Talmon prefaced his remarks with the following: 'You need not be a heart-and-soul Zionist to admit that the act of establishing the State of Israel is the most salient creative achievement of the Jewish people – as a cohesive collective – in the past two millennia and one of the mightiest feats in all of human history.'[13]

Shmuel Ettinger, a student of Dinur's and a colleague of Talmon's, carried forward the attitude that traced the Holocaust to the historical hatred of Jews and the nature of the past century, which Talmon termed the age of violence. However, Ettinger added another layer to the debate. In his opinion, the ascendancy of antisemitism was also rooted in changes in the Jews' status among the peoples of Europe, which he attributes to three kinds of political activity: political actions by Eastern European Jews laden with revolutionary tension, especially in the Russian Empire; the buildup of political strength of the new Jewish center in the United States; and the advent of Zionism as an autonomous national movement.

For various reasons, says Ettinger, these political developments aggravated the tension between the Jews and the surrounding peoples, thereby whetting historical antisemitism. This, under the specific social and political conditions of the time, greatly facilitated the Nazis' drive to implement their scheme in the European continent that they had occupied.[14]

These formulations of Talmon, Dinur, and Ettinger concerning the Holocaust, and their sense of mystery in pondering the formation of the State of Israel, were carried forth by Lucy Dawidowicz, the doyen of Holocaust historians in the United States. The title of her famous book, *The War against the Jews*,[15] speaks for itself. The book stresses that two factors converged to bring about the Holocaust: the antisemitic pathology of Hitler and the German people, and the organized system of the modern state. Dawidowicz was not a Zionist in the sense that Dinur and Talmon were; her national worldview and positivistic historical perceptions approximated the outlooks of Simon Dubnow. As such, she condemned the approach of certain Zionist historians who, although she did not cite them by name, must have included Dinur who, she says, deemed Jewish statehood a historical necessity.[16] Just the same, she, like Talmon, departed from the straight path of positivism and empiricism when she assessed the long-term progression of modern Jewish history. In this context, she was willing to accept the views of Yitzhak Baer, a great historian with a Zionist outlook, who argued that Jewish history has its own laws that move – especially in the modern era – between poles of destruction and deliverance. Such poles are Holocaust and statehood, the exodus of the Arab countries' Jewish communities and the miracle of the Six-Day War, and the devastation of Jewish life in Soviet Russia and the redemption of this Jewish community from Communist coercion. Dawidowicz concluded this lecture with the following pronouncement: 'Whether we are believers or skeptics about providential destiny, we must admit that Baer was right: that Jewish history follows its own laws.'[17]

There is undoubtedly a connection between this historical perception and Lucy Dawidowicz's affiliation in the 1980s with the Jewish neo-conservative current, which stressed Jewish singularity in both the substantive sense and in terms of national interest.[18]

Among the second generation of Holocaust historians, the one closest to Dinur's doctrine is Israel Gutman, a leading figure at Yad Vashem and a crafter of its academic doctrine. In the early 1990s, undoubtedly in response to the escalating debate over the singularity of the Holocaust – which had moved into the public domain – and the controversy surrounding the establishment of the Holocaust museum in Washington, Gutman summed up several basic assumptions in Holocaust research at Yad Vashem. First,'The Holocaust is perceived, above all, as an event in Jewish history and should be examined in view of processes of continuity and change among the Jews.' This argument allows scholars to explore the uniqueness of the Holocaust relative to previous violence and destruction that had befallen the Jews and to link these events with the general development of modern society. Second, 'The uniqueness of the Holocaust is based on an elucidation and analysis of the role of racist antisemitism in the *Weltanschauung* of Hitler and National Socialism and the phases in which the Nazi Third Reich put this perception into practice during the war.'[19] Thus, racist hate that targets only the Jews is one of the fundamentals in the pathological intellectual world of Hitler and National Socialism. Therefore, it (along with other factors) helps us attain a comprehensive understanding of the Nazism phenomenon. Consequently, Gutman upheld the singularity of the Holocaust but did not object to linking it with general developments. To reinforce this stance, he explained that the *a priori* emphasis on the singularity of the Holocaust does not rule out – and actually encourages – a comparative research method that examines 'the responses and behaviors of other peoples in similar if not identical situations'.

Four years later, when the fashion of public debate about the meaning of the Holocaust came to Israel and prompted a dispute in the newspapers between historians and non-historians concerning this singularity, Gutman wrote an article whose headline needs no elaboration: 'There's No Escaping the "Singularity" of the Holocaust'. In this article, he discusses how difficult it is to define the Holocaust as unique precisely because recent general interest has mounted so vigorously as to have universalized the event. Universalization occurs in two contexts: expansion of the act of annihilation during World War II to other peoples and other social groups, and use of the term holocaust to denote all acts of killing and genocide in history. Gutman stresses that with its proliferation of meanings, the term holocaust has eroded in the sense of a historical phenomenon in time, setting, and intent. Therefore, even when he displays understanding of the universalization of the Holocaust, and even when he seems to exude some satisfaction with the evolution of a topic that had been the esoteric concern of a handful of scholars into one of the most important issues in Western academia and intellectual debate, he does not retreat from his basic sensibility, as professed by his great mentors. Therefore, Gutman adds:

However, it seems to me that in the consciousness of modern man and in the meaning given this term in every dictionary worthy of the name, the reference is to the sufferings of the Jewish people, to the plan to exterminate the entire people, and to the killing of these millions by the Germans.

Nevertheless, within the contours of his basic assumptions for historical assessment of the Holocaust, Gutman categorizes the Holocaust among those universal historical events 'whose impact has left its mark and is penetrating paths of thought and emotion that are difficult to judge but that gather a strength of memory and a substance of significance for generations'.[20]

Professor Saul Friedlander, the historian of Nazism, has stationed himself alongside Gutman. Unlike Gutman, who as a member of Ha-shomer ha-Tsa'ir in the Warsaw Ghetto and a former kibbutz member in Israel has deep Zionist roots, Friedlander came to Eretz Israel and Zionism as an outsider, from universal Western culture and an assimilated Jewish family, with which he continues to wage an indecisive dialogue. On the singularity of the Holocaust as a historical phenomenon, however, he entertains no uncertainties. He believes that the uninhibited ambition of Nazism to annihilate the Jewish people sets the Holocaust apart from all the Nazis' other killings and defies rational explanation in the context of ideational and political developments in modern society, such as fascism, totalitarianism, imperialism, etc. In sum, Friedlander regards the Nazis' actions as a novelty that nevertheless fits into the continuity of persecution of Jews over the generations.[21] Thus, from this standpoint Friedlander is even more radical than Gutman, or the other way around: since Gutman expressed himself ten years after Friedlander, one may say that he rendered Friedlander's *Weltanschauung* more moderate.

Two scholars who have spoken at greater length than others on the issue of Holocaust singularity are Steven Katz, professor of the history of modern Jewish thought and philosophy, and Professor Yehuda Bauer, a founding member and doctrinal guide of Yad Vashem.

Steven Katz, a third-generation American Jew, has been laboring on a vast and comprehensive research enterprise that has one goal only: to prove that the Holocaust is unique relative to the other mass killings in history and, especially, in the modern era, which he dates from the discovery of America. In this enterprise, which compares the annihilation of the Indians in South America, the Armenians, and the Gypsies, Katz also describes the methodical killings perpetrated in the Soviet

Gulag – all for the purpose of contrasting them with the Holocaust of European Jewry.

The entire project is supposed to be published in three volumes, of which only the first has come out thus far. The first installment in this trilogy of gore, along with publications that preceded it, allows one to pinpoint Katz's intent but not to discuss his final conclusions.[22] For the time being, one may say that Katz is attempting to define the Holocaust by process of elimination, i.e., by demonstrating what it is not or what is not unique about it. First, in comparison with other historical cases, he does not consider the Holocaust quantitatively unique either in the number of its victims and their share in the population or in the obliteration of population concentrations and cultural centers. It is not unique, he says, in political terms or in its imperialistic economic intentions, such as enslaving a population group to exploit its labor. Neither is it singular in its Christian religious motives, because the victims were not given the option of out-conversion. All that remains – this being Katz's evident point – is the Nazis' unique *intent*, the likes of which human history has never witnessed.

Katz's Nazi-intention doctrine is unquestionably related to his Zionist worldview, which, parenthetically, is more than slightly aberrant among American Jews in the vehement public enunciation that he gives it. In his opinion, Zionism is the only correct answer to all the Jews' disillusionments with the hope of progress, especially in Europe: the Emancipation, the Haskalah, assimilation, cultural patriotism, Marxism, and anti-Zionist Jewish socialism. All these hopes were consumed in the pyres of Auschwitz. Zionism, in contrast to all of these, even when it does not attain all its goals and evokes disenchantment among not a few of its supporters, is the only Jewish answer that promises Jews a collective or national life. Therefore, Zionism and Zionism alone has frustrated Hitler's intent and plan to obliterate the Jewish people.

Thus, the Holocaust, an expression of Hitler's general intent, and Zionism, which frustrated this intent, converge in Katz's thinking. By propagating this view, Katz carries on and develops the thinking of Emil Fackenheim and Irving Greenberg, two theologians on whose teachings he wrote a comprehensive historical study. In this sense, he is undoubtedly one of the most visible scholars who probed the unique contours of the Holocaust in order to perfect this point of view.

In contrast to Katz, an American Zionist who has immersed himself in a mammoth effort to demonstrate what is unique about the Holocaust, Yehuda Bauer, an Israeli Zionist, has moved, following

years of research and intellectual effort on Holocaust history, from a
particularistic stance toward a universalistic view: from staunch public
stipulation of the Jewish uniqueness of Holocaust to obtuse distinctions between Holocaust and genocide.

Bauer took up this matter publicly as early as 1980, after President
Jimmy Carter decided to appoint a public commission to commemorate the Holocaust in the United States. He warned against the trend,
evinced in the remarks of the president and those who influenced him
and encouraged him to make them, of expanding the concept of
Holocaust to include all the victims of the Nazi regime, half of whom
were not Jewish. The problem with this trend, Bauer believed, is that
'the Holocaust is in danger of becoming de-Judaized and
Americanized'.[23]

Thus, Bauer called attention to a trend that would gain much
momentum in public thought and legitimacy: the Americanization of
the Holocaust. As he did so, however, he developed the ideas of Dinur,
Baron, Talmon, and especially Dawidowicz. He, like they, considered
the Holocaust unique in its overall genocidal intent, its painstaking
planning, and its resolute effort to obliterate a specific national group.
He stressed in particular that the Nazis perceived the Jews as their
sworn enemies because of their vast influence on those Western
governments belligerent toward Germany. Thus Bauer, like
Dawidowicz, believed that Hitler, in theory and in practice, embarked
on a war against the Jewish people worldwide. Moreover, Bauer stated,
Nazism espoused a quasi-religious apocalyptic ideology that justified
the genocidal act.

From this standpoint, Bauer maintained that the genocidal actions
perpetrated against the Armenians in World War I and the Gypsies in
World War II do not resemble the Jewish Holocaust. The Armenians
were massacred for nationalistic reasons; the Gypsies were murdered
for motives that were not racial but social. In both horrifying cases, the
genocide was not total. Its intended victims could avoid their fate: the
persecuted Armenians by embracing Islam, the Gypsies by joining a
more respectable socioeconomic class. Furthermore, Gypsies were
considered to be of Aryan racial descent and, in certain cases, were
actually drafted into some units of the Wehrmacht.

That same year, Bauer expressed this idea with greater vehemence
in a debate with the former 'Canaanite' intellectual Boaz Evron, differ-
entiating clearly between mass killings among other peoples and the
Holocaust of European Jewry. The Nazis, he said, regarded the Jews
neither as human beings, for only they were such, nor as subhumans,

like the Slavic peoples. Instead, '[viewing] the Jew as the "anti-race", the "anti-human", … they regarded the Jew as the devil'.[24]

Nevertheless, he is troubled by the Turkish government's genocide of the Armenians during World War I. For nearly twenty years, he has repeatedly taken up comparisons between the two tragedies.[25] The more he does so, the more one senses that he finds similarities between them. Underlying the internal dynamic of Bauer's thinking is his progressive Zionist worldview, his leadership of a group of intellectuals that established an association for humanistic Judaism, and his personal involvement in American academic circles that show a growing tendency to universalize the Holocaust.

Thus Bauer's worldview led him to gradual recognition of the universal meaning of the Holocaust. He took the first step seven years after he spoke vehemently against the Americanization of the Holocaust and warned about the implicit danger of this trend. In 1987, he attempted to construe the Germans' motives in exterminating the Jewish people as a global ideology of sorts that purported to liberate European society and all of humankind, not only Germany, from the Jewish menace.[26] In other words, it is in fact the Germans' intent that makes the Holocaust universal, and because of this universal intent, with its unparalleled absolutism, scale, and fixity of purpose, Bauer proposes to subject genocide to rankings. He distinguishes between total annihilation, which he terms holocaust, and annihilation that is partial in both intent and extent, which he terms genocide. Thus, every act of mass killing resides somewhere on the universal continuum between genocide and holocaust. On this continuum, the slaughter of the Armenians is the act most similar to the Holocaust but is not identical to it. Beyond holocaust, a total event vis-à-vis the Jews, there lies only one possibility, the product of modern society: annihilation of all of humankind. According to this ranking, it is the 'war against the Jews', to use Lucy Dawidowicz's term, that makes the Holocaust universal. This prompts Bauer to conclude that 'those Jewish commentators who wish to diminish the horrific dimensions of the Holocaust by slipping it into the context of Jewish history, in which it refuses to be ingested, are utterly mistaken. The work of explaining the Holocaust does not mean it can be subjected to exercises like these.' Instead, he considers the Holocaust 'a singular and special event in human history, one that was perpetrated against a certain people, for certain reasons, at a certain time, and one that also presents a universal threat to humankind'.[27]

Bauer's opposition to the confinement of the Holocaust in a cell of

Jewish history and his argument that the Holocaust is unique because it was perpetrated against a certain people for certain reasons seem mutually exclusive. Since this certain people is the Jewish people and none other, the Holocaust must belong to its history above all. The same may be said about the certain reasons, some of which are in fact general but others are very specifically Jewish. These reasons include not only the pathological, pseudo-religious messianic attitude of Nazism, which aspired to liberate human society from the Jews – as Bauer correctly stresses – but the attitude toward the Jews of other European peoples, those which the Nazis enslaved. Transcending this, however, is the blind-eye behavior exhibited toward the murdered Jews by the governments that fought the Nazis. Nor can one disregard the hostile and antisemitic cultural residue toward the Jews that these peoples had accrued over the generations. The uniqueness of the Holocaust resides here, in the Jews' exceptional historical condition.

There is no doubt that Bauer's views changed direction signifi-cantly in the ten years following his attack on the Americanization and universalization of the Holocaust. To probe this fully, I shall cite his remarks in full, as he expressed them in his aforementioned article in the early 1990s. After Bauer, like Steven Katz, rejects by process of elimination the uniqueness of the Holocaust in terms of its casualty toll and the proportion of the Jewish population that perished; after he compares the extent of murderous brutality against the Jews with the Turks' treatment of the Armenians in World War I and the Germans' abuse of Poles and Russian Communists in World War II; and after he noted the Nazis' mistreatment of the terminally ill among their own people – he concluded that 'The murderers' motivation was unique since Nazi ideology regarded Jews everywhere as a satanic force that, if not eradicated, might corrupt and sunder humanity and obliterate the entire population of the globe. ... This type of pseudo-religious, pseudo-messianic idea was unique.' On the basis of this premise, he states with authoritative fervor: 'I maintain that what made the Holocaust unique was the murderers' motivation.'[28] In his remarks on the Nazis' pseudo-religious pathology, Bauer followed the lead of his late friend, Professor Uriel Tal, who was the first to explore the Nazis' perception of Jews as the carriers and emblems of anti-Nazism in the sense of 'spiritual values, conscience, and morality'. From their stand-point, Tal argued, 'to vanquish the Jews was ... tantamount to evidence of a victory over monotheism and its heritage in human civilization'.[29] However, Tal also commented on the equilibrium between the pan-human significance of the Holocaust and its specific lesson for the

Jews. Shortly before his untimely death, he explained:

> The historical lesson is … an organic lesson for Jewish history. The Jews' fate is a particularistic one, unique to the Jewish people, and their suffering is a singular suffering. What makes this special, however, is that this historical singularity is instructive of all of human history, and just as Judaism contributed monotheism to the world, so it has contributed a lesson to history that is neither enclosed in a ghetto nor limited to the fate of the Jews. Instead, its crux is that the Holocaust came upon a people at a time when political trust had been given exclusive, sanctified, and absolute authority, and at a time when relative values had become absolute and vice versa: when absolute values had become relative.[30]

These remarks reflect Tal himself. Because his consciousness, faith, and life were altogether those of a particularistic Jew and a universalistic personality, Tal was the first Israeli Zionist historian who saw a universal moral mission, apart from Jewish historical singularity, in the lesson of the Holocaust. His idea – that this universalistic lesson of abysmal evil on the one hand and horrific human suffering on the other hand must serve humanity – underlies the worldview that justifies the establishment of the Holocaust Museum in Washington.

Yehuda Bauer adopted Tal's approach and brought it into clearer focus. This is what prompted him to abandon his reservations about the idea of the Holocaust Museum at its outset, ten years ago, and to become a fervent supporter of this enterprise. His initial opposition to the Americanization of the Holocaust gave way to a view of uniqueness and universality as two sides of one coin where the Holocaust is concerned. However, his remarks leave one with the impression that the particularist-Jewish component and the universalist-global element are not fully in balance. After all, the Jewish suffering displayed at the museum is not an object in itself; it is a teaching aid of sorts, meant to warn society against the recurrence of actions such as these, which may assail any collectivity, not only the Jews. Underlying this perception, which strongly underscores the universal element of the Holocaust, are Bauer's objections to attempts by theologians and ideologues on the Israeli and American far Right to transform the Jewish people into the eternal victims of a hostile surrounding world, with the implications of this posture for the behavior of Jews among Gentiles, Jewish–Gentile relations, and Israeli government policies toward the Arabs.[31]

Here we believe it important to stress the difference in the views of

the two leading historians in Holocaust research in Israel, who helped
lay the methodological foundations of this discipline: Yehuda Bauer
and Israel Gutman. For Gutman, the uniqueness of the Holocaust lies
in Jewish history; for Bauer, it lies in the history of German Nazism.
Gutman examines its implications for the present, foremost in the
meaning of Jewish existence; Bauer – today – regards it as a matter of
pan-human consequence. Gutman applauds the expansion of
Holocaust teaching and scholarship from the narrow confines of
Jewish studies into a topic of worldwide concern, but he does not
consider this a universalistic mission as Bauer does. This difference
between them mirrors the symbolic difference between Yad Vashem in
Jerusalem and the Holocaust Museum in Washington.

In 1997, as the World Zionist Organization marked its centenary
and as Holocaust scholars, including his own students, honed their
universalistic leanings, Yehuda Bauer reiterated forcefully and lucidly
the stance he took twenty years before in two articles in the newspaper
Ha'aretz.[32] The titles of these articles speak for themselves: 'Why Did
They Murder Jews and Not Cyclists?' and 'The Holocaust Is Indeed
Unique!' In the first article, he seeks the answer to his question in the
specific historical situation in which a specific people, the Jews, was
placed. 'It is simply impossible', he wrote, 'to understand this act of
genocide without dealing with the Jews' station in European society,
their relations with the peoples of Europe in pre-Holocaust periods,
their community organizations, and their responses to the encroaching
danger, not to mention their responses during the Holocaust itself.' In
the second article, Bauer restates, one by one, his arguments in the
1980s concerning the uniqueness of the Holocaust relative to other
instances of genocide, and from this point of departure he arrives at a
dialectic approach of sorts between singularity and universality. In his
opinion, there is no contradiction between the two, because

> the very fact that the Holocaust befell a certain people because of
> a very specific history and very real causes gives it general human
> significance. It means that, at least theoretically, it can happen to
> others, although surely not in exactly the same way. It is the real
> assault on the population of a specific people that lends the
> Holocaust an element with which every human being can
> identify.

Although this view is indisputable, the uniqueness of the situation
– its dissimilarity from relations among other peoples – stems from the

unequivocal history of Jewish–Gentile relations over the centuries. I am referring to the stepwise continuum, which one dare not disregard, from the murder of the Son of God to racial purity to the international Jewish conspiracy based on the myth of domineering Jewish power, despite – and perhaps precisely because of – the Jews' lack of political sovereignty.

The shift of emphasis on the question of Holocaust uniqueness, from Jewish history to the nature of German Nazism, was further explicated by the Canadian-Jewish historian Michael Marrus. While Bauer regards the pseudo-messianic pathology of Nazism as the source of the uniqueness, Marrus finds it in the bureaucratic organization of the genocide process, especially in the concentration camps, where people were dehumanized before they were put to death.[33] Marrus outdid Bauer by attributing no importance to that certain situation in which the Jewish people was immersed. This stands out in his discussion of the Nazi ideology as one of the motives for the genocide, as he regards the antisemitic nature of this doctrine as quite unimportant.

The historian Michael Marrus, who reduces the uniqueness of the Holocaust to the inhuman regime in the extermination camps, is the thinker closest to the group of scholars, mostly in the social sciences, who consider the Holocaust foremost a universal phenomenon. Generally speaking, one may say from the outset that the methodology and the ideology are much clearer and unequivocal to social scientists than to historians. For the latter, the particularistic event and the universalistic process are in constant tension; even when the emphasis is on the singular and the specific, it is always set within the general context. Social scientists, in contrast, not only hold the opposite attitude but give much less weight to particularism, by its very nature, than historians give to universalism.

The nexus of methodology and ideology also flows from this. Historians of the nationalist and Zionist persuasion refer to the uniqueness problem in different ways that originate, to no small extent, in how they understand the role of Zionism in Jewish history. In contrast, for sociologists and historians of civilization who view matters from a non-nationalist perspective, this nexus comes across in one hue and is coterminous.

The doyen and most prominent member of this group is the sociologist Irving Horowitz, the Hannah Arendt Professor of Sociology at Rutgers University. Horowitz describes himself frankly as a universal man, a Jewish-American whose parents came from Russia. As such, he obviously does not feel like an exile. On the basis of this worldview, he admits to 'sensing multiple obligations and marginal affiliations to nation, ethnicity and religion'. To put it differently, these obligations are universal because of their human, liberal, and progressive nature, among other reasons. The affiliation, however, is particularistic because it expresses an identification with a part at the expense of the whole. Furthermore, he recommends in so many words that this ideational principle be applied in scholarly research: 'It is my fervent opinion that all authentic scientific generalizations have to remain multiple and marginal in the above stated sense.'[34]

The principle of strong commitment and weak affiliation also determines Horowitz's attitude toward Israel. He does not repudiate his affiliation with it but describes it as minimal. As a Jew, he portrays himself figuratively as a shareholder in a company called the State of Israel. Any rational stockholder, he says, knows that the value of shares is not constant, that it oscillates with changing market conditions or, in this context, with changes in the historical situation. Therefore, 'Being a spiritual holder of a volatile national stock, I am fully aware of the risks as well as rewards of marginal stock participation.'[35]

Notice that Horowitz set forth his doctrine of limited or marginal affiliation in a book published in 1974, one year after the Yom Kippur War – a conflict that undermined the confidence of many Jewish intellectuals in Israel's existential stability. Horowitz personally believed that the Jewish people could not withstand another Holocaust should it occur in Israel; the people would disintegrate into fragments that would eventually disappear. Only the Ultraorthodox sects would survive, carrying on in their traditional way because this further disaster would not have the same meaning for them as it would for the rest of Jewry. The Jews in Israel might integrate into a broad Arab federation, where eventually they might resume Jewish community life. Another possibility for Israeli Jews would be a UN protectorate regime.[36]

The weighty doubt that Horowitz expressed about Israel's survival prospects flows not only from the military and political realities that the country faced after the 1973 war but also from his own worldview. Horowitz is an admirer of Simon Dubnow, and following his lead, believes in the existential strength of the Jewish national entity as a Diaspora phenomenon. He wishes to stress a basic difference between peoplehood, with reference to Diaspora Jewry, and nation-statehood, as in Israel. As an objective scholar, he admits that Jewish collective existence today is bound to the State of Israel. From the ideational standpoint, however, he does not consider this an advantage for Jewish continuity. By creating a bond with and a dependency on the state as a territorial-political entity, the Jews, he believed, lost what Dubnow called the consciousness of a supra-territorial, non-governmental national identity. This, plus the fact that the Jewish state, as such, is no different from any other normal state entity, submerges Diaspora Jews in many moral dilemmas for which they are not responsible. This leads Horowitz to two conclusions, one of them personal: that it is better to belong to a minority than to a majority, and one should beware of the extreme perception of majority rule that holds sway in Israel; and more generally, 'as Jews, we have the requirement to transcend nationalism and to outlive all nation-states'. As such, endowed with the ability to outlast the nation-state, the Jews should return to their original role as the bearers of the idea of social equality.

These remarks do not suggest marginal involvement, as Horowitz defines it, in Jewish ethnicity or nationhood. On the contrary, Horowitz, following Dubnow and much like Hannah Arendt, believes in the existence of a Jewish entity invested with peculiarity although not uniqueness, and it is manifested in their having 'a nationality in their minds'.[37] From this Dubnowian perspective, he espouses a Diaspora ethnic worldview that parallels, and even contrasts with, the Zionist view that Israel as a Jewish state commands centrality in all matters Jewish. This, of course, is not a philosophy of marginal importance; rather, it essentially offers an alternative.

Equipped with this Dubnowian perspective in its liberal-radical Western rendition, Horowitz set out ten years later to confront the issue of Holocaust uniqueness. Of course, one who argues that Simon Dubnow attributed oddities, not peculiarities, to the Jewish people cannot accept the argument that the Holocaust of the Jews is socially unique even as genocidal actions are being perpetrated against other peoples. In a book that went through three printings – a smashing success in scholarly research – Horowitz attempted to refute the historians and theologians, particularly Emil Fackenheim, who traced the roots of the Holocaust to modern antisemitism.[38] In contradistinction to this particularistic view, Horowitz promotes the universalistic factor: the power of the modern nation-state, atop which rests racism as a universal pathological *Weltanschauung* – of which antisemitism is only a part, and not a special part at that. In Horowitz's social conception, the historical order – what preceded what, antisemitism preceding racism or vice versa – is utterly unimportant.

Horowitz's anti-singularistic ideological zealotry and methodological extremism lead him into an argument reminiscent of the views of Ernst Nolte, who ignited the historians dispute in Germany in the second half of the 1980s, about five years after Horowitz's book appeared. In Horowitz's opinion, Fackenheim was mistaken in striving to prove that the uniqueness of the Jews' disaster stems from an additional factor: their non-belligerence in the war against Germany. Horowitz, the sociologist, held a totally different view. As he understood matters, the Jews, as part of the economic middle class and members of the liberal professions, represented the democratic civil legitimacy against which the Nazis fought. Moreover, as activists in the proletarian and intellectual movements that helped shape the ideology, they were Nazism's foes. 'The Jews', he rules flatly, 'posed a threatening challenge to the legitimacy of the Nazi regime.'[39]

Although this sounds like the argument of Lucy Dawidowicz, Uriel Tal, and Yehuda Bauer – that the Nazis waged a war against the Jews – it is substantively different. In the opinion of the others mentioned, the Nazi pathology originates in having made the Jews into enemies; Horowitz maintains that the Jews' objective social role and status made them the enemies of Nazism. By inference, the origins of the Nazis' profound, murderous hatred were not peculiar to them alone but reflected a general social condition. Indeed, Horowitz believes that only parochial thinkers, like most Jewish historians, can assume that the Holocaust, as an act of systematic genocide, stems exclusively from the nature of the Third Reich regime. It has been shown since the Holocaust and World War II, he maintains, that most societies have adopted similar genocidal policies against national minorities and other peoples. Therefore, Horowitz says, one should not project from the singularity of Jews' lives onto the singularity of their death: 'Dying is a universal property of many peoples, cultures and nations.'[40]

According to Horowitz, even when one cannot disregard several singular features of the Holocaust, which all other scholars have already noted – such as its methodological organization and its perpetrators' ideological staunchness – these are, after all, but manifestations of the potency of the bureaucratic apparatus that sought to cleanse the country of all undesirable impediments. In other words, the murderous hatred was a superstructure imposed on the bureaucratic mechanism of the modern state. Thus, he rejects as utterly inapplicable Yehuda Bauer's distinction between genocide as mass killing and holocaust as total obliteration. It is unimportant and merely interferes, for reason of its sectarian, parochial approach, with positioning the Holocaust as a universal, cross-cultural model, broad in perspective, of genocidal actions in the modern era, foremost in the twentieth century.

We devote considerable space to Horowitz's thinking here for two reasons: first, his obvious connection between ideology and methodology; and second, his radical approach which dismisses both the uniqueness of the State of Israel and of the Jewish Holocaust out of a consistent if not militant sociologism (as a parallel to historicism) in his thinking and his statements.

Even those who share this view such as the New York sociologist Helen Fein, who three years before Horowitz devoted an entire book to the de-singularization of the Holocaust,[41] could not match his consistency. As the head of a research institute for genocide studies, Fein could not disregard what she considered a very meaningful phenomenon that had surfaced as the Jews were being massacred. It referred not to the Nazis' plans but, of all things, to the Christian regimes that had been warned of the Germans' intent to obliterate the Jews before and during the war – and took no meaningful action to prevent it. Fein also argued that by not offering the Jews asylum before the onset of the war and the genocide, the Western governments proved that they had adopted the Nazi belief that an influx of Jews would aggravate the Jewish problem that already beset these countries. Therefore, torn between sociology and history, between conception and reality, Fein defines the situation by way of compromise: one must differentiate between 'the historical singularity – as opposed to the metaphysical uniqueness – of the Holocaust, [which] arises out of its unveiling of the grotesque yet paradoxical implications of the state system'.[42] In other words, if there is anything singular about the Holocaust, it originates not in the Jews' special situation in Europe but in the paradoxical if not grotesque implications of the modern state system. As for the factors that distinguish one modern state from another – why one becomes murderous and the other remains liberal – Horowitz and Fein make little effort to express uncertainty. Unlike Horowitz, however, Fein as a researcher of genocide does not remain completely loyal to this generalization.

In an expository piece written three years later (1987),[43] Fein points to antisemitism as a factor in the genocide of the Jews. However, she attributes this factor only to the countries of central and eastern Europe, where discrimination against Jews is a historical attitude. She stresses that in western and southern Europe, such as Italy, where Jews had equal rights, the local population not only refrained from cooperating with the Nazis but helped save nearly half of their Jewish citizens. These remarks amount to a compromise of sorts between factual history and Fein's ideology, because her intention is to disprove to her readers persuasively that the whole world was against the Jews. Therefore unbalanced remembrance of the Holocaust must not be allowed to foster a hostile, aggressive, 'never again' attitude toward the Jews' non-Jewish surroundings.

Fein's new argument, in which she acknowledges the role of anti-semitism in the Holocaust in certain countries, definitely undermines her previous conception, shared by her colleagues, of the bureaucratic apparatus of the modern state as the forebear of genocide. Concurrently, however, she attempts to reinforce the universalistic ideology by virtue of which the democracies granted Jews equal rights and status. Perhaps for this reason she overlooks the considerable equality and general social influence that the Jews enjoyed in pre-Nazi Germany. Neither does it surface in her remarks that the Jewish population in all countries where the local population helped save them was not particularly large, whereas Eastern Europe had millions of Jews concentrated in specific territorial sectors: central Poland; the western Soviet Union; and the Ukraine. It is amazing to see a researcher in the social sciences disregard the quantitative factor in the attitudes of Gentile peoples toward the Jews. Nevertheless, it is worth stressing that Fein covers half the distance between the two disciplines, history and social science, and between the all-inclusive theory and the partic-ularistic approach. This compromise, of course, is not intended to nullify the universal message of the Holocaust.

Sociological thought in understanding the Holocaust continued to develop, and extended the cause from the modern bureaucratic state to the comprehensive cultural phenomenon of modern society. The sociologist Zygmunt Bauman refined this approach by augmenting it with a universal and individualistic moral message. Bauman, born in Poland, deeply imbibed the Marxist culture in which he was raised. Forced to leave Poland in the late 1960s, he thought momentarily to seek his homeland in Israel, but he quickly found a home at the University of Leeds in England. There he launched, or accelerated, the process of exchanging the universalistic ideology and methodology – Marxist and collectivist – for a universal, liberal, and individualistic one.

Bauman neither engaged in Holocaust research nor took an interest in the subject until the 1980s, when his wife began to write her memoirs about her childhood spent in a ghetto and in hiding with a Polish family. Having belatedly discovered the Holocaust, Bauman set out to study it in order to integrate it into general sociological theory. The interesting thing about Bauman's approach is that, in contrast to the sociologists who preceded him and the young historians who followed him – whom we discuss below – his point of departure is the Jewish singularity of the Holocaust.

In the introduction to his book, Bauman states emphatically: 'The Holocaust was indeed a Jewish tragedy', even though its six million Jewish victims were fewer than one-third of the twenty million whom the Nazis put to death. In so stating, he accepts the basic premise of the Jewish thinkers and historians: that among all peoples, only the Jews were singled out for annihilation. Nevertheless, it is clear to Bauman that the Holocaust was not only a Jewish problem and does not belong solely to Jewish history:

> The Holocaust was born and executed in our modern rational society, at the high stage of our civilization and at the peak of human cultural achievement, and for this reason it is a problem of that society, civilization and culture.[44]

Thus, Bauman's well-spoken remarks express nothing new vis-à-vis the arguments of the sociologists who preceded him, who said that the Holocaust is a phenomenon of modern society and, especially, of the bureaucratic state. However, his approach is novel in a certain sense. For Bauman, the Holocaust flowed from the Jews' peculiar status in modern society. Bauman spoke on the issue of the special Jewish status in modern European society in the past – and in the future – in a symposium on the future of the Jewish people,[45] where he attempted to explain the essence of the Jewish tragedy in modern society. In his very first sentence, he asserted: 'For the last two centuries or so, *ambivalence* was the glory and the misery of the Jews.' The ambivalent station that has typified the Jews since the French Revolution stems from their very unsuitability for the national society that has come about in Europe. Other peoples define themselves in terms of borders, governments, official languages, national histories, laws, and armed forces. The Jews, in contrast, remain apart in their ambivalence – not only in their unsuitability for the partitioning into nation-states but also in their unsuitability for a partitioned world. However, the very ambivalence that keeps the Jews apart from other peoples has led the Jews directly into the center of modern society. Because the Jews became an archetype or paragon of the 'altogether human' in the world, 'this uniqueness of typicality was also the ambivalence of the Jew'. In this modern society, according to Bauman, the Jews' existential difference is deemed a sin, and their wish to blur this difference is deemed by others to be a crime. Therefore, modernity offered the Jews only two options: sin or crime. The Jew's existential dualism of insider–outsider makes him a perpetual defendant, upbraided for the 'sin' of being different and indicted for the crime of wishing to integrate. This, says Bauman, explains the radicalism of the Jewish revolution-aries who attempted to destroy the society that isolated them and replace it with a different society, an open society that would no longer exclude them. It also explains the Holocaust, Bauman argues in his book, as the modern nation-state decided to invoke its bureaucracies to expunge the different Jew from its midst. Therefore, the singularity of Jewishness lies not in a consistent historical wish on the Jews' part to be separate but in the unwillingness of the national societies to let the Jews integrate. At a certain stage, this unwillingness escalated into a murderous craving for riddance, and here lies the singularity of the Holocaust. Bauman, however, speaks in the name of modern Jews, some of them assimilated or universalistic, who wished to have no relationship with their people. They included intellectuals and revolutionaries, among whom Bauman was also enumerated in various phases of his life. However, these Jews – Kafkaesque tragic heroes who wished to enter the Gentiles' national castles and were turned away – whom Bauman makes into existential symbols of all of Jewry, were but a minority, however prominent, among the Jews. The majority – Orthodox, national-Zionist, and non-Zionist – did not wish to dissolve into the Gentile world without leaving a trace. Indeed, they aspired to find different ways, some traditional and others revolutionary (such as Zionism), to live apart from others. Even the Marxist Bund, which demanded cultural-national autonomy, did not correspond to Bauman's typical pan-human Jew. However, Bauman, following his erstwhile Marxist *Weltanschauung* and his present liberal-universalistic worldview, cannot regard this reality as important, since it clashes with his conception. Like many important figures in his circle, he exchanged faith in the Marxist utopia for faith in the post-modern utopia, in which the tragic and (as he said) ambivalent clash between Jews and their surroundings would be resolved.

In an open and diverse post-modern society which acknowledges the value of difference with equanimity, worships innovative ideas, and opposes unidimensional ideologies; in a society in which everyone belongs and there are no strangers; in a society that has converted the Kafkaesque castles into open homes, the Jews have finally found themselves at home. Thus, 'their distinctiveness ceased to offend the eye; but only because the state of "being distinct" has turned into the only truly universal mark of the human condition'.

Then, in the best tradition of the dialectic method, all the peculiarities that the aggressive, particularistic national society condemned as parochial, odd, strange, and even threatening – peculiarities that in fact were essentially universal – are finally being acknowledged. In this world, which is ascending and advancing toward a pan-human world culture, human society may for the first time admit its true essence 'in the mirror of Jewish experience'. In other words, as Bauman argues explicitly, in contrast to the views of Jewish intellectuals who dread the loss of Jewish identity and its replacement with a universal identity, 'it is not that the Jews in the modern world have surrendered to an un-Jewish universality. It is rather that in the modern world ... Jewish universality has been fulfilled.' Following this dialectic doctrine, Bauman considers it the Jews' unique opportunity in post-modern society to lend this society their specialness, not as paragons of parochiality but as the standard-bearers of the prophetic utopian vision of universal humanism.

This outlook, which ignores the resurgence of aggressive nationalism and religious fundamentalism in the past decade and which, like the Marxist outlook that preceded it, may result in disillusionment because of its utopian and rationalistic perspective, has a dual significance that pertains to our theme. First, as an opponent of nationalism, Bauman clearly opposes Zionism; he avoids the issue of the Jewish state and does not mention it as a factor in contemporary Jewishness. Second, as a bearer of the universal vision, he transforms Holocaust consciousness into a moral mission vis-à-vis the world, into an educational device. After all, in the open post-modern world, the Holocaust no longer belongs to any people or group – neither the victims, who seek special treatment due to their suffering, nor the hangmen, who face punishment for the evil they have wrought. The Holocaust belongs to all of humankind: 'The present-day significance of the Holocaust is the lesson it contains for the whole humanity.'[46] This message is primarily individual. It is the individual's mission, even if he is one of a few, to make the moral choice, even – and specifically – when this choice conflicts with the rational calculus of self-preservation. The number of people who have chosen this path does not matter; what counts is that a few have done so.

We discuss Bauman's *Weltanschauung* at such length because it embodies the most extreme attempt to break the Holocaust–state nexus, an attempt manifested in pronounced indifference toward and disregard of the state with respect to the Holocaust and its results. The same applies to Bauman's attitude toward Jewish nationalism in both its Zionist and its Diaspora–ethnic senses. Rather than ruling out this nationalism, he simply ignores it. In so doing, he effectively dismisses it in the name of his individualistic, universalistic vision. This indifference, exceptional in view of the strong criticism of Jewish nationalism and the Jewish state expressed by Bauman's universalistic colleagues, is deeply rooted in factors that need not be discussed here except for one remark: Bauman himself admitted how profound his estrangement from Jewishness had become. After all, only after fifty years had passed since the Holocaust did he begin to study this, the central event in modern Jewish history, and even then only because of his wife's personal experience.

The universalistic trend in these discussions steadily became more radical during the 1990s, developing from the ethnic universalism represented by the Americans, Horowitz and Fein; through Bauman's transnational individualism; to the acrid anti-Zionist version of anti-nationalism coupled with aggressive criticism of the State of Israel expressed by the young generation of historians and philosophers in the United Kingdom and in Israel.

Mark Mazover, the modern-era historian who has been conducting research on World War II, opposes any attribution of uniqueness to the Holocaust. He rejects the very concept of singularity, Fein's synonym for uniqueness, because he considers such concepts utterly meaning-less. Because every historical event is unique, he says, the crucial property of an event is not its uniqueness but its historical context. Therefore, the proper field of inquiry in examining the genocide perpetrated against the Jews is its context. From this juncture, he takes Bauman's analysis farther afield. In fact, he rejects Bauman's argument that the Jews' ambivalent status encouraged others to hate them in a way that escalated into antisemitism and, ultimately, the Final Solution. In his opinion, antisemitism is neither part of Western Christian culture nor an expression of the *volk* spirit of German nationalism. Instead, it is but one facet of the racial doctrine and the racial prejudices that have typified the West since the early twentieth century.

Therefore, following Raphael Lemkin, who coined the term 'geno-cide' and to whose memory Mazover dedicated his article, he urged scholars to stop dealing with the singularity of the Holocaust and to focus on its lesson for this century in general. The war ended half a century ago, he explained, but the struggle against intolerance and racial discrimination continues.[47]

The historian Mark Levene, who probes genocidal actions in the modern era, pursued the same policy in the quarterly that printed Mazover's article. In Levene's writings, however, the principled argument against the singularity of the Holocaust becomes pronouncedly and overtly anti-Zionist. The doctrine of uniqueness, he says, serves the myth of Jewish unity. Remove it, and there will be no further point in memorial days, no special reason for the existence of the State of Israel, and no room for what he terms the nationalistic slogan and battle cry, 'Never again'.

Levene is afraid to depict the Holocaust as singular not only because of his anti-Zionist views but also because of the negative message, in his opinion, that this myth communicates to Jews and other peoples. In a world where genocidal actions are foreseeable, the only refuge for individuals is the nation-state, as the only mechanism of deliverance in general and for the Jews in particular. As for the other: 'Those who can't help themselves can literally go to hell.'[48]

Two kinds of thinking underlie this choleric expression: not only an anti-national ideology that rules out Zionism but also a degree of intellectual fear that nationalism, of which the Holocaust was one of the terrible climaxes, will gather strength. Therefore, in his opinion, only when we understand the Holocaust as part of, or a stage in, a set of genocidal actions in the modern era can it serve as a lesson and a warning of the horrors that may follow.

The outlooks emanating from these articles, and the spirit of others in the same quarterly that pertain indirectly to the matter at hand, beg the question: Why did this radical universalism originate in England, of all places – a society that is still considered quite insular? First it is worth noting that the changing of the generational guard and changes in trends of thought turned the *Jewish Quarterly*, once a moderate intellectual Zionist journal, into a forum for radical Diaspora ideology. The forces behind this publication regard England as a liberal multicultural society, in which Judaism will find its place as an English subculture alongside other subcultures that do not necessarily stem from the Anglo-Saxon majority culture. This is said to explain the collective ideological and cultural background of their attitude toward the Holocaust.

As for the issue itself – the universalization of the Holocaust – I believe we should accept the views of the historian Tony Kushner, who explored the attitude of liberals in England toward the distress of European Jewry before and during World War II. Kushner traces this approach to a profound liberal tradition – because of which they could hardly grasp, let alone understand, what was happening in Europe – and, to no small extent, an *a priori* attitude tainted by antisemitic sentiments that led to a disregard of the Jews' plight. In the conclusion to his book, Kushner asks why discussion of the Holocaust and its lessons began about twenty years later in England than in the United States and, of course, in Israel. In his opinion, England's liberal principles were an encumbrance to discussion of the Holocaust as it occurred and afterwards. It is ironic, he says, that precisely when the debate began, 'it is universal aspects of the Holocaust which have made it accessible to the liberal imagination in a country as removed from its horrors as Britain'.[49] Thus, on the basis of this assessment, the universalization of the essence and lesson of the Holocaust also serves as an additional calling card that liberal Jews may use to enter British society. However, instead of its being the personal calling card that Heinrich Heine proclaimed some 180 years ago – such a document is no longer needed; Jews are no longer barred from university chairs – it is a passive calling card for the Jewish collectivity, which is fated to lose its national identity and assimilate or integrate totally into the multicultural society.

This phenomenon of opposing if not repudiating nationalism is not limited to Jewish historians and sociologists in the Anglo-Saxon culture of the US and the UK. In Israel, too, these views have moved to the forefront of the public discourse. The historian Henry Wasserman, who concerns himself with German and German-Jewish history in the modern era, enunciated this stance so clearly and sincerely that one cannot doubt the ideology that underlies the methodology. 'It is among the most famous of matters', he said, 'that insistence on the uniqueness of a phenomenon, even when expressed in reference to universal meanings – and often for that very reason – is a salient characteristic of patterns of thinking in modern nationalism, which dwells at length on the uniqueness of virtues and the suffering of "its" nation.' His conclusion: 'Overinsistence on the uniqueness of the Holocaust, as evident in Israel and various parts of the globe, usually occurs in accordance with parochial national needs.' Thus, he says, American Jews use it to reinforce their Jewishness, and Jewish historians 'are doing what national historians have always done well: endowing the sufferings of their people with metahistorical significance'.[50]

This generalization concerning metahistory is difficult to accept, because it is intrinsically inaccurate and incorrect with respect to each of the aforementioned historians in the context of the Holocaust. This is not the place to take up the matter, except to remark that, importantly, Wasserman's remarks reflect a genre of academic thinking that has become entrenched in Israel, especially among a group of relatively young scholars who concern themselves with the philosophy of science. We shall discuss them below.

In the meantime, however, let us explore a discourse that runs parallel to that of the historians and the sociologists – a discourse of philosophers, some in the humanities and sciences and others from the realm of *litterateurs* and essayists. At this level, too, one finds a nexus of ideology and attitude with respect to the uniqueness of the Holocaust. Here, however, the nexus does not always overlap, as with the historians and especially the sociologists, and sometimes it contains phenomena that are inconsistent with our methodological model.

The most unequivocal scholar in this discourse is Professor Nathan Rothenstreich, considered the most important Zionist philosopher in the statehood era. In an article that counters the views of Ernst Nolte – written pursuant to the famous historians' dispute in Germany that Nolte's book ignited – Rothenstreich vehemently stresses the uniqueness of Hitler's Nazi regime as against the Bolshevik regime of Stalin and emphasizes the unique causes of the genocide perpetrated against the Jews. The Soviet regime's motives for mass killing, Rothenstreich argues, originated in class war and therefore in a socio-historical situation that, by being particular, is variable. In the Nazi regime, in contrast, the racial doctrine – which not only distinguished among people but sorted them by their moral qualities – is constant and unchanging. Accordingly, Rothenstreich asks Nolte a crucial question about the motives of the Nazi state: 'If this policy was not a catastrophic contribution of traditional antisemitism and [was] just a copy of the Gulag, why were the Jews singled out?'[51]

In contrast to Rothenstreich, who traces the singularity of attitudes toward the Jews to totalitarian regimes, Eliezer Schweid, the uncompromisingly Zionist philosopher, points to the singularity of the Holocaust in the string of devastations that have visited the Jews in their history. Addressing himself to the idea of unifying the mourning of the Ninth of Av with Holocaust Remembrance Day in a package of national bereavement – denoting the tragic cycle from the destruction of the Temple to the obliteration of one-third of the Jewish people in the Holocaust – Schweid seeks to distinguish between the two. In his opinion, the Ninth of Av marks an event that created the state of exile that still exists, both in times of distress and in times of relative well-being, whereas 'Holocaust Remembrance Day tells us that the era of

Jewish existence as a people in exile has ended. In exile, the Jewish people has no future. It awaits perdition.'[52] For him, perdition means not necessarily the certainty of a further Holocaust but only the possibility of one, which is improbable in view of the nature of modern society. From this standpoint, his analysis is no different from those of the anti-Zionist sociologists and historians. However, the main thing for Schweid is the people's loss of power to resist the assimilation process, in view of the thinning out of its national potency because of the Holocaust. Therefore, his conclusion is 'simple and unequivocal, and it affirms the Zionist viewpoint staunchly. ... The people Israel should be made into a strong people, capable of protecting itself by means of its own strengths, i.e., it should be taken out of exile and granted a territorial political framework like that of any other people.'[53]

Schweid, although an ideological successor to Dinur, differs from Dinur in methodology. For Schweid, as stated, the Holocaust is not another segment or phase in a sequence of exiles, each of which ended in devastation, although it is distinct in the act of destruction it involved. The Holocaust stands apart from all other disasters in that it totally transformed Jewish history by terminating the state of exile.

This view, with its implications for the status of the State of Israel among the Jews and the Jews among the Gentiles, was deemed unacceptable by the most prominent Diaspora philosophers. The most interesting and complex of them is the researcher and philosopher George Steiner, who lives in constant tension between his extreme Jewish universalist worldview and his profound dread of a recurrence of the Holocaust. It is this stance, between two poles, that determines his attitude toward the State of Israel. On the one hand, Steiner rejects the state on principle as a manifestation of Jewish nationalism, to which he is opposed. On the other hand, he regards it as the last refuge for Jews, should they be visited with another Holocaust.

In an essay he published in the 1960s, 'A Kind of Survivor', dedicated to Elie Wiesel, Steiner disclosed that even though he had fled with his parents from France to the United States in 1940, he considers himself a survivor who experienced the terror of death face to face. This feeling not only besets him relentlessly but has become an ideology of sorts:

> That fear lies near the heart of the way in which I think of myself as a Jew. To have been a European Jew in the first half of the twentieth century was to pass sentence on one's own children, to force upon them a condition almost beyond rational understand-

ing. And which may recur. I have to think that – it is the vital clause – so long as remembrance is real. Perhaps we Jews walk closer to our children than other men; try as they may, they cannot leap out of our shadow.[54]

Steiner still harbors this fear. A generation after these lines were written, on the fortieth anniversary of Israeli independence, he published an article in *The Sunday Times* entitled 'Why a Jew Can Only Grieve'. The article subjects Israel to harsh criticism but also makes explicit remarks on its connection with the Holocaust. Steiner attacks liberal-radical Jews who argue that Israel's fate has nothing to do with theirs: 'I take this to be nonsense. There is tragically, proudly, not a Jew anywhere whom Israel does not, be it only in a spiritual sense, hold hostage.'

In other words, not only must Steiner, as a conscious Jew, maintain a spiritual relationship with Israel, but 'there is [no one among the Jews] who does not know, deep inside himself, that it is in Israel that he or his children have their only guarantee of refuge should the night come again (in South Africa, in Argentina, in the Marseilles of Le Pen)'.[55]

Until this point, the Zionist, Schweid, and the anti-Zionist, Steiner, are amazingly alike. Neither dismisses the possibility of another Holocaust in the modern state, and both regard the Jewish state, as a political and territorial framework, as a refuge for persecuted Jews. Beyond this, however, they are separated by an ideational abyss. Schweid regards the state not only as a refuge but as a creative center of Jewish culture, whereas Steiner considers the Jewish nation-state diametrically opposed to the Jewish spirit. Explaining in the 1960s why he did not apply the logical conclusion warranted by his sense of existential dread and move to Israel, he stated sadly, 'The State of Israel is, in one sense, a sad miracle' because of the tragic circumstances under which it was formed. The danger of annihilation that threatens Israel has turned the country into a clenched-fist society beset by unsurpassably extreme national tension. However, the Israeli must be resolute, 'if his trip home is to survive the wolf-pack at its doors. Chauvinism is almost the requisite condition of life'. Indeed, the Jews are deeply conscious of the State of Israel and may have no chance to continue existing without it. But, 'The nation-state bristling with arms is a bitter relic, an absurdity in the century of crowded men. And it is alien to some of the most radical, most humane elements in the Jewish spirit.'[56] This is the spirit in which Steiner, like Bauman, envelops the great Jewish thinkers and *litterateurs* in the West, from Marx, Freud, and Kafka, to the poet Paul Célan, whom Steiner considers one of the greatest of post-Holocaust muses. It is a spiritual Judaism that needs no framework, be it national, cultural, or territorial. It is the only Judaism that has no roots anywhere. After all, in a metaphor that he repeats at every opportunity, people are not trees:

> Trees have roots; men and women legs. The possibilities which this opens seem to me peculiarly pertinent to the Jewish condition, which is to learn new tongues, to cross frontiers, to contribute wherever he is given breathing space to the life of the mind, to that of moral argument.[57]

If so, Steiner's Jewish messianic vision is that of the circuit intellectual who enriches and revitalizes every stop, whether he wanders of his own volition or under duress. For such a Jew, a nation-state represents not redemption but a death trap. However, Steiner's maskilic Ultraorthodoxy bumps against two constraints. One is the fear of another Holocaust, for which reason this nation-state is needed even though it menaces the spirit of Judaism as he construes it. The second constraint pertains to the very existence of the Jewish collectivity, which he values highly. Therefore, Steiner, the territorially rootless Jewish intellectual, sinks his roots in the Jewish Holocaust. Moreover, he lends it a singular symbolic and metaphysical significance, since it has become crucial to contemporary Jewry. 'The presumed uniqueness of the Shoah has become vital to Judaism now', he proclaimed in a lecture at the University of Haifa in the 1980s. Only the unbearable memory of the Holocaust unifies the diverse segments of the Jewish people: Orthodox and atheist, religious and secular, Israel and Diaspora, Zionist and anti-Zionist. 'To normalize that understanding would, very precisely, signify an abandonment of the appalling yet also ennobling justifying mystery of our Jewish identity.'[58]

This is why Steiner stopped using the term Holocaust and replaced it with *Shoah*, thereby symbolically substituting the Jewish meaning of the disaster for the universal meaning. This positions the Jewish identity between the appalling and the ennobling, against the background of the infathomability of the Holocaust. In this respect, Steiner's outlook closely approximates that of Elie Wiesel, to whom he dedicated his essay 'A Kind of Survivor'. It may have been Steiner's influence that prompted Elie Wiesel, several years later, to conclude that the term Holocaust should be replaced, from the Jewish standpoint, with a term of primeval Jewish connotation and meaning. What separates them, however, is the attitude toward the Jewish-spiritual meaning of the State of Israel. Both thinkers are bound to Israel, each in his own way. Wiesel, by taking a demonstrably favorable attitude toward it, is a perpetual defender of sorts, although he notes Israel's faults. Steiner, in contrast, is a prosecutor and a harsh critic. This is so because Wiesel treats the establishment and existence of the state as a metaphysical mystery at the opposite extreme of another metaphysical mystery, the Holocaust. For Steiner, the state is a brutal necessary evil occasioned by aggressive nationalism. Therefore, even when its existence is crucial, its comportment, especially toward the Arab population, is illegitimate. For Wiesel, the state is a manifestation of the post-Holocaust Jewish revival; for Steiner, its very political and national essence clashes with the Jewish spirit. The Jews need the state not as a source of spirituality but as a physical refuge from whatever woes may befall them. Despite these profound differences, both philosophers agree that the Holocaust ethos and the state myth are the building blocks of the contemporary Jewish collective identity. In the opinion of both, however, the Holocaust has left a stronger imprint on Jewish existence than the state has, and the Jewish people exists by its own virtue, its existence not totally hinging on that of the Jewish state.

The British-born author and essayist Fredric Raphael approximates Steiner's outlook on the essence of the Holocaust as part of Western culture. In an essay with the provocative title 'The Necessity of Antisemitism', and in a Baroque-style flow of thought, Raphael explains in the third person that 'he sees the Jews as both like and unlike other men, both part of Europe and external to it, both assimilable and indigestible. ... Surely we are supposed to recognize an attempt at least to indicate why antisemitism is not a sad contingency or even a disagreeable contagion, but a constant and essential working part of Europe's sombre unreformed logic.'[59] Raphael arrives at the uniqueness of the Holocaust from the uniqueness of antisemitism as an integral part even of the rational manifestations of European culture, among people who cannot be accused of harboring a tradition of hating Jews. Thus Raphael, like Steiner, prefers to invoke this concept rather than the one already put to universal use, Holocaust. However, unlike Steiner, Raphael, who was never a child refugee, does not relate to the Holocaust as a traumatic phenomenon. His style is ironic, not dramatic; he avoids the almost-tragic political or moral reckonings with the State of Israel. He is simply a non-Zionist *and*, in the style of the generation that succeeded him, a non-universalist. He is a

European Jew whose existence is ambiguous; he is an insider *and* an outsider, and he accepts favorably the situation that Zygmunt Bauman regarded as the source of the Jews' tragedy and confidently expresses the possibility of their vanishing into post-modern society.

However, the young generation of philosophers is closer to Bauman's sociological–philosophical worldview than it is to the literary–philosophical perspectives of Steiner and Raphael. At roughly the same time that Raphael made his remarks, two students of Western culture published an article entitled 'The Unlearned Lesson of the Holocaust',[60] in which they go farther than any of their predecessors. Following Bauman, they trace the Holocaust to the nature of modern society, but they surpass him in dismissing anything specifically Jewish among its causes. Recognition of the nexus that binds the two, presents the cult of secular progress with a challenge. In other words, modern society brought disaster upon the Jews not because it forced them into a special ambivalent situation, as Bauman believes, but because the murder-lust, which the modern state employs as an instrument under certain conditions, is embedded in the modern secular cult itself. Therefore, the only lesson one may adduce from the Holocaust is the need to hold in doubt the principles of modernity that underlie Western civilization.

The two authors' argument against the secular cult of modernism is quite reminiscent of Edmund Burke's famous evaluation of the French Revolution, which inaugurated the modern era, as a religion of heretics. Our concern here is not to delve into sweeping assessments of modernity so typical of the past generation of sociologists, political scientists, and philosophers. We merely remark that modern culture has developed in more than one direction and has not necessarily led to mass murder by means of the nation-state or modern bureaucracy. The proof of this is that the countries where the denouncers of modernity live – the United States, England, and France – have displayed modernity's other face, the humane, democratic, and relatively equitable one. However, one aspect of the matter does pertain directly to our theme. There is undoubtedly something of a secular cult in the all-out worship of modernity that occurs in contemporary Western society. It is equally true, however, that a post-modern secular cult is taking shape, a cult of universal moral mission, borne no longer by peoples, classes, or parties, but by individuals or groups of individualists. It is no coincidence, of course, that the Jews are well represented among them. The Jews who bear the idea of post-modern universalism have replaced their coreligionists who, a century ago, brought the tidings of modern universalism. The earlier efflorescence was of a socialist–collectivist complexion; the contemporary version is liberal-individualist. The object of the struggle, too, has changed: war against discrimination, racism, prejudice, and conceit has replaced class warfare, the economic exploitation doctrine, and faith in the all-redeeming process of revolution. From this standpoint, these Jewish intellectuals have replaced the socialist revolutionary ethos as a universal moral message, espoused by members of previous generations, with consciousness of the Holocaust.

Thus far, we have sorted Jewish universalists into two groups in terms of their attitude toward the Holocaust: the American group, which cannot overlook the singular ethnic features of the genocide, and the English group, which, for reasons stemming from the British liberal tradition, wishes to disregard these peculiarities altogether. However, a third group should be added, that of Israeli radicals who, in view of the national struggle between the Jewish and the Palestinian peoples, have integrated ideological politics into moral consciousness of the Holocaust.

This ideationally united group, most of whose members deal in the philosophy and history of science, congregates around the quarterly journal *Theory and Criticism*. The ideological tendencies of this group are anti-Zionist, anti-nationalist, and supportive of a binational Jewish–Arab state. Therefore, they regard Holocaust consciousness as a component of identity in the collective Jewish national consciousness, and the connection between it and justification of Israel's existence, as fundamentally illegitimate.

Moshe Zuckerman, one of the most prominent voices in this group, argues:

> The Holocaust has become the most pronounced ideological legitimization of Israeli and Jewish society and provides a secular historical 'proof' of its right to have been founded, to exist, and to have developed as it has developed in all of its phases, including the occupation since 1967, with everything this implies. ... In this sense, Israel has never confronted the universal, trans-Jewish meaning of the Holocaust *as a singular historical event* [emphasis mine – Y.G.], but usurped it functionally to fulfill its ideological goals, which are fundamentally alien to the universal essence itself. [Furthermore,] not only has existential dread grown in view of the Holocaust, but so has the ideological use of this dread. The collective Holocaust experience – in its sense as an existential

dread – has been gradually transformed, to the point that nothing remains of it but a political-ideological die that uses the Holocaust as a code. The myth of the Holocaust has supplanted the Holocaust itself, and the existential dread has become a fossilized ideological imperative. ... Thus, the Zionist collective makes a dual demand of itself: to dislodge the Holocaust from existential reality so that a 'new leaf' can be turned on the one hand, but concurrently to sustain the *zakhor* [remembrance] so that this 'new leaf' can be ideologically anchored on the other hand. Thus, the Holocaust line has to be nurtured without allowing the Holocaust to have too penetrating an effect in fashioning the collective's self-definition.'[61]

Even more politically emphatic was his partner in these views, Amnon Raz-Krakockin.[62]

Beyond the concrete politicization of the Holocaust, addressed to the Israeli government's policies toward the Arabs – which we take up again in the next chapter – this group also elaborated an idea that, paradoxically, turns Holocaust consciousness into a faith of extremists. Thus, just as we found political theology in the theological discourse, so do we find theological politics among members of this group. Both seek the meaning of existence: the religious with the assistance of politics, and the secular with the assistance of theology, even when the latter group is unaware of it.

Adi Ophir, editor of *Theory and Criticism* from the time it was founded until recently, presents a typical example of this trend of thinking. In a stylistic, boldly phrased, challenging, and stimulating essay – 'On Reinventing God [In the Hebrew: *Hiddush ha-shem*, a pun on *qiddush ha-shem*, martyrdom] – The Holocaust, an Anti-Theological Tractate'.[63] Ophir enunciates the principles of a secular theological tractate of the Holocaust. He directs his harsh criticism at the intellectual mythology and theology of the Holocaust – as expressed in the writings of Holocaust theologians and in the emotive, cultic grass-roots sense – that prompts the public to feel that 'the Holocaust is God'. This expression certainly makes readers' ears ring, as Ophir says. In his opinion, this vulgar theology of the Holocaust is based on four commandments: *Thou shalt have no other Holocaust save that of European Jewry*, in other words, the uniqueness of the Holocaust is a theological imperative; *Thou shalt make no graven or molten image*, that is, make no artificial, external efforts to understand the Holocaust by employing rational scientific and academic tools – by implication, anyone who did not experience the inferno personally cannot grasp its essence and meaning; *Thou shalt not take its name in vain*, the Holocaust must never be likened to any similar tragedy in the history of the Jews or of other peoples; finally, *Remember*, since this is an existential imperative at the national collective level, disregarding it is tantamount to the sin of assimilation.

On the basis of this mythology, Ophir asserts, a vulgar grass-roots and political culture of remembrance has taken shape – one that even academia has failed to avoid. Both factors, mythology and vulgarity, 'belong to this process of "sanctification" that adds an important layer of religiosity to our lives, however areligious and secular we may be'. Then, through associative dialectic reasoning, Ophir says, 'it may well be that the more developed one's secular self-consciousness is, and the more profound the disengagement is from the necessary conclusion from the revelation that I have beheld, the stronger are the connection with and the use of the modern revelation, that of absolute evil'. The danger, then, lies not only in the mythologization of the Holocaust by religious theologians and right-wing political functionaries, but also, and perhaps precisely, in the secular public's sweeping gravitation toward this cult, which Ophir, like others before him, characterizes as anti-rational, anti-universal, and even anti-human in its refusal to make the lesson of the terrible suffering the property of all humankind.

Because this is the problem, Ophir spins a web of secular theology that presents his set of imperatives parallel to the traditional ones, wholly based on universal critical and moral assumptions. In this web, 'thou shalt have no other Holocaust' means that one should acknowledge the possibility of another Holocaust and take action to prevent it vis-à-vis each and every people. 'Thou shalt make no graven image' actually means that an attempt should be made to understand the Holocaust by means of rational tools and exploration of its day-to-day details and its manifold human facets. 'Thou shalt not take its name in vain' really means that one should not compare the Holocaust with other similar occurrences. 'Remember' represents, above all, the imperative of attempting to understand and taking action that would facilitate such understanding.

Thus far, these rational commandments add nothing new to the conventions in academic study of the Holocaust. Even the theologians and politicians whom Ophir criticizes venomously would not deny this. However, when we examine the explicit ideology that lurks behind the methodology of this deconstruction – or 'reduction to factors', as he calls it – its secular theological nature becomes visible.

The first reason, as Ophir and those of like mind note with considerable justice, is that 'the process we take up for judgment here is the
political institutionalization of a shared national remembrance and, in
fact, the limits of the self-consciousness of the modern Jew, the self-
identity of post-Holocaust Judaism'. In their opinion, the
national-religious theological web determines their collective identity
by driving a wedge between Jews and the society that surrounds them.
Therefore, the alternative to this introverted and hostile approach is
the conclusion that 'a different gospel should come forth from that
inferno, the crux of which is the humanness of the atrocity, its being an
existing human possibility, i.e., a possibility of ours'. It is difficult to
ignore the Judeo-Christian religious symbolism, evidently inadvertent,
that emanates from this quote – devastation and a redeeming gospel
that emerges from it, the sin embedded in the human personality, and
the human suffering and the humanness of the horror as a way of
spreading the sin around. The sole purpose of this presentation is to
show that 'the contemporary meaning of the Jew's moral confrontation
with the Holocaust is the humanization of the genocide act and the
universalization of its possibilities. The universalization of the
Holocaust has become a crucial component in the self-consciousness of
the Jew a generation after Auschwitz, and an essential condition for his
moral being.' Doesn't this unequivocal statement – this categorical
imperative – express a rationalistic, universalistic faith rooted in the
secular religion of the eighteenth century? I would say that it does. *A
fortiori* there is no moral or political difference between Ophir's
outlook and the 'Jewish theology of liberation' preached by Marc Ellis,
as discussed in the previous chapter. Furthermore, it is hard to avoid
the ostensibly paradoxical thought that the far Right's nationalistic
slogan 'Never again' has something in common with the Jewish ultra-
liberals' quasi-universalistic expression 'Never again'. Not coinci-
dentally, the radicals were not indifferent to this slogan in the late
1960s and early 1970s.[64] Both slogans are ahistorical: the former disregards the limits of national power and the latter shuts its eyes to the
painful, stinging failure of humanistic universal messages in history,
from the French Revolution to the present time. In other words, both
have legs planted in faith and heads immersed in a hope that resonates
with messianic intonations. After all, both advocate and hope for a
thoroughgoing change in the order of human society and, as a part of
it, the status of the Jewish people. It is this faith that integrates these
political attitudes so thoroughly that one can hardly tell them apart. We
encountered this phenomenon in the theological discourse, in extreme

statements concerning the theology of power and the theology of liberation, by Richard Rubenstein and Marc Ellis, respectively. The next chapter in our study will deal directly with this question in its overall sense – with respect to both internal and external relationships.

To sum up the academic discourse, we can say that with respect to the Holocaust singularity issue we have found ideology and methodology to be related at two levels. At the personal level of scholars and thinkers, there is an almost total reciprocity between the perception of Jewish national uniqueness and the uniqueness of the Holocaust. From this standpoint, the Zionist Dinur and the anti-Zionist Steiner are connected by a single line. For both, either emphatically or implicitly, the state has historical meaning in that the disaster that befell the Jewish people has left an imprint on it. Hence, the farther one drifts from acknowledging the uniqueness of the Jewish people, the more universalistic an interpretation one gives the Holocaust. Only the ethnically aware are still willing to deem the Holocaust unique in several senses, but those for whom ethnicity is alien, those who espouse post-modern cultural pluralism to the exclusion of everything else, disregard these few uniquenesses. What counts for them is the absolute universalistic message of the Holocaust.

The relationship between worldview and research is reinforced at the non-personal level, in the very separation of those who deal in disciplines associated with Jewish studies such as history, philosophy, and critical study from those who concern themselves with general sciences in the same disciplines.

At both levels, the strength of the connection with the Jewish nation and the extent of the occupation with the Jewish cause are the factors that influence the perception of Holocaust uniqueness and its implications for the existence of the State of Israel. The particularistic or universalistic significance of the Holocaust and, of course, its relationship with the State of Israel rise and ebb commensurably.

NOTES

1. On historical research on the Holocaust generally, see Dan Michman, 'The Holocaust in the Eyes of Historians: The Problem of Conceptualization, Periodization, and Explanation', *Modern Judaism*, 15 (1995).
2. Benzion Dinur, *Galuyot ve-hurbanan* (Jerusalem: Mossad Bialik, 1964), Vol. 8, 1933.
3. Benzion Dinur, 'Our Fate and War at the Present Time' (1943); ibid., *Zakhor, Remarks on the Holocaust and its Lesson* (Jerusalem, 1958), pp. 40–1.
4. Benzion Dinur, 'Fate and Destiny in Educating Our Generation', *Zakhor*, p. 52.

5. Benzion Dinur, 'What We Should Remember on Holocaust and Heroism Remembrance Day', *Zakhor*, pp. 144–5.

6. Benzion Dinur, 'Our Fate and War at the Present Time', *Zakhor*, pp. 35–6.

7. Salo W. Baron, 'Queries in Retrospect', in *Colloquium on the Holocaust* (Dropsie University and Villanova University, USA, 1973), pp. 11–12.

8. See Yosef Gorny, *The State of Israel in Jewish Public Thought: The Quest for Collective Identity*, pp. 24–5.

9. J. L. Talmon, 'European History in View of the Holocaust', in *In the Age of Violence* (Tel Aviv, 1975), p. 26 [Hebrew].

10. Ibid., pp. 267–8.

11. Benzion Dinur, *Zakhor*, pp. 80–96.

12. Talmon, 'European History', p. 291.

13. Jacob Talmon, 'The Six-Day War in Historical Perspective', in *In The Age of Violence*, p. 294.

14. Shmuel Ettinger, *Studies in Modern Jewish History, I: History and Historians* (Jerusalem, 1992), pp. 256–66.

15. Lucy Dawidowicz, *The War Against the Jews 1933–1945* (New York, 1979).

16. Lucy Dawidowicz, *The Holocaust and the Historians* (USA, 1982), pp. 140–1.

17. Lucy Dawidowicz, *What Is the Use of Jewish History?* (New York, 1992).

18. Yosef Gorny, *The State of Israel in Jewish Public Thought: The Quest for Collective Identity*, p. 147.

19. Israel Gutman, 'The Holocaust and Its Imprint on Jewish History', *Yalkut Moreshet*, April 1991 [Hebrew].

20. Israel Gutman, *Ha'aretz*, 29 September 1995.

21. Saul Friedlander, 'On the Possibility of the Holocaust', in Y. Bauer and N. Rotenstreich (eds), *The Holocaust as Historical Perspective* (New York, 1981), p. 2.

22. Steven T. Katz, 'The Holocaust and Mass Death before the Modern Age', *The Holocaust in Historical Context*, Vol. 1 (USA: Oxford University Press, 1994); 'The "Unique" Internationality of the Holocaust in Post-Holocaust Dialogues' (NYUP, 1985); 'Quantity and Interpretation: Issues in the Comparative Historical Analysis of the Holocaust', *Holocaust and Genocide Studies*, Vol. 4 (1989); 'Defining the Uniqueness of the Holocaust', in *Historicism, the Holocaust, and Zionism* (NYUP, 1992).

23. Yehuda Bauer, 'Whose Holocaust?', *Midstream*, November 1980.

24. Yehuda Bauer, 'An Attempt to Clarify,' *Iton 77*, September–October 1980.

25. See, for example, his debate with the Armenian intellectual Pierre Papazian in *Midstream*, April 1984.

26. Yehuda Bauer, 'On the Place of the Holocaust in History,' *Holocaust and Genocide Studies*, Vol. 2, No. 2, 1987, pp. 209–20.

27. Yehuda Bauer, 'Is There an Explanation for the Holocaust?' *Yalkut Moreshet*, April 1992, p. 133.

28. Ibid., p. 128.

29. Uriel Tal, 'Remarks on Holocaust and "Genocide" Research', *Political Theology and the Third Reich* (Tel Aviv, 1991) [Hebrew], pp. 200–5.

30. Uriel Tal, 'The Historical and Spiritual Meaning of the Holocaust (A Conversation with Gideon Greif)', *Yalkut Moreshet* [Hebrew], December 1985.

31. Y. Bauer, 'Judaism After the Holocaust', *Humanistic Judaism*, Winter 1986–87, pp. 15–18; Y. Bauer, 'The Holocaust, Religion, and History', idem, Spring 1990, pp.

10–15; and Y. Bauer, 'A Response', idem, pp. 31–2.

32. *Ha'aretz*, 2 and 30 May 1997.

33. Michael R. Marrus, *The Holocaust in History* (Canada, 1987), p. 23.

34. Irving Louis Horowitz, *Israel Ecstasies, Jewish Agonies* (New York, 1974), p. viii.

35. Ibid., p. 80.

36. Ibid., p. 82.

37. Ibid., p. 84.

38. I. L. Horowitz, *Taking Lives: Genocide and State Power* (USA, 1982).

39. Ibid., p. 197.

40. Ibid., pp. 201–2.

41. Helen Fein, *Accounting for Genocide* (New York/London, 1979).

42. See her remarks at the symposium, 'Was the Holocaust Unique?', *Midstream*, April 1984.

43. Helen Fein, 'The Holocaust – What It Means, What It Doesn't', *Present Tense*, November–December 1987.

44. Zigmunt Bauman, *Modernity and the Holocaust* (Cambridge University Press, 1989), p. x.

45. 'At the Crossroads of History: Is There a Future for the Jewish People?', *Jewish Quarterly*, Summer 1993.

46. Zigmunt Bauman, *Modernity and the Holocaust*, p. 206.

47. Mark Mazover, 'After Lemkin', *Jewish Quarterly*, Winter 1994/5.

48. Mark Levene, 'After Rwanda', *Jewish Quarterly*, Winter 1994/95.

49. Tony S. Kushner, *The Holocaust and the Liberal Imagination* (Oxford, 1994), p. 278.

50. Henry Wasserman, '[An Argument] against the "Uniqueness" of the Holocaust', *Ha'aretz*, 8 September 1995.

51. Nathan Rothenstreich, 'The Holocaust as a Unique Historical Event', *Patterns of Prejudice*, Vol. 22, No. 1, 1988.

52. Eliezer Schweid, '"And You Shall Choose Life ..." The Holocaust in the National Reckoning', in *From Judaism to Zionism, From Zionism to Judaism: Essays* (Jerusalem, 1984), p. 123 [Hebrew].

53. Ibid., p. 135. In the same context, see Eliezer Schweid, 'The Spanish Exile and the Holocaust: A Study in Jewish Spiritual Response to Catastrophe', Background Papers, Memorial Foundation, 3 July 1990.

54. 'A Kind of Survivor: For Elie Wiesel' (1965), *George Steiner, A Reader* (Harmondsworth: Penguin Books, 1984), p. 221.

55. 'Why a Jew Can Only Grieve', *The Times*, 14 May 1988.

56. Ibid., 'A Kind of Survivor', p. 223.

57. Ibid., see Note 52.

58. George Steiner, 'The Long Life of Metaphor: A Theological-Metaphysical Approach to the Shoah', in A. Cohen and Ch. Wardi (eds), *Comprehending the Holocaust* (New York/Paris, 1988), pp. 50–1.

59. Fredric Raphael, 'The Necessity of Antisemitism', *Jewish Quarterly*, Spring 1992.

60. Alan Milchman and Alan Rosenberg, 'The Unlearned Lesson of the Holocaust', *Modern Judaism*, May 1993.

61. Moshe Zuckerman, 'Had the Great Genocide Never Occurred', *Theory and Criticism*, No. 3, Winter 1993 [Hebrew].

62. Amnon Raz-Krakockin, 'Exile amidst Sovereignty', *Theory and Criticism*, 5, Autumn 1994 [Hebrew].

63. *Politika*, June–July 1986 [Hebrew].
64. See my book, *The State of Israel in Jewish Public Thought: The Quest for Collective Identity*, Chapter 6, 'Revolutionary Radicalism'.

4

The Ideological Discourse

INTRODUCTION

The ideological discourse coincided with the academic discourse. The difference between the two was not personal, since many participants in the former also took part in the latter. The issues discussed, too, sometimes covered the same ground. The difference is that while ideology hid behind methodology in the academic discourse, the contours and purposes of the ideological discourse concerned matters of worldview. Thus, the connection between ideational principles and political perceptions and stances, which the participants in the academic discourse wished to dull, were discussed at length and with unadulterated frankness in the ideological discourse. Consequently, whereas the question of *uniqueness* stood at the forefront of the previous discourse, the problem of *identity* is central in the discourse to be discussed. In other words, participants in the ideological discourse treated the Holocaust not as a historical phenomenon of partial or overall uniqueness but mainly as a component of the collective Jewish identity. Hence, the place of the Israel–Holocaust nexus was more natural and comprehensible in this discourse of ideological complexion, as in the theological discourse, than in the academic discourse. Furthermore, the exceptional importance of the State of Israel in this discourse gave the country's political problems a role in it and allowed them to add a political and existential layer to the discussion both in the United States and in Israel. It was under these circumstances that spiritual and political conservatives and liberals in both countries, all perturbed by the question of the Jews' identity vis-à-vis themselves and their surroundings, squared off against each other.

To explore the public ideological discourse in the two countries, one must distinguish between awareness and consciousness in the public sense of these terms. *Awareness* is a situation in which the public's attention is drawn to a phenomenon because information about it has been disseminated systematically. In *consciousness*, a historical, ideational, national, or social lesson has been adduced from the awareness. The distinction between the two situations is not always clear, especially in the present context. In this sense, when we deal with discussions of the Holocaust and the State of Israel and their nexus in pan-Jewish thought in Israel and the Diaspora, we should draw several distinctions within the discourse.

The first distinction pertains to time. In this sense, as this chapter will make clear, a taxonomy of three periods should be set forth: from the end of World War II until 1952, from 1953 until 1976, and from 1977 until 1993 – when the United States Holocaust Memorial Museum in Washington opened its doors.

The second distinction belongs to the field of culture. It pertains to differences between writings in the Jews' national languages, Yiddish and Hebrew, and their writings in other languages, especially English. The Hebrew and Yiddish press, influenced by the Eastern European political culture, was ideological as a matter of essence. Therefore, the distinction in this press between awareness and consciousness is not always clear and not always especially important. In contrast, in the non-ideological English-language press, all writings on the subject during the time in question belong mainly to the domain of awareness.

The third distinction is territorial and political – between the Diaspora, especially that in America, and Israel as a state. One may say that until 1953, when the government of Israel enacted the Remembrance of Holocaust and Heroism – Yad Vashem Law (here-inafter: the Yad Vashem law), the public domain in both societies repressed the subject.[1] Since then, as we shall see, the scope and contents of the discussion have been different in each country.

The fourth distinction pertains to contents. In this sense, the discourse in the two countries resembles two diagonal lines that originate at distant points but subsequently converge until they intersect. The distance between them stemmed from the different natures of these two Jewish societies; their convergence was inspired by a growing similarity between them. The collective national complexion of Israeli society, in contrast to the civic/individual nature of American society, is the factor that determines the points of origin relative to the Holocaust in each country. In Israel, it took on the nature of public state remembrance; in the United States it was buried – in the first generation after the Holocaust – in the memory of individuals.

The *rapprochement* of the two societies, prompted by universal cultural processes and the strengthening of their political relationship after the Six-Day War, has also had a two-way effect in regard to the Israel–Holocaust nexus. Israel conveyed to American Jewry the perception, subsequently articulated in the slogan 'Never again', that was embedded in the very pairing of Holocaust and heroism: now that the Jews have a state, they will never again be helpless as a people, and there will never again be Jewish refugees in whose faces the rest of the world will slam its gates. This perception, as we shall see, became fundamental in the worldview of American neo-conservatives. On the other (American) side, the universal perception, which sought to cleanse Holocaust consciousness of its national element, began to flow to Israel in the 1980s – for reasons that we explore below.

ISRAEL

The ideological discourse in Israel on the essence of the Holocaust–State relationship preceded that which took place in American Anglophone Jewish culture by about twenty-five years. This happened for three reasons: statist, political, and national. The state institutionalization of Holocaust remembrance by means of the Yad Vashem law positioned the relationship, as Holocaust and heroism, within the pantheon of the Jewish people's memorial days. Since the Holocaust-and-heroism combination became a national value, political parties have sought to underscore their role in and contribution to it, both to strengthen their worldview internally and to advance their political interests outwardly.[2]

Beyond commemoration and politics, the public had a sense and an awareness of the existence of an overt *and* a covert relationship between the Jewish people's disaster and its rebirth. Therefore, it made room for them in the public discourse that took place in the press, most of which was of a party-political nature. Even the discourse in non-partisan press, such as the newspapers *Ha'aretz* and *Maariv*, was not free of ideology.

This discourse, which lasted for nearly thirty years – from the early 1950s to the early 1980s – took place within the political establishment and corresponded closely to the Zionist worldview of the parties and personalities involved. In the mid-1980s, the scene of the discourse shifted from the political establishment to the academic and intellectual establishment, although the transition did not cost it its ideological complexion. On the contrary, the academization and intellectualization of the discourse made it even more ideological and, for this reason, aggravated the ideational disagreements and schisms of the discussants.

The factor that typified the public discussion throughout the daily press was the Zionist-educational message. This prompts us at once to ask whether the educational nature of the message invested it with worldview differences of principle, since most of the press, as in the Yishuv period, was political and ideological. From the political stand-point, the adversaries were the labor camp, organized under the Histadrut (General Federation of Labor) and its constituents, and a shaky coalition comprised of the parties and groupings that made up the civilian camp. From the Zionist ideological standpoint, a different dichotomy prevailed. At one end were the moderate center and factions to its left, for instance various liberal circles and the social-democratic Eretz Israel Labour Party (Mapai); at the other were parties that espoused radical Zionist prescriptions, arrayed from left to right – the socialist United Workers' Party (Mapam), the nationalist Herut, and the national-religious camp.

Despite the political and ideational overlappings, a consensus of sorts coalesced during that decade concerning the essence and meaning of the Holocaust–State nexus. It was expressed symbolically by a liberal member of the central committee of the General Zionist party, Member of Knesset Elimelech Rimalt. In a speech he gave during the debate over the Yad Vashem law in 1953, Rimalt said:

> There is a relationship between the Holocaust and the establish-ment of the state. The relationship exists for a very profound reason, one of cause and effect. Who knows if it were not this Holocaust that gave the [Jewish] people, not only [Jews] in Palestine, the supreme impetus to liberate themselves and estab-lish their state? Who knows what would have become of the entire Jewish people had the state not come into being?

Then Rimalt, a secular Zionist, asked himself the question that two Zionist theologians, Emil Fackenheim and Eliezer Berkovits, asked twenty years later:

> Is it blind fate – pointless, reasonless, purposeless – that rules the history of this people? Is it possible that all the victims, the murder, and the burnings were for nothing, without compensa-tion? Without recompense? Apparently, there was a fateful historical reaction by the nation to the Holocaust – to establish the state.[3]

These comments, which, as stated, represented a Zionist common denominator, undoubtedly reflected excitement about the alternative that the fighting, statebuilding Yishuv offered to the extermination and extinction of the Jewish exiles. One may of course trace this feeling to the negation of the Diaspora perception that underlay its elitist and Palestine-centric essence. Evidence of this is not lacking. One need only read the remarks of the national leader of Polish Jewry in the 1920s, Yizhak Gruenbaum, who left this community in the early 1930s, embittered and disenchanted. In the opinion of Gruenbaum, who contemplated his failure to merge Polish Jewry into a political force that would struggle for Jewish rights, this failure was connected with the Jews' behavior in the Holocaust. 'Jewish Warsaw', he stated, 'entered the Second World War under the domination of a strategy of submissiveness and accommodation, masses having despaired of the strategy of fighting for their rights.' The outgrowth of this was the Jewish leadership's tragic illusion that it 'would manage to rescue a portion of the people by means of surrender ruses'. Then, after all else had failed, came the rebellion that saved 'the soul of the people and its sense of self-respect'. This led to 'the timeless legend of heroic death that would commit future generations to a life of sacrifice and struggle'.[4] Gruenbaum, of course, was not alone in holding this view. Therefore, Weitz argues correctly that in the thinking of the leaders of that decade, the fighters' valor was 'perceived as the only model [of behavior] worthy of remembrance and commemoration'.[5] However, in retrospect and reconsideration, one may give these matters an additional interpretation and discover covert facets that took years to become overt.

Elimelech Rimalt spoke of the establishment of the State of Israel as the enterprise of the entire Jewish people, 'not only [Jews] in Palestine'. Yizhak Gruenbaum, not always noted for balanced assessments and remarks, spoke – after condemning the leadership of Polish Jewry – of the rebels who would commit future generations to the heritage of uprising and heroism. In other words, the people that struggled for statehood, as Rimalt said, and from which the heritage of valor emanated, as Gruenbaum said, resides in the Diaspora. On this subject, the Left-leaning newspaper *Al Hamishmar* stated that 'the rebirth of the Jewish people in this country has come about as a continuation of the same struggle'.[6] Yehuda Gotthalf, in the Histadrut newspaper *Davar* – actually the mouthpiece of the dominant party, Mapai – outdid himself by elevating the struggle of the Warsaw Ghetto fighters to a valor unmatched anywhere or by any people in World War

II: 'We would probably not be overstating the case by asserting that at no stage and on no battlefield was the anti-Nazi struggle revealed in its full purity and splendor as in the desperate war in the ghettos.'[7] The Religious Zionist organ *Hatsofe* was unable to credit movements affiliated with its camp with leadership in the uprising. Nevertheless, or perhaps for this very reason, it linked the rebels' valor to martyrdom, and stressed that they had 'derived their inspiration from their profound messianic faith, the faith that makes us special, [the faith] by virtue of which we have established the State'.[8] Even *Ha'aretz* – non-partisan, liberal, moderate, and consistently critical of many kinds of government actions – argued that the Yad Vashem law, although not flawless, 'honors the martyrs and heroes who, in their death, sanctified the name of God and the Jewish people for the world to see and imposed the duty of honor, including self-honor, upon the State of Israel, which came into being by their virtue'.[9]

In other words, the very Diaspora that Zionism negated gave an edifying lesson to posterity in the Jewish state that, all these writers agree, represents the opposite of exile. Even if they stipulate that this admirable heroism is the opposite of the Diaspora spirit, it sprouts from the midst of exile and thereby creates a sort of dialectical unity between them. Even if we further argue that only a handful of Diaspora Jews exhibited heroism while the multitude practiced submission, the same may be stated about Palestine: the Palmah and Irgun fighters were in the minority, and activists in both of these camps subjected the passive majority, which tended to accept the situation, to no shortage of entreaties and furious criticism. Admittedly, this is a belated view, of which the 1950s generation was hardly conscious. However, even writers who posit only the handful of rebels as worthy models for emulation and admiration admit explicitly that the Jewish masses also contributed to the resurrection of Israel in the way they died and behaved. Therefore, it hardly seems possible to speak of an all-inclusive 'negation of exile'. Thus, it appears that the time has come to adopt a less habitual approach – more critical and more dialectical – toward understanding the relationship between negation of exile and the approach taken toward the murdered Jewish masses. Within this framework, the expression 'like lambs to the slaughter' – coined in Poland and imported to Palestine – which wields a power that stuns the intellect and outrages the psyche, should also be given more balanced treatment in the dialectical relationship between Holocaust and rebirth.

This adds yet another dimension to the bottom-line Zionist common denominator of Holocaust and heroism. Historically speaking the Zionist movement, as a volunteer political entity internally compartmentalized into political and social affairs, could function only by virtue of several basic principles that were amenable to its ideological complexions. These were, first, Palestine as a territorially irreplaceable national goal and the center of the Jewish people, followed by achievement of a Jewish majority in Palestine and, thereby, transformation of the Jews' historical minority status into that of a majority in its homeland. Economic restructuring of Jewish life for the purpose of social normalization, and the revival of the Hebrew language and Hebrew culture as an expression and a symbol of the return to the historical roots also constituted basic principles. Thus, the awareness that the Holocaust had contributed to the establishment of the state became an additional fundamental in the Zionist consensus in the 1950s. In this sense, the ultimate justification of the inauguration of statehood – the Holocaust, the tragic proof of the 'negation of exile', and heroism, beginning with the ghetto uprisings and continuing in the War of Independence – are not contradictory but complementary.

The tendency to contemplate the substantive linkage of the Holocaust and the state gained strength about ten years later in the aftermath of the Eichmann trial. Newspapers at the political extremes – *Al Hamishmar* on the Left and *Herut* on the Right – continued to accent heroism and juxtapose it with the Diaspora mentality;[10] *Ha'aretz* and *Davar*, organs of the liberal and social-democratic center, expressed a balanced view. *Ha'aretz* repeatedly stressed the glory owed to the minority of rebels in the extermination camps and the ghettos, ruling that 'we are duty-bound to transmit their glory to posterity'. From this standpoint, it is the very fact of the struggle, and not its results, that counts in shaping the collective consciousness. Therefore the 'military failure [of their struggle] in no way diminishes its moral value'. After emphasizing the nation's moral debt to the rebels, *Ha'aretz* re-assesses a phenomenon that, ostensibly, is the very opposite of the spirit of the rebellion – the passivity of the masses: 'To honor the minority that had clear and bold awareness, must we really disparage the majority that could not foresee the indications of the bleak future?' The newspaper blames this lack of foresight and failure to prepare for the imminent horrors not on a Diaspora mentality but on the universal folk characteristic of attempting to make peace with any situation in the natural hope that somehow the fury will pass. To buttress this argument, the newspaper states that 'None of the peoples that came under German military occupation rose against the occupier *en masse*, even though they knew their countries … and hundreds of thousands of them knew how to use arms.'[11]

In *Davar*, the newspaper of the ruling party, such matters were expressed more explicitly and clearly: 'The first and highest national ethical imperative in consecrating the memory of the millions who were slaughtered and burned, and of the tens of thousands who fell while carrying the colors of the uprising, is to foster the consciousness of partnership in Jewish faith, unity, and identity.' Thus, *Ha'aretz*'s apologetics in explaining the behavior of the Jewish masses are no longer necessary. Their behavior in death is deemed equivalent to that of the rebels, and their memory is mobilized in the service of the aspiration to Jewish unity. Furthermore, the main targets of these messages are the youth – those formerly educated to reject the Diaspora and to stress heroism as against the Holocaust. With regard to these young people, 'who were educated to defend themselves, we must find a way to induce them to identify consciously, not only emotionally, with that portion of the [Jewish] people that was slaughtered'. These remarks, written after the Eichmann trial, were meant to transform an emotional awakening and identification with the suffering of individuals, as arose from the testimonies given in the Eichmann trial, into a conscious collective lesson.

> We must understand and remember that each of the six million died for his Jewishness, was loyal to his Jewishness, and kept his ember burning – and in his death he contributed to the existence of Jewry and the Jewish state, which [reference to the state] has but one function: to serve the Jewish people.[12]

Thus the secular *Davar* seconds the views expressed in the Orthodox *Hatsofe* a decade earlier. Going like lambs to the slaughter has become a collective martyrdom which, even if carried out for lack of choice – after all, the victims could not avoid perdition by leaving the faith – remains meaningful in the sense of educating the nation.

An interesting phenomenon in this context is *Lamerhav*, the organ of the activist movement led by Hakibbutz Hameuhad. In 1953–69, *Lamerhav* articulated inclusively and lucidly the Holocaust-State nexus, the chain that links the rebels' valor to the warriors of 1948, and the relationship that should exist between life in the Jewish state and 'our exterminated brethren', both as a memorial and as a lesson to the nation.[13] After the Six-Day War, this newspaper, like the Revisionist *Herut* and the Orthodox *Hatsofe*, warned about the Arab countries' intentions, stressed that 'Nazism has not vanished from the world', and ruled that 'Our strength is the one and only answer to those who scheme to perpetrate a "final solution" against Israel'.[14]

What brought about the transition from hesitant acknowledgment of the dialectical relationship between Holocaust and rebirth to an explicit acknowledgment that gives both equal status in the national ethos and thereby indirectly obliterates the 'negation of the Diaspora' principle in the national ethic? The reason, which I consider to be obvious, indisputable, and alluded to even in written texts, is the painful impression created by the testimonies – neither of Zionist leaders nor of glory-wreathed underground fighters but of ordinary people at the grass-roots level. This impression evoked feelings of guilt and regret toward those who had been forgotten in the passion of the struggle for statehood and the coalescence of the state's image during its first decade. The transition to an emotional response may also have been an expression of ideological regret. This is manifested in an article by Eliezer Livne in a nonpartisan newspaper, *Yedioth Ahronoth*. Livne, an erstwhile political intellectual who had been ousted from the Mapai leadership in the late 1950s for his independent and critical attitude toward the party, was the first to note this phenomenon, which certain historians transformed into an important factor in understanding the attitude of the Yishuv and the Zionist leadership toward the Jews who had been murdered in the Holocaust.[15] Livne, formally released from the yoke of party discipline, confessed that the Palestine-centric Zionist worldview had inspired him and his comrades to continue to focus on events in Palestine and invest their efforts in the Zionist state-building enterprise. As he expressed it, this decision

> was backed by three generations of Zionist tradition, including the one I imbibed at home. I accepted their judgment. There was something fundamentally flawed about this tradition. We paid a terrible price for it. Disregard of the recent past led to many defects, distortions, and ugliness. We ought to resurrect [that past] and make it confront the fullness of our consciousness, in order to cure the national psyche of its illnesses.[16]

Livne referred to two matters: Zionist education in Palestine, which persistently rejected the entire Diaspora reality, and the behavior of the leadership during the war.

It is not my concern in this book whether Livne assessed the matter correctly or overstated himself. The historical research that develops this line of thinking is accompanied by studies that display a more balanced attitude toward the Palestine-centrism phenomenon and its political and psychological aspects.[17] All we shall say is that Livne's remarks point to several factors that contributed to the perceptible turnabout that occurred in the 1960s – one that may also be defined as a transition from the Palestine-centric Zionist perception to a pan-Jewish Zionism that views the Zionist activism displayed in the Yishuv and Israel not as a contrast to the Diaspora, the setting of the Holocaust, but as its extension.

Notably, too, Israel's second decade, the 1960s, is different from its first, the 1950s. The first decade was dominated by a protracted state of emergency. In each of the crises of this period – coping with mass immigration, a shaky security situation that led to military reprisals, the Egyptian–Soviet arms deal, and the Sinai Campaign – the ethos of heroism was needed as a device for educating and molding the people. In the second decade, that following the Sinai Campaign, the society of old and new immigrants had shown itself capable of passing the national test. Life began to look more normal and a more balanced and conciliatory attitude toward the past came into being. Consequently, the ideational tension between Israel and the Diaspora ebbed. The Holocaust-and-statehood consciousness moved into its next phase: from exaltation of the rebels' valor to the sanctification of the murdered Jews, and thence to concern for the Jewish unity in the here and now. In the late 1970s and the 1980s, in view of antisemitic manifestations in Europe and the advent of those who would deny the Holocaust, the value of Jewish solidarity in Holocaust remembrance became more important. From this standpoint, the remarks in *Al Hamishmar,* which for a generation had been a principal disseminator of the message of Jewish heroism that, in its opinion, should be used to educate future generations, are typical. Now, however, the same newspaper states:

> It is our duty to raise and educate a new generation that will understand Israel's partnership of fate with Diaspora Jewry. ... In the past few years a turnabout seems to have occurred in this field, as in others; the Israeli sabra is now aware of the horrors of the Holocaust not as a foreign horror story but as a chapter in the history of his people.[18]

Davar and *Ha'aretz* expressed the same line. *Davar* stated with emphasis that 'in our confrontation with the heritage of the Holocaust, we must carry on in profound identification with the fate of the Jewish people in the recent past and strengthen the sense of Jewish unity, for even today, [Jewish] existence faces grave dangers, be they physical, spiritual, or cultural'.[19] *Ha'aretz* carried the same idea to greater lengths by stating that the Holocaust era has not ended: 'It continues as a collective experience that we feel not as a matter of history but as an existing thing that refuses to lose its currency. It cannot and should not be otherwise. ... It is our sacred duty to speak about the Holocaust as one of the experiences that will shape the image [of the Jewish people] in this century.'[20]

The political Left and Right still accepted this stance as a matter of broad national consensus, despite the peacemaking controversy that erupted between them after Labour's 1977 electoral defeat that brought Menachem Begin's Likud to power, despite the war in Lebanon that Prime Minister Begin initiated, and despite Begin's attempt to stimulate Holocaust consciousness and transform it into an existential national imperative – a gambit to which people took exception even then. Nevertheless, there was consensus between two long-standing Zionist intellectuals on the two extremes: the Right-wing pundit and former member of the Stern Group, Israel Eldad, and the moderate liberal Zionist and editor of *Ha'aretz*, Gershom Schocken, both used the context of Holocaust Remembrance Day to warn Diaspora Jewry about the menace of assimilation. Eldad, with his well-known penchant for extremism, cited two menaces that threaten Diaspora Jewry: neo Nazism, which again aimed to obliterate them, and the Jews' own 'neo-exilism', which hastened the assimilation process 'to the extent of mass annihilation through intermarriage in the West'. Eldad, the radical Zionist, carried out a similar reckoning with Orthodoxy, 'which is continuing as in the past to sit in exile, chirping like starlings as they pray'.[21] An editorial in *Ha'aretz*, written by or under the inspiration of Gershom Schocken, expresses the same stance in more moderate language, stating explicitly that 'The destruction of the Third Reich did not eliminate the problematique of Jews' existence as a minority amidst a non-Jewish majority. The message of Holocaust Remembrance Day should be aimed no less at the Diaspora than at ourselves in Israel.'[22]

It is evidently not by chance that the heroism concept has been deleted from Remembrance Day, leaving only the Holocaust to be commemorated. The omission reflects the general trend of thought that places ever-growing emphasis on the Holocaust as a lesson of current, and future, significance. Thus, Holocaust consciousness became a mainstay in the inclusive national Zionist perspective, the one shared by both the liberal Left and the nationalist Right. However, at this of all points in time, the two approaches and the two camps attested to the Zionist complexion of this controversy by parting ways. Just as the pre-state Zionist movement conducted an acrid debate on spiritual, social, and political issues, on the basis of the minimum common denominator, so in this matter, on the basis of the shared acknowledgment of the meaning of the Holocaust and the state in the Jewish collective identity, there developed a controversy about the political lesson to learn from this nexus in view of the outside world's attitude toward the Jews and the State of Israel.

Two approaches can be discerned in this matter: that of the nationalist Right and that of the national Left. Because both rested on the Zionist consensus, their clash was less than a frontal collision. Even the partial differences between them, however, were of vast importance in the perception of the Jewish collective identity.

The nationalist Right, which consecrates the national interest in word and deed, turned the lesson of the Holocaust into a perpetual state of national emergency predicated on historical antisemitism, the new antisemitism that had surfaced in various parts of the world, and the Arab countries' hostility to the State of Israel. The most extreme and consistent articulator of this policy was *Hatsofe*, the organ of the National Religious Party. In view of antisemitic manifestations in various parts of the world – some overt and others, in the opinion of the NRP newspaper, camouflaged as anti-Zionism – it is befitting that 'on Holocaust and Heroism Remembrance Day we should remember anew that the world still evinces eternal hatred for the Eternal People'.[23] It is this nexus of eternal hatred and an eternal people that gives the Jews the identity of a collectivity ever-aware of the dangers that envelop it, and that invests this collectivity with a sense of constant suspicion vis-à-vis its surroundings. This identity is essentially non-Zionist, since all hues of Zionism intend, directly or indirectly, to destroy the ramparts of hostility and suspicion that separate the Jews from other peoples.

Cognizance of perpetual hostility toward the Jewish people becomes a perpetual and all-inclusive sense of emergency that obliterates the distinction among manifestations of anti-Jewish hostility. Thus, after a bomb went off in the Vienna synagogue in proximity to Holocaust and Heroism Remembrance Day, the nonpartisan *Maariv* wrote that the identity of the culprits – neo-Nazis or Palestinian terrorists – does not matter. What matters, *Maariv* said, is this:

> The fact that this criminal act may be traced to either of them points to the similitude of these players and their shared goal. The

ideology invoked in attempts to murder Jews is of no account. What counts is that the thirst for Jewish blood survives.[24]

Hatsofe, too, draws a direct connection between the Nazi Germans' genocide against the Jews and the murder of children by Arab terrorists. In its opinion, these children were murdered 'because they are Jews', and only the existence of a strong Jewish state guarantees that the murderers' schemes will fail.[25] Israel Eldad expressed this line even more explicitly and resolutely. For him, Hitler's *Mein Kampf* and the Palestine National Covenant are one and the same. Both have the same intent: to obliterate the Jewish people.[26]

The attitude of the national Left was not the opposite, although it was different. It neither ignored the existence of neo-Fascist and neo-Nazi antisemitism nor abandoned its concern about the Arab states' enmity toward Israel, but it refused to invest this dual hostility with the quality of eternity. Thus, it refused to accept the tension that stems from a constant sense of emergency as a perpetual feature of the collective identity. *Al Hamishmar* did agree with *Hatsofe* that 'the existence of the State of Israel is a historical response to the Nazis' plot', but maintained that the 'consolidation of the state, its security, and the ordaining of peaceful relations with its neighbors are the guarantee that the Holocaust will not recur and descend on our people's heads'.[27] The three newspapers of the national Left, in contrast to the nationalist Right, also participated in an effort to reduce tension between Jews and surrounding society by arguing that the Western media and governments had recently been inclined to fight the menace of Fascism vigorously. They also attempted to lend the Holocaust, as *Hatsofe* does not, a universal meaning without forsaking its Jewish particularism.[28]

Summing up, the discussion of some thirty years of Zionist public thought, in its ideational and partisan senses, brings three characteristics to the fore. First, the various ideational currents maintained a lowest common denominator with respect to the Zionist national lesson that Israelis should learn from the Holocaust and the rebirth. This common denominator served as a framework within which disputation took place; it also kept the disputation within limits. Even when the cleavages among political rivals became deeper, especially after the Likud rose to power in the late 1970s, all players continued to share this minimum basic perception. Second, the emphasis shifted from appreciating the rebels' valor to understanding the behavior of the Jewish masses and, thence, to concern for the existence of Jewry at large. Finally, a schism took shape between the national Left and the nationalist Right in appraising the attitude of the non-Jewish world toward the Jewish people. Here, in terms of the Zionist common denominator, the demarcation line ran between socialists and liberals, who took a more optimistic and liberal view, and the nationalist conservatives, who expressed a pessimistic and fatalistic approach toward anything associated with this nexus.

Another change in public thought began to occur in the mid-1980s with the advent of two trends of thought that clashed with the minimum Zionist historical consensus without forming a new consensus that would embrace the former one. One of the new perceptions is post-Zionist; the other may be termed neo-Zionist. The Israeli ideological polemic concerning the lesson of the Holocaust for the nation, especially in its implications for the historical role of the State of Israel, had been acrid because of its pronounced political complexion. Here, as stated, two new perspectives clashed with the old. Both of them, the former essentially anti-Zionist and the second ultra-Zionist in its own eyes, diverge from the historical Zionist national mainstream – the post-Zionist perspective in the attire of secular and universal liberalism, the neo-Zionist outlook dressed in the garb of power-centric, selfish, messianic nationalism.

The two perceptions developed and pulled apart from each other in response to the shocks that jolted Israeli society in the past generation – the Yom Kippur War, the war in Lebanon, the Intifada, and peace talks with the Palestinians. Each, however, derives its doctrine from different ideational sources in Zionist ideology, sometimes in parallel, sometimes in contrast, and sometimes in concert. Post-Zionism carries some of the universal-liberal, democratic, and humanistic ideas that belonged to the spiritual baggage of part of the Zionist movement; neo-Zionists cultivate the particularistic national and political elements that all Zionist currents once shared. Both, however, have taken these principles to such extremes as to have distanced themselves, deliberately or not, from the Zionist common denominator in its original sense. This has brought about a new situation in the internal Zionist dispute: the absence of a national consensus. With respect to the common denominator, both approaches are ideologically anti-Zionist and politically anti-historical. This is manifested, on the one hand, in the views of the negative post-Zionists, who wish to cleanse the State of Israel of its Jewishness, and on the other hand, in the ambition of the positive neo-Zionists to impose their will on another people. Both approaches are contrary to the aspirations, wishes, and beliefs of the population to which they address themselves – both Jewish and Arab – and therefore fall outside the scope of history in our times.

The nexus of Holocaust consciousness and state consciousness stands at the forefront of the discussion and the controversy in this debate. Indeed, the combination of Holocaust and rebirth is the crux of the dispute between the national particularistic and the liberal universalistic approaches. When the debate takes place in view of a political controversy – which is steadily becoming more acrid – concerning Israel's status in the region and the status of the Arab civic minority in Israel, the intellectual debate, like the intellectual discourse, becomes an existential struggle to determine the image of Jewish society. Thus, for both sides the Holocaust has ceased to be a historical memory and has become a lesson for the present and an imperative for the future, and the two sides, each from its own radical perspective, arrive at clashing conclusions. One may therefore say that post-Zionists and neo-Zionists are intellectually identical in their non-historical approach and that an unbridgeable gap exist between their national ideologies.

Beyond that, they are vastly different in the sociopolitical sense. Neo-Zionism, stationed on the right flank of Israeli society, is national-collectivist in worldview and bases itself on political parties and social organizations such as the Likud, the National Religious Party, and the settlement enterprise in Judea-Samaria. It has affiliated journals, such as the monthly *Nativ* and the weekly *Nekuda*. In contrast, post-Zionism is essentially an individual phenomenon that lacks an official, formal organization. It has no regular organ, let alone a political party that disseminates its ideas. Even Meretz, the party that represents political liberalism in Israel, does not meet this criterion. Thus, post-Zionism influences the public indirectly – through the liberal press, the critical electronic media, and the academic freedom available in the universities.

Positioned between nationalist neo-Zionism and anti-Zionist post-Zionism is a third approach that one may call dialectical Zionism. Unlike the mono-dimensional nature of the previous two, this third way is diverse and multifaceted. Dialectical Zionism is espoused by those who accept Zionism not as an ideal but as a historical necessity and those who once considered it an ideal but believe that the new Jewish reality has rendered it invalid. Other exponents of dialectical Zionism are those who cling to classical Zionist concepts and 'Canaanite Zionists', so to speak, who consider the State of Israel the only possible habitat of the Jewish national future. Dialectical Zionists, unlike the zealous ideologues of neo-Zionism and post-Zionism, are cautious about making unequivocal historical assessments and tend to change their worldviews. Some of them used to be pronounced post-Zionists.

In 1986, the ultraliberal journal *Politika* devoted an entire issue to the three-way nexus of the Holocaust, Zionism, and the aggressive policies of the Israeli Right. The authors of the major political articles in this issue had once belonged to the 1950s 'Canaanites', the social-ist–Trotskyist Matzpen group, or the Communist Party, and were currently affiliated with radical anti-establishment groups. Most of them belonged to academia by sectoral affiliation, although some did not hold positions in important Israeli universities. This issue of *Politika* criticized Zionism in an attempt to challenge its historical justice and moral validity from three directions: to dismiss its value as the agent that made it possible to create a safe haven for the Jewish masses; to convict it of having nationalized the Holocaust for political purposes; and to accuse it of invoking the Holocaust to create a warped myth concerning the crux of the Jewish–Arab conflict.

Boaz Evron, a pundit, essayist, and leading Canaanite in the 1950s, argues that Palestinian Jewry would have shared the fate of European Jewry had Montgomery's British forces not defeated Rommel's German forces at El Alamein. Thus, he claims, the entire Zionist ethos concerning Palestine as a potential haven for the Jewish masses is a myth; if such was the case in the past, it is no less so in the present. In the event of nuclear war, worldwide dispersion would be better for most Jews than concentration in Israel. In addition to alleging that Zionism could not have helped the beleaguered Jews, he opposes the Zionist depiction of the Holocaust as a unique or a Jewish phenom-enon in history. Notably, ten years before the German revisionist historian Goetz Aly[29] attempted to prove that the Holocaust is no way unique and should be understood as part of the overall Nazi intent to create a largely depopulated *Lebensraum* in Eastern Europe, Evron expressed the very same argument, perhaps with a stronger revisionist slant than in Goetz's version. The problem, Evron said, was rooted in European imperialism and not the German problem: 'The Nazis' intention in Eastern Europe was to import European colonial methods of the previous century (such as liquidating the native populations of North America, Australia, and parts of South America and Africa) into the European community of nations.'

The point of this dubious theory, which cites as support the number of Russian losses – between 25 million and 30 million – is clear. If the

Holocaust is not essentially Jewish, then there is no justification for the Zionist ideology, let alone the policies of the government of Israel under Menachem Begin, and anyone who sustains these policies artificially is risking Jewish lives. Evron argues that if the Holocaust was merely a Jewish and not a universal phenomenon, it has nothing to do with other peoples, who are therefore absolved of the need to resist the antisemitic manifestations that erupt from time to time. Therefore, he states by way of summary, 'One must struggle to learn the correct lessons of Nazism and the Holocaust not only in order to understand history correctly but also to prosecute the domestic political and cultural struggle in Israel.'[30]

The trend of thought that links the Holocaust with the Jewish–Arab conflict and thereby adds the Palestinian Arabs to the roster of its victims, was carried forward by Dan Diner.

His article, 'Israel and the Trauma of Genocide', focuses on the Israeli perception, as he defines it, of the Arab–Israeli conflict.[31] Of concern to Diner, who held a professorship in a German university at the time he wrote the article, was how the Israel–Holocaust nexus affects the Jewish–Arab conflict. Unlike Evron, the ideologue, Diner the historian does not ignore the Jews' special historical memory of being a landless and persecuted people that tends to regard the Jewish–Arab conflict as a continuation of its existential struggles with other peoples. In his opinion, however, the Jewish–Arab conflict is totally different from the Jews' previous ordeals. It is a demographic and colonial conflict, he asserts – a struggle in which one people, the Jews, has banished another people, the Arabs, from its land and thereby created a new demographic reality. From this perspective, the Holocaust consciousness deliberately and naturally masks the true nature of the conflict by means of metaphors and similes from the Jewish disaster in Europe.

Zionism, in Diner's opinion, applied great sophistication in exploiting the situation that came about after World War II – not only in what it asked the world powers to do but in capitalizing on the feeling that had gripped Jewry as a people abandoned by the ostensibly enlightened world. Thus, the world accepted the establishment of the Jewish-Zionist state not only as a solution to the Holocaust refugees' plight but as an assurance to the Jews against the possibility of further persecution in the future. Thus, the Holocaust has become a myth that unifies the Jewish people in its struggle against the new carriers of the genocidal virus (the Arabs) and a binding existential ethos. This, in his opinion, is the source of the misleading, artificial, and historically and ideationally false integration of the Holocaust and the existence of the state. 'This peculiar state of affairs', he writes, 'thwarts almost any possibility of confronting the true causes of the conflict. Any such attempt encounters a barrier: the memory of the suffering of European Jewry.' So firmly has Holocaust remembrance been inserted into the Israeli Zionist consciousness that 'while the Germans – who bear the burden of guilt for the genocide – wish to regard the past as done with and to assume that biology will put the past to rest, the Jews have kept the German past alive and well in the Israeli–Arab conflict, whose end is not in sight'.

For the historian Henry Wasserman, the instrumental treatment of the Holocaust in the context of the Jewish–Arab conflict, as noted by Evron and Diner, is a total educational and organizing device that the State of Israel uses to subject the Jewish people to Zionist reeducation. In his article 'Nationalizing Remembrance of the Six Million',[32] the author takes aim at Ben-Gurion's Zionist statism, which deliberately unhitched Holocaust remembrance from traditional historical remembrance of the destruction of the Temples, observed on the Ninth of Av. It is the painstaking effort to render the Holocaust utterly unique, relative both to Jewish tradition and to genocidal actions against other peoples, that, in Wasserman's view, makes this remembrance into an instrument that serves the state in various ways: to educate Israelis in national heroism as a contrast to the Diaspora Jews' helplessness during the Holocaust; to obtain reparations from Germany; and, especially, to invoke its lesson in the Arab–Jewish conflict.

These intentions were also expressed in governmental and academic forums – memorial ceremonies, establishment of university departments, and formation of public research institutes for Holocaust teaching and research. This nationalization transforms the Holocaust not into a national cultural asset but into an instrument for governmental use, like the nationalization of any other asset or means of production. This makes the memory of the Holocaust, communicated to the people simplistically so as to be comprehensible to all, a device in the hands of a regime that intends to control remembrance in a totalitarian fashion. When the nationalized, statist Holocaust also becomes a way to justify Israel's attitude toward the Arabs, then the state, according to Wasserman, is behaving like the Soviet Communist regime, which nationalized the memory of the victims of Fascism for political exploitation, and Israel's ultranationalist elements espouse ideas of deporting Arabs that recall the Nazis' Madagascar plan.

One who reads these three writers' remarks gets the impression that they ranked their arguments by degrees of extremism. Thus, Evron's criticism of the national and historical perceptions of Zionism ascends to Diner's demographic colonialism ('ethnic cleansing', in current terminology) and, finally, to Wasserman's perception of the Bolshevik intentions of the government of Israel and the Fascist if not Nazi ideology of Jewish Rightist circles.

It is hard to avoid defining these remarks as a dehumanization of the Holocaust for the purposes of Zionism and the government of Israel. The remarks are made despite the great enterprise of Holocaust-related historical research in Israel – at Yad Vashem, the universities, and the kibbutz movements' institutes – that over the past decade has probed the daily realities of life in hell, and despite public encouragement to publish personal memoirs pertaining to that era. However, we suspend our discussion of the phenomenon of post-Zionist criticism in this regard until the end of the chapter.

The opinions expressed in this issue of *Politika* attracted a much broader public reverberation following an article by Professor Yehuda Elkana about two years later – 'In Affirmation of Amnesia'.[33] Elkana, a teacher and the patron of a group of radical universalistic intellectuals who centered on the quarterly *Theory and Criticism*, is himself a Holocaust survivor who, like Elie Wiesel, underwent the horrific experience of the death march as a child.

Elkana's opus on the virtue of amnesia, aimed at the collective Holocaust remembrance fostered in Israel as Henry Wasserman describes it, was preceded and prompted by the Intifada, which drove many young Israelis who underwent the traumatic experience of enforcing the occupation and repression of Palestinians to despair – for which they blamed both the policies of the Israeli government and the rejectionist extremism of the leadership of the Arab national movement. In Elkana's opinion, these harsh feelings stemmed from different factors. 'Recently I have become convinced', he wrote, 'that it is not personal frustration, as a socio-political factor, that impels Israeli society to treat the Palestinians as it does, but rather a profound existential dread, fueled by a particular interpretation of the lessons of the Holocaust and the willingness to believe that the entire world is against us and we are the perpetual victim.' Elkana, of all people, a survivor of Auschwitz, 'regard[s] this ancient belief, which has so many partners today, as Hitler's tragic and paradoxical victory'. Auschwitz, in his opinion, is the source of a partitioning of the Israeli population between the rational, universalistic minority that takes pains to ensure that 'it will not happen again' and the frightened, anxious particularistic majority that shouts, 'It will not happen again *to us*'. 'In my estimation', Elkana concludes, 'had the Holocaust not been driven so deeply into the national consciousness, the conflict between Jews and Palestinians would not have led so many to act "aberrantly" and the political [peacemaking] process might not have reached an impasse.' Furthermore, 'I see no greater danger to the future of the State of Israel than systematic and powerful injection of the Holocaust into the consciousness of the entire Israeli polity, even the very great portion of this polity that did not experience the Holocaust.' The Holocaust is imprinted in children through the education they receive – in lessons about the Holocaust, in visits to Yad Vashem, and in marches to the extermination camps. Therefore,

> It may be important for the great world to remember. I have my doubts about this, too, but either way this is not our concern. Every people, including the Germans, should decide in its own way and from its own considerations whether it wishes to remember. We, in contrast, should forget. I see today no political and educational function more important for the construction of our future than this, and to avoid dealing day and night with symbols, texts, and lessons of the Holocaust. We must uproot the dominion of the historical [command to] 'remember' over our lives.

Elkana admits that he deliberately phrased his remarks in extreme either/or terms. He did so because of the gravity of the problem that he is calling to the public's attention. Thus, his article actually reflects symbolically the attitude of the post-Zionist radical liberalism toward the Holocaust–State relationship. The nexus of Auschwitz and Jerusalem, thus explained, acquires a negative if not monstrous significance and content.

Six years later, Professor Uzi Ornan, like Boaz Evron a leading member of the Canaanite group of the 1950s, carried Elkana's argument to a greater extreme. Like his comrade in thought, Ornan dismisses the existence of a Jewish nation and regards the contemporary manifestation of this idea, Zionism – the only player that still espouses this idea – as a distortion meant solely to warp the souls of young people by teaching them 'to identify only with what happened to the Jews of Europe and to know only one truth: The whole world's against us.' Three years after the insolent Iraqi dictator Saddam Hussein evoked associations with the crematoria of Auschwitz by threatening to incinerate the Jews and launching murderous missile barrages at Israel's civilian population, Ornan wrote that 'this education', which links the existence of the state with the tragedy of the Holocaust, 'is the main culprit in the injustice and the discrimination between "Jewish blood" and "non-Jewish blood" that have surfaced among us recently'. What Israel needs, he concludes, is a public educational thrust in the opposite direction of that in evidence thus far; the country should 'desist from the Holocaust addiction that is destroying generations of young Israelis. Do not wallow in the terrors of the past; turn your thoughts to the future.'[34]

Professor Yehuda Elkana's department colleague, Dr Moshe Zuckerman, even found a connection between the assassination of Prime Minister Yitzhak Rabin and the politicization of the Holocaust. In Zuckerman's opinion, 'the instrumental use of the Holocaust was not invented by the Right. It has existed in the Israeli political system since the system came into being, every single day. The political culture is utterly suffused with codes of Holocaust remembrance. Therefore, the right-wingers' utterances were not created *ex nihilo*.' Use of Holocaust remembrance cannot be avoided; the choice is between coupling remembrance with a universal lesson and coupling it with a particularistic lesson. The latter option, Zuckerman says, is usually accompanied by ethnocentric values:

> The State of Israel cannot boast of universalistic remembrance of the Holocaust. By choosing the second type of remembrance, the particularistic one, it has legitimized the creation of more and more victims. Thus, an essence that set out against repression has become a repressive essence. ... In the political dispute between Left and Right, the latter sometimes invokes the victims of the Holocaust to justify the reality of the occupation.

Zuckerman then uses intellectual gyrations to argue that the use of the Holocaust as a tool in political struggle by the Left – by Professor Yeshayahu Leibowitz, for example, who coined the odious term 'Judeo-Nazi', or by Professor Moshe Zimmerman, who likened the Jewish children in Hebron to the Hitlerjugend – is positive, not negative. This is because its intent is to liberate and not, as in the manner of the Right, to repress. What troubles him, then, is not the use of the Holocaust as such but the intent that prompts it – occupation of the territories and repression of the Arab population, or departure from the territories and liberation of their population from the yoke of foreign rule. The issue here, in Zuckerman's opinion, concerns 'two worldviews, one based on repression and the other attempting to cleanse itself of it. These two perceptions cannot be reconciled – as the assassination of Rabin shows.'[35]

The focus of the post-Zionist discussion, which has attracted our attention here – not to mention the critical barbs of all the discussants, each in his/her own language and rationale – is the concept of nationalization of the Holocaust. However, this nationalization, which the post-Zionists identify as the root of all cultural, ideational, political, and even academic-historiographic evils, is substantively related to Zionism as a national movement. Because they are unwilling to recognize this movement as such, they struggle to acknowledge it at all. Every national movement that has arisen since the origins of such movements in the nineteenth century, including Zionism, has appropriated the history of its national group, including defeats, tragedies, and victories. The Poles, for example, surely nationalized their years of repression by Czarist Russia after their country was partitioned. The African Americans' awakening and auto-emancipation movement definitely nationalized their period of suffering in servitude, both before and after emancipation from slavery. The post-Zionists' opposition to Jewish nationalism estranges them from any notion related to the uniqueness of the Holocaust. In this respect, they are not only universalists but also of one mind with Orthodox circles that reject the differentiation of the Holocaust from the other Jewish devastations and disasters – all of which, including the Holocaust, tradition commemorates on the Ninth of Av. Thus, in the consensus between the ultra-secular and the ultra-Orthodox in opposition to Israel's nationalization of the Holocaust, their historical anti-Zionist alliance was restored.

Since the Holocaust, the Jewish people has had no national movement other than Zionism and has fulfilled its national aspirations, in struggles, failures, and downfalls, nowhere but in Israel. In this constellation of ideas and actions, the Holocaust has indeed been used as an instrument to expose the collective powerlessness of the Jewish people during the Holocaust, both where the slaughter occurred and in the free countries that fought the Nazis. The argument of all post-Zionists – that it was not Zionism that saved the Jews – actually demonstrates the collective powerlessness that Zionism fought with only partial and small success. The issue here is not the ability of Zionism to have rescued the Jewish people even had it succeeded in establishing a Jewish state in Palestine before the war. Although all post-Zionists cite this argument recurrently, no Zionist leader did so, and such a rescue was impossible from the outset. Instead, had there been a Jewish state during the war, and had this state pledged an army of 100,000 or 200,000 soldiers to the Allies, the Western powers would have treated the genocidal actions against the Jews differently. Had the organized Jewish people been a genuine ally in the war against the Nazis – so believed even the anti-Zionist Hannah Arendt when she favored the idea of a Jewish army – it is very likely that the Western leaders would have offered the Jews who were murdered in the extermination camps protection in ways that transcended rhetoric. However, it would be difficult for post-Zionists to accept this view, with which, by the way, George Steiner concurs[36] – the same George Steiner who shares most of their criticisms of Israel, Jewish nationalism being as much an anathema to him as it is to them. Therefore, their lexicon of the Israel–Palestinian struggle contains entries such as a 'demographic', 'colonial', and 'imperialistic' problem – as distinct from *nationalism*. After all, recognition of Jewish nationhood implies recognition of a *Jewish collective* problem, not a problem of *Jews* as human beings. This collective problem as a national issue can be resolved only in the historical country in the national sense. The lesson of the Holocaust is embedded in this premise, because Jews were murdered not only as people but as *a* people. This makes the lesson of the Holocaust part of the memory, the ethos, and the collective myth. These, of course, reside in the background of this collective, which is embroiled in a bloody conflict with its neighbors. The rationalist urgings to separate the two – some of which are correct – reflect a misunderstanding of the folk spirit that emanates from excessive intellectualization and an elitist, condescending culture that is not only reluctant but also unable to fathom the origins of the grass-roots feelings. Many intellectuals – especially Jews in universal, anti-nationalist radical movements – have experienced this inability to grasp popular particularist nationalist sentiments and have paid a heavy public and personal price for this shortcoming.

As noted, the reverse of this radical post-Zionist mentality is the neo-Zionist state of mind. Those who attempt to explore the neo-Zionist approach in relation to the Holocaust–State nexus find that the neo-Zionists have written much less on this matter than the post-Zionists have. Furthermore, the more extremist the neo-Zionist groups or organizations, like Gush Emunim, are, the less intellectually preoccupied they are with the lessons of the Holocaust.[37] This reflects neo-Zionism's ask-no-questions, harbor-no-doubts attitude toward this matter. It is this that leads to the articulation of ultra-radical views. Although these views are few, so are the more moderate attitudes.

The neo-Zionist perception traces a direct line between murderous Nazism and the Arabs' hostile actions against Jews. The intellectual foundation for this mono-dimensional approach was laid down in the 1970s by Ariel Fisch, professor of comparative literature at Bar-Ilan University. Several years after the murder of the Israeli athletes at the Munich Olympiad in 1972, Fisch asserted that, 'in fact, the ghostly spirit of the Holocaust appeared a year before the Yom Kippur War, in Munich (of all places), in September 1972, when the world looked on as eleven Israeli athletes were led out of the Olympic Games, bound and helpless, on route to murder at the hands of their Arab captors'. From Fisch's perspective, the fate of the Jews in Europe in 1942, when the mass annihilation began, is indistinguishable from that of the Israeli athletes in 1972. In total disregard of the extreme change in the status of the Jewish people that occurred following the establishment of the State, which renders even the most brutal terrorism incomparable with the attempted genocide perpetrated in the Holocaust, Fisch rules firmly and unequivocally, 'The State of Israel was meant to be an antithesis of the Diaspora with its suffering, its hopeless faith in the justice of the Gentile world, a justice that was denied to the Jews. Instead, Israel itself has evidently inherited the very same situation.'[38] Thus, utterly rejecting the regime that preceded the political upheaval in 1977, Fisch substantively belittles the Jewish state as a phenomenon that has changed the course of Jewish history.

Fisch's status as the mentor of many members of Gush Emunim may explain how the editorial board of the monthly *Nekuda*, the ideological organ of Gush Emunim, agreed in 1991 to publish an article by a doctoral student at Bar-Ilan University, born in Germany after World War II, whose major premise is that 'the Arabs as a collectivity are morally inferior today to the Germans during the Holocaust. If they only could, they would eradicate us without feeling guilty after the fact and without any guilt complex and guilt feelings among the next generation, as happened to many Germans.' The racist generalizations in this article reduce matters to absurdity. Just as the Holocaust consciousness is part of the identity of Jews, Holocaust-scale hatred of the Jews is so entrenched in the Arab identity that it defines their collective identity. As the article says, this is not the kind of hatred that exists between two hostile peoples that have engaged each other in war; such an antipathy leaves room for eventual peacemaking. Instead, 'this is a hatred of a different type – the hatred of an entire collectivity, whose culture is based on hate and cannot exist without it'. This hate serves as a determining, constant internal need of sorts, 'because it plays an important role in the coalescence of the modern Arab identity, an offended identity, which after the golden era in the Middle Ages found itself devoid of genuine content'.[39]

These remarks are exceptional in their racist content and sweeping derogatory generalizations about the Arabs. However, the fact that the editorial board of *Nekuda* saw no reason to take exception to them, let alone to refrain from publishing them, tells us much about its opinion in the matter. One may adduce the feelings of the Jewish inhabitants of Judea-Samaria on the Holocaust–state nexus from an article by Zvi Mozes of Karnei Shomron, a settlement in the territories.[40] The article, moderate in approach, may be considered a counterpoint of sorts to Seidler's rantings. As a psychologist, Mozes discusses the collective trauma that the Holocaust inflicted upon the Jewish people and its influence on extreme attitudes on the Left and the Right regarding how to solve the Jewish–Arab conflict. In reference to the Right, especially his comrades and neighbors – several of whom he treats as patients – he notes that they distrust Arabs because Arab violence reminds them of the Nazis' brutality. Mozes wishes to rectify this situation not by forgetting the past but by understanding history differently. He proposes adopting a dialectical assessment of the Holocaust and, like many of his comrades – he says – regarding it as a 'pre-redemption crisis'. Accordingly, he comes out against his comrades' catastrophic perspectives and security-obsessive policies, which they justify by citing the horrors of the Holocaust. In his opinion, his associates' politics of death should be replaced by a politics of life, which 'may shatter political conventions and concepts and place the individual at the center of the political negotiations'. This changeover from politics of death to politics of life, he says, arouses hope for a settlement between the two peoples.

One of the most extreme and blunt expounders of the politics of death on the far Right is Arye Stav, the editor of *Nativ*, who orchestrates a group of right-wing intellectuals. After Prime Minister Yitzhak Rabin visited Poland, he expressed himself in words that leave little need for exegesis. He described it as an occasion of contrast, in which, on the one hand, 'an old, tired Jew stands in his people's killing field' and explains that the Holocaust teaches Jews not to be weak anymore, 'and at the very same time he dispossesses his people of their few assets and hands them over to the worst of their enemies, the successors of yesterday's oppressor'. Were this not enough – if the hand doing the writing is not trembling – according to Stav, the political formula of 'territories for peace' is the direct continuation of the inscription over the entrance gate to the Auschwitz extermination camp – *Arbeit Macht Frei*. Thus, the 'territories for peace' policy, by pushing Israel back to the 'Auschwitz borders' (a phrase coined by Abba Eban in 1967), is actually leading the Jewish people into a death trap.[41] In a 1995 interview with Yona Hadari-Ramage, Stav, following Erich Fromm, characterized the government's policy as 'a flight from freedom on the part of the individual Jew, who, terrified of sovereignty, flees from it as from a plague, willing to do anything to return to the embrace of the protective ghetto, to exile at its best'.[42]

Eliav Schuchtman, professor of Jewish law at Bar-Ilan University, expresses himself similarly in the same journal. In Schuchtman's opinion, the government's attempt to conclude political agreements with those 'whom historical experience prove to be untrustworthy endangers the very existence of the state ... and [shows] total contempt of the lessons of the Holocaust and the inescapable lessons of the Jews' other disasters in history. Accordingly, it is, in a sense, an unforgivable crime.' Schuchtman then adds what he considers an important lesson: 'the indifference of the whole world as the death mill operated relentlessly in Europe, without interfering'. Hence, he concludes firmly, when it comes to settling the Jewish–Arab conflict, one must not forget this lesson of the new world attitude toward Israel if the Jewish state must again fend off the danger of annihilation.[43]

The style and content of these remarks may lead one to conclude that neo-Zionism is in many senses a negative image of post-Zionism. After all, in reverse fashion it dismisses the erstwhile efforts of the Zionist movement and Israeli government policies no less vehemently than their opponents do. As for using the lesson of the Holocaust and its relationship with the Jewish state-ethos, both doctrines induct both of them, overtly and demonstratively, in the service of their ideology.

Between the radical approaches – the negative post-Zionism and the catastrophic neo-Zionism – rests the positive post-Zionism. In essence, and in contrast to those previously discussed, this post-Zionism is neither unequivocal nor mono-dimensional. In its basic view of the past and the present, its ideational attitude, and its political conclusions, it is more dialectical and empirical. In the intellectual and psychological senses, one may state that while for the negative post-Zionists the triple nexus of Holocaust, state, and the Arab problem carries a manipulative and malicious connotation, and for the neo-Zionists its significance is apocalyptic, the positive and dialectical post-Zionists endow it with a tragic aspect. Its tragedy stems from its historicity, from the recognition that it cannot be divorced from the historical circumstances that brought it into being and that were not under the total control of the forces that acted on them. Although it is not a fatalistic historical approach, it carries a layer of ideational confusion in view of the strength of the reality and the changes occurring in it.

Pronounced indicators of this attitude and all its traits may be seen, of all places, in Boaz Evron's article *Medina ke-hilkhata*.[44] A radical negative post-Zionist in the mid-1980s, as we recall, Evron changed and softened his views a decade later. He remains firmly opposed to the Zionist doctrine of natural traits shared by all Jews, but he stresses his acknowledgment of the existence of a Jewish nation in Eastern Europe. Thus, paradoxically, from a 'Bundist' stance, he also recognizes Zionism indirectly as a Jewish national movement; after all, it was born and raised in that region. Parenthetically, most Bund intellectuals in the United States after the Holocaust and the establishment of Israel came around to this way of thinking.[45] Furthermore, as an exponent of the principle that the liberal state belongs to all its citizens, he rules out Israel's definition as a Jewish state in all respects. However, he recognizes the historical necessity, upon the proclamation of statehood, to create and sustain a policy that discriminates in favor of Jews. Finally, despite his principled opposition to Zionism, he acknowledges its revolutionary historical role – a favorable one from his standpoint – in creating the Hebrew nation and giving it its political and cultural contours.

Following Boaz Evron, and in view of his outlook and doctrine, perhaps one should wonder how greatly, dialectically and even unconsciously, the myth and ethos of the Holocaust contributed to the coalescence of the Hebrew nation. After all, history teaches us that nationalism transforms primordial trends of thought and yearnings into an entity, a well-formed nation, under conditions of stress and external siege. Holocaust consciousness and Israel's regional political situation are nation-shaping pressures of these kinds.

The most conspicuous and direct example of the change in historical assessment is the turnaround in the views of Dan Diner, also over a decade or so, after his return from Germany to Israel and the European national awakening that followed the disintegration of the Soviet Empire.[46]

Diner both modified and refined his assumptions concerning the problematic trinity of the Holocaust, the Jewish state, and the Israel–Arab confrontation. In his revised opinion, the dispute between

Zionist and post-Zionist historians lies not in different mythologies but in cultural-value confrontation between the Eastern European tradition and the Western European tradition. The Eastern tradition places greater emphasis on collective values and national interests; in the Western tradition, personal rights and humanistic values hold sway. Both traditions are manifested in the Zionist attitude toward the Holocaust and the Arab problem. The Eastern tradition attempts to link the two, using the Holocaust, to justify the existence of the State and its power-politics behavior; the Western tradition rules out this nexus and condemns use of the Holocaust to provide moral justification for repressive actions.

However, Diner moderated the definition of the Jewish–Arab conflict and made it more flexible. Instead of the pairing of concepts that characterizes the conflict as *colonialist* and *demographic*, he now proposes to define it as a 'colonial conflict between two nations'. Although he struggles to accept Zionism as a national movement of the Jewish people before World War II, he acknowledges it as a national solution for the Jews after the war and the Holocaust. These matters resonate clearly from the epigram of his article, a quotation from Max Horkheimer, who in 1961 described Zionism, as a response to the anti-semitism that had begun in the late nineteenth century, as in fact an extreme manifestation of loss of faith in 'the prospects of pluralism and individual culture in Europe'. Horkheimer, a non-Zionist, reached the conclusion that 'a history-shaping aspect that has occurred since – in terms of both the Jews and Europe – is the factor that vindicated Zionism'.

In other words, Diner the historian has made his peace with the sad justice of Zionism, but as an intellectual he refuses to accept its tragic justice as its political justification. This, of course, touches upon the Jewish–Arab conflict, in which, he believes, the Arabs are already willing to acquiesce in the existence of Israel but not to recognize its Biblical rights or to make peace with the matrix that links Israeli nationhood to the Jewish Holocaust. Not so the Western world, which in view of World War II and the Holocaust recognizes the state and its frontiers as they came about. Paradoxically, these frontiers, which Abba Eban disapprovingly termed the 'Auschwitz borders' shortly before the Six-Day War, are no longer in dispute. In contrast, Diner finds the post-1967 frontiers unacceptable. Thus, according to Diner, the Holocaust and the state are intertwined from two different directions, with both of which he agrees, in the order given. He regards the establishment of the state as a necessary outgrowth of the postwar progression of history, and he rejects the use of the Holocaust as a source of moral legitimization for Israeli government policies. Summing up his moderate post-Zionist reckoning, Diner accepts the Jewish state *post factum*, after the Holocaust, but not as the fulfillment of a historical aspiration of the Jewish people.

The confusion of Diner, who, following Horkheimer, acknowledges the victory of Zionism but knows it is a sad victory, recurs in the confusion of the historian Yigal Elam. Elam also believes that Zionism has won – not because of the treachery of Western civilization, as Diner believes, but because it knew to strive for its goal with the relentlessless, the resolve, and even the brutality of a revolutionary movement. However, this victory, in Elam's view, came at the price of abandoning Diaspora Jewry during the Holocaust. When asked the troubling question of whether the Zionist movement could have saved at least some of Diaspora Jewry, Elam replies by arguing that,

> From the outset, Zionism did not undertake to fight Diaspora Jewry's war against antisemitism. From the outset, Zionism neither believed in the likelihood of [winning] this struggle nor showed an interest in it, for such a struggle would be the antithesis of the Zionist idea, which rejects Jewish existence in the Diaspora and demands the ingathering of the exiles and the construction of a new Jewish national home in Palestine. Zionism as a solution to antisemitism proposed a new path in which Jews turn their backs on the Diaspora and focus on the Palestinian enterprise. Zionism quit the Diaspora scene and left the Jewish masses there to their fate.

Elam traces all of this to the two-edged Zionist conception of negation of the Diaspora and Palestine-centrism – fixation on building the new Jewish society in Palestine. 'Just as this conception determined the vigor of Zionist action in Palestine', he believes, 'so did it determine Zionist inaction in the Holocaust.' It was so strong and resolute that it thwarted any possibility of a reassessment on the part of the Zionist and Yishuv leadership as to what was happening in Europe. Thus, it also ruled out any serious mobilization of the Yishuv to save whatever could be saved of European Jewry.[47]

In other words, if in Diner's opinion the state was sired by the Holocaust, for Yigal Elam it came into being because Zionism disregarded the disaster of the Holocaust. Thus, Elam, who for years has advocated the normalization of Jewish nationhood not by means of a

Jewish state that belongs to the dispersed Jewish people but by a state that belongs only to its citizens – Jewish and non-Jewish – concurrently criticizes and congratulates Zionism for its behavior during the Holocaust. He criticizes the leadership for its anti-Diaspora conception but stresses that only by virtue of this conception, of amassing power in Palestine, did the Jewish state come into being. Therefore, the implication of Elam's remarks, from both the ideational and political standpoints, is the need to uncouple the Holocaust myth from the state myth. The connection between these two myths lies in Israel's existence as a Jewish state. Only as such does Israel join the chain of the Jewish historical heritage, of which the Holocaust is part, and only as such, as an organized, powerful Jewish state, does it maintain the contrast that also represents a continuation of the continuum and the historical causality. However, Elam's ultra-Zionism, which paradoxically may be defined as 'Canaanite Zionism' in view of its political prescriptions – such as a binational state, a confederation, or an American-style civil state – leads of necessity to the undoing of this dialectical nexus.

The most representative historian in this dialectical group is Saul Friedlander, a Holocaust survivor who settled in Palestine at the age of fifteen to take part in the Yishuv's struggle for Jewish statehood. Since then, however, he has remained, in both the cultural and the political senses, between 'here', in Israel, the Jewish nation-state, and 'there', Western European civilization. In his memoirs, *Im bo ha-zikaron* (When memory comes), he describes the passage of a Jewish boy from Prague, the offspring of an affluent assimilated family, through his rescue in Christian institutions in France, to his return to Jewish society and relocation to Palestine in 1948. The book ends after the visit of Egyptian President Anwar Sadat to Israel, the prospects of a regional peace settlement in sight. The hope thus expressed is accompanied by doubt about the political denouement of this dramatic historical step and some confusion about the future of the state in view of the historical fate of the Jewish people.

Despite the prospects and the hope, Friedlander never rids himself of the thought that the rare, nonrecurrent historical opportunity will be wasted. Today, some ten years later, he still believes that unwillingness to strike a political compromise, nourished by the Jews' abiding anxieties and fears from the past, will influence the peacemaking process. However, he hopes that these existential anxieties will eventually fade away and lead the Jews to a sense of normality to some extent. 'Such an evolution', he adds, 'will of necessity have an impact on the centrality of the Shoah on the narration of Jewish past.'[48] This lack of confidence concerning the Jewish political future originates in factors that transcend fleeting moods that correspond to changes in political moves in the Middle East. His perplexity is rooted in his view of Jewish history: 'The uncertainty that grips us is different in meaning and occupies a different dimension. It has always characterized the Jewish reality, and in many respects – for better or for worse – it has made us what we are.' Therefore,

> when I reflect on our history – not that of these past few years but its entire progression – I sometimes conjure a picture of perpetual tumbling, of striving for rootedness, normalization, and security, a striving that again and again, generation after generation, is punctuated with a question mark; and I tell myself that perhaps the Jewish state is also one stage in the progression of a people that, with its unique fate, symbolizes the relentless bewilderment, the ever-hesitant and ever-renewing bewilderment, of all humankind.[49]

Friedlander belongs neither to the universalist school that dismisses the uniqueness of Jewish existence nor to the circle that asserts a doctrine of a Jewish mission and a universal message in the name of the disaster that visited the Jews in the Holocaust. However, he regards the uniqueness of Jewish existence, as he construes it, as a symbol of general human existence. This positions Friedlander on the narrow border between Zionism and non-Zionism. By recognizing Jewish historical uniqueness, he sides with the Zionists, but in his confusion about the historical future of the accomplishment of Zionism and in his reflections on the fate and history of the Jewish people, he is not one of them. Therefore, the dialectical process is also the path of Friedlander's life – from the boy, the offspring of an assimilated family, to the teenager and young man who identifies with Zionism and fulfills his identification with it by joining it, to an adulthood and maturity in which he embodies a synthesis of here and there, of Israel and the West (or the United States), not only spiritually but in the concrete sense as well.

The historian David Vital is another dialectical Zionist. However, the trend of Vital's thinking is the opposite of Friedlander's. Both agree that the Holocaust is unique; both object to making it the determining event in Jewish history, an event that for this reason affects the Jews' collective identity and their attitude toward their surroundings.

However, their rationales are different. For Friedlander, the objection stems from his fear of the influence of an excessive sense of the Holocaust on the Jewish–Arab conflict; for Vital, the apprehension originates in his concern for the Jewish people's image in its own eyes.

Vital's concern stems from his pessimism about the ability of Diaspora Jewry to sustain itself as a national collective.[50] He even argues that the interests of the Diaspora are crucially contrary to those of Israel; this is why the Jewish world, battered by assimilation on the one hand and susceptible to the dangers of an antisemitic revival on the other hand, is pulling apart (see Ahad Ha'am). The weakness of the Diaspora is the result of the destruction of its national center in Central and Eastern Europe during the Holocaust, at the very time that the Gentiles were showing, in a proliferation of indications and manifestations, that their ancient conflict with the Jews was not over. Accordingly, Vital vehemently rejects the universalist attitude toward the Holocaust, that is, that the Holocaust is not unique in itself, as ahistorical with respect to both Jewish and general human history. However, he also opposes the contrasting approach. In his opinion, Holocaust remembrance should be an auxiliary factor in reorganizing Jewish public life and shaping individual and collective consciousness. It is a much different matter, he believes, when this remembrance becomes the prime motivating force in internal Jewish community life. This, he says, makes the Jews the victims of death in the eyes of others and, step by step, in their own eyes. Such a conviction may be very dangerous, because 'little can be so destructive of the inner life and stability of Jewry, of its sense of self as an old and, despite everything, honored member of the family of nations, or of its capacity to sustain the manifold pressures which the present and the future surely hold in store'.[51] Therefore, Vital's point of departure is the opposite of Friedlander's. Vital rejects the Diaspora as a moral phenomenon – because of dependency on others – and expects the Diaspora to disintegrate into fragments that will steadily lose their interconnections until total dissociation occurs. His dialectical approach to the Holocaust is manifested in regarding its lesson as a factor that may impede the parting process and promote an effort to create unity. From his standpoint, however, the best guarantee of the survival of Jewry as a national entity is its independent state, which, unlike Friedlander, he does not regard as but one phase in the Jewish people's unpredictable course. In this sense, the lesson of the Holocaust may also buttress, to some extent, the state's ability to withstand the dangers that the future 'surely holds in store'. However, the lesson must not imprint Jewry with the mark of the perpetual victim, because this would interfere with the process of normalization.

Thus, ultimately, Friedlander and Vital pour their personal history into their perspectives on history. Friedlander, the man who straddles two worlds – Judaism and the assimilation of his childhood, Israel and the West, particularism and universalism – cites the abnormal progression of Jewish history in his arguments. Vital, who grew up entirely within the Jewish national culture and still adheres to the classical premises of Zionism, argues in favor of normalization. Thus, in their historical view, Friedlander places German fascism and the Holocaust at the forefront of research and academic endeavor. Vital, in contrast, treats these as secondary factors; what counts for him is the State of Israel as a Jewish national entity.

The dialectical Zionist approach is especially salient among *litterateurs*. Gershon Shaked, who since childhood has carried the scars of dread from the trauma that Nazi thugs inflicted on him in Vienna in 1939, articulates it with special vehemence. In his opinion, 'it is impossible to understand the Jewish and Israeli mentality without the Holocaust'.[52] This is the origin of his dialectical Zionist perspective that 'there is nowhere else',[53] the expression that forms the title of his book. After all, the Holocaust proved brutally, once and for all, that there is no possibility of sustaining a collective Jewish culture in the Diaspora. Hence, too, the understanding he displays in accepting the dialectical nexus of Zionism, the State of Israel, and the Holocaust. He believes that

> Zionism needed Holocaust consciousness in order to steer people toward the revolution. ... It is true that Zionism emerged from the menace of annihilation, but it sought to overcome the anxieties and illusions of the Jewish people and to eradicate the ambivalent condition between destruction and Messiah. ... Zionism also attempted to replace the main symbol of the destruction, the Western Wall, with a new national symbol, Massada, as an expression of a nation that fights for its freedom to the bitter end, its world not including the option of exile.

This contrast between the Holocaust – after which the option of exile exists, and which places an entire people in a state of mind of lamentation and Messianic hope – and the option of struggle, which rules out the option of exile, is the pivotal contrast through which Zionism attempted to absorb and interpret the experience of the third destruction, the Holocaust. The initial absorption of the annihilation of European Jewry in the Israeli consciousness was linked to negating the Diaspora and identifying Diasporism with the cliché 'like lambs to the slaughter', in contrast to 'Israelism' and the Warsaw Ghetto uprising.[54]

However, Shaked says, the Eichmann trial, the Six-Day War, and especially the Yom Kippur War

> led to an internalization of *hurban* consciousness as part of the Israeli identity. The Jewish dread of total annihilation has totally transformed Israelis' attitude toward the Holocaust and caused the consciousness of the destruction to be internalized as part of the Israeli identity. ... Eretz Israel was no longer perceived as a safe refuge and a final solution to the risk of the various 'final solutions'. Existential dread has become part of the Israeli identity and it dictates the basic ambivalence in the political behavior of Israeli society. The prospect that Massada may fall again has instigated a physical and psychological re-searching for 'tools of exile'. Awareness of the Holocaust experience has restored the consciousness of the Destruction *dialectically* and left the imprint of this consciousness on the Israeli Jewish identity.

Thus, paradoxically, the very state that was supposed to be the diametrical opposite of the Holocaust reinforces the Holocaust consciousness through the fact of its threatened existence. Consequently, 'those who assimilate into the *sabra* Zionist reality have returned, as it were, to the historical Jewish consciousness that they had sought to flee. The historical memory overcame all the ideological attempts to obliterate it. It rose phoenix-like and began to leave its imprint on the Israeli identity across the whole political spectrum.'[55] For this very reason, in the opinion of Gershon Shaked, whose psyche carries the experience of his childhood terror, it is this dialectical nexus of Holocaust and rebirth that strengthens his Zionist awareness. Therefore, from his standpoint, there is nowhere else; he is 'convinced that Eretz Israel is the one place where a Jewish person may maintain his complete and independent identity, if only he struggle for this identity and not be tempted to [accept] an imaginary identity'. This is because Eretz Israel represents 'the optimal solution for independent Jewish existence. I am convinced of this to the bottom of my soul, perhaps because I watched ... European Jewry fail in its attempt to assimilate and pay an unsurpassably heavy price for its failure.'[56] A. B. Yehoshua, whose life experience as a sabra is different from that of Gershon Shaked, shares the feeling of 'nowhere else' as a dialectical conviction stemming from the tragedy of the Holocaust.

Yehoshua wishes, first of all, to separate the Holocaust from the establishment of the state both politically and ethically. The state, he believes, would have been established even were it not for the disaster of the Holocaust because of the national development of the Yishuv. It is unethical to justify its formation by citing the destruction of six million, since their plundered lives are a greater loss than Jewish statehood is an attainment. Nevertheless, the two are related after the fact. 'The Holocaust has shown us', Yehoshua says,

> how dangerous an abnormal existence among the nations is: how dangerous illegitimacy among the peoples can be in our world. [This is because] we were outside of history. We were not 'like all the peoples'. Since we were 'others' in our ways of life, different from everyone else, it was easy to regard us as subhuman and to deem the shedding of our blood permissible.

Furthermore, if the issue concerns the relationship of the Holocaust to sovereign national life, then, in his opinion, in addition to demonstrating the danger of being an aberrant national collectivity among the peoples, the Holocaust also shows that 'the solution lies not in changing the world and adjusting it to the special nature of our existence but in changing the nature of Jewish existence and adjusting it to the world – in the normalization of Jewish existence'.

Dialectically, based on his desire for normalization, Yehoshua attempts to separate the Holocaust from other disasters that have visited the Jewish people in its history. One who likens these disasters to the Holocaust, he states, 'is in fact saying that this model of relations is irreparable, that we have no control over our fate, that we are moving about in a cul-de-sac. ... [To say this is] to blur the substantive difference between the destruction of the Second Temple and the loss of independence, and the Holocaust as a failure of existence in the Diaspora. The former, the destruction of the Temple, expresses our failure in administering our independence' – an idea that recalls Spinoza's opinion about how and why Jewish statehood was destroyed back then. 'In contrast, the Holocaust expresses the failure of our terrible passivity in dispersion, among the nations.' Therefore, as a lesson of the distant Diaspora past and the Holocaust in the recent past, Yehoshua demands and stresses that 'between these two colossal failures we must find a third path, a more correct path, toward existence among the nations of the world'.[57] About fifteen years after these lines were written, in a conversation with Yona Hadari, Yehoshua defined the Diaspora condition as a formidable disease, of which the Holocaust was, of course, its most terrible symptom. The disease is called 'Jewish abnormality', and 'Zionism is the name of the remedy for the cure of the disease. The disease is exile; the medicine is Zionism.'[58]

Thus, David Vital, Yigal Elam, and A. B. Yehoshua are of like mind, in a sense. All three reject the Diaspora and regard the Holocaust as a result of the Diaspora situation, which is marked by collective helplessness. All three understand the Zionist revolution primarily in terms of political sovereignty and national normalization. None of the three dismisses the remembrance and lesson of the Holocaust as a component of the collective identity, but all object to treating it as overly important. Therefore, all three, inadvertently, are subjective negators of the Diaspora, to follow the taxonomy of Ahad Ha'am, because they realize that the Diaspora will neither become extinct nor disappear in the objective sense.

In contrast, Diner and Friedlander, the bearers of Western European civilization, accept the State of Israel as the result of the Holocaust tragedy. They accept it as a reality forced upon the Jewish people by its disaster, and they assume responsibility for this reality. However, they neither identify with it totally nor rule out the Jewish Diaspora condition. On the contrary, sometimes they even regard it as a historical reality worthy of appreciation and continuation. Israel-born Haim Guri and the Holocaust survivor Gershon Shaked view the matter differently. For them, the Holocaust is more than a motive and a causative factor; it is embroidered into the national reality. In 1962, at the end of the Eichmann trial, Guri asked:

> Can the Jews maintain two realities any longer? Can they forget that they are dispersed among peoples who did not spare them from extinction? Among innumerable people who lent a hand to the genocide or who stood aside? It is not a disgrace when the weak die for lack of choice and for lack of a savior, but an existence that does not exercise the right to live differently is ignominious.[59]

Gershon Shaked positions himself between the two approaches. For him, the Holocaust is a component of angst in the Jewish and Israeli national identity. As such, it links the Diaspora to the state, even though each has its own intrinsic and separate existence. From this standpoint, even though he continues to espouse his 'nowhere else' formula, he is closer to Diner and Friedlander than to Vital, Elam, and Yehoshua, because 'nowhere else', to which he first attached an existential-national meaning, has now acquired cultural-national content. In other words, only in Israel can a Jewish collective or total culture come into being.

Amos Oz, the most politically involved Israeli author, has a very similar outlook. The war in Lebanon prompted him to object to Menachem Begin's identification of PLO Chairman Yasser Arafat with Adolf Hitler. In an open letter to Begin, he wrote, 'Hitler has already died, Mr. Prime Minister! ... Again and again, Mr. Begin, you reveal to the public a strange urge to revive Hitler in order to kill him anew every day.' Hitler, Oz says, materializes before Begin in different forms, in the personae of the enemies or opponents of the State of Israel. 'This urge to resuscitate and wipe out Hitler again and again is the result of a psychological burden that poets can articulate but that for statesmen represents a danger that may lead them down a horribly risky path.'[60]

There is no doubt that precisely because he fiercely protests the use of the Holocaust lesson in Israel's military struggle with the Arabs, Oz, in contrast to his colleague, A. B. Yehoshua, refrains from discussing its national lesson. At the end of a series of articles he wrote on Claude Lanzmann's film, *Shoah*, in 1986, Oz did not specify response to the Holocaust, instead contenting himself with citing the clashing views and conclusions of the ethical universalists and the power-flushed particularists, juxtaposing them without ruling in favor of either side, and identifying with the message of Lanzmann's film. As he expresses it:

> Claude Lanzmann's film says much less 'Auschwitz existed', and even Auschwitz was not inconceivable. The camera, the words, and the silences are capable of grasping that the past is still the present. Nothing has ended. Here is the murderer and here is the person who's been saved from the murderer's claws, and here are the trees, and here something happened, and here things took place, just so.[61]

In other words, the Holocaust is still an objective and ineradicable *substance*, although its *meaning* lends itself to subjective assessment – a matter with which Oz does not wish to deal. As with Shaked, however, the past is still the present, and the erstwhile dread still exists. For this very reason, the Holocaust must be kept out of the Jewish–Arab conflict, because even if it exists, it belongs to another place and dimension, and mingling them may falsify its meaning.

Let us sum up the three types of attitudes toward to the Holocaust and the State of Israel in the dialectical post-Zionist perception, as we have defined it. According to the first dialectical formula, the political Zionist solution is accepted *de facto*, for practical purposes, in the aftermath of the Holocaust. Friedlander and Diner are estranged from the Hebrew culture that came, and was brought, into being by the Jewish-Zionist national movement. They chose the Zionist solution because the failure of Western civilization had vindicated it. Nevertheless, their migration from West to East does not mean that they repudiate the West culturally and ethically. Therefore, paradoxically, with reference to Israel's domestic and foreign political issues, they attempt to fulfill in Israel what failed in the West during World War II. Humanistic liberalism at its best, the doctrine that went up in flames in the crematoria of Auschwitz along with the millions of Jews, is re-applied in Israel with respect to civil rights and Jewish–Arab relations – not only as a fair and just, if not essential, solution, but as a manifestation of the Western humanistic spirit of which the Jews and Judaism that emanated from the West were inseparable parts.

From this standpoint, the second dialectical approach, that of Vital, Yehoshua, and Elam, differs in its point of origin, the aspiration to normalize the Jewish condition. In this approach, Zionism is above all a revolutionary movement that aspires to revise the historical condition of the Jewish people by giving it national territory and political sovereignty. Therefore, it does not need the Holocaust as a justification; its linkage to the Holocaust is by negation only. The Holocaust attests to the disease of exile, a state of collective helplessness against the danger of annihilation or extinction. From this standpoint, even Elam, who disagrees with Yehoshua about the comportment of the Zionist movement during the Holocaust – arguing that it could have done more to save the Jews – admits practically and theoretically that Diaspora Jewry would have been helpless without Zionism. Thus, the exponents of this approach rule out the Diaspora in favor of normalization, and for them the Holocaust is a horrific attestation of the abnormal state in which European Jewry was immersed. In other words, without disregarding humanistic values and – while aiming to attain a Jewish–Arab peace settlement and without belittling the importance of the Holocaust in Jewish history – it is the sovereign state that will determine the future progression of Jewish history. Therefore, Israel and the Holocaust are not equivalent. This attitude disregards the fact that, from the popular perspective, the separation of the two – the state and the Holocaust – is still unrealistic and may remain so forever.

The third approach merges the fundamentals of the other two. On the one hand, Oz and Shaked are standard bearers of and great believers in Hebrew culture. On the other hand, they – especially Shaked – mourn the loss of Western culture. Shaked, who once believed that because of the Holocaust there is 'nowhere else' but Israel and debated with Friedlander fiercely on this point, concluded that, after all, there can be somewhere else for Jews as individuals though not for the Jews as an independent cultural entity. Jewry as such has nowhere other than Eretz Israel.

Amos Oz, in contrast, continues to stand apart, not choosing among the lessons of the Holocaust and not choosing between the universal and its opposite, the particularistic.

The difference between the dialectical Zionist and the post-Zionist approaches, as manifested in Israel, boils down to how much distance to place between the state and the Holocaust. Post-Zionists want a total divorce between them; dialectical Zionists, while acknowledging the dangers that arise from too close a relationship between the two, cannot separate them completely. They allow proximity and distance to intermingle and keep the two in tension.

Thus, despite differences of attitude among those of dialectical mind, all of them have something in common. Those born in Palestine/Israel and those who settled there reconsidered the modality of their affiliation with the Jewish people in view of their attitude toward the Holocaust and the attempt to elucidate the Israel–Holocaust relationship. Hanoch Bartov aptly expressed this situation by warning, 'I'm not a mythological sabra', as he sought for himself and his contemporaries – and those of the successor generation – 'wings to fly with, far from the mythological sabra [and] back to the two-sided Jew, the real Israeli'.[62] The question of the Holocaust–statehood relationship is embedded in this two-sidedness, or in Isaiah's well-known metaphor (Isaiah 6:2) 'Each [seraph] had six wings; with two he covered his face, and with two he covered his feet, and with two he did fly', whence the title of his book, *Each Had Six Wings*. They are the wings that cover the past and that elevate the future. Will these two functions exist separately or are they one?

THE UNITED STATES

Public discussion of the Holocaust and the State of Israel among American Jews, in terms of time, scope, and content, has been quite similar to that in Israel. Here, too, one may distinguish two main periods: from the end of World War II to the mid-1970s, and from then on. The difference between the two periods is that during the first, as in Israel, there was a consensus about the meaning of the Holocaust and the state, whereas in the second period this consciousness became disputed and fragmented. However, when the debate in Israel was shifting from the center of public consciousness to the domain of intellectual discourse, in the United States it moved from the Yiddish cultural fringes into the mainstream of American Jewish culture.

The crux of our discussion concerns the second period, but to make the picture clear and to elucidate the changes and the continuity in the development of the public debate and the interest it commanded, the complexion of the discourse in the first period should be sketched out.

The thirty-year period between the mid-1940s and the mid-1970s may be divided into two subperiods: from 1945 to 1960, the year Adolf Eichmann was captured in Argentina, and from then until the second half of the 1970s, when our discussion begins. Notably, the debate of the mid-1960s and that which erupted in the late 1970s are topically continuous. Even in the earlier period, opinions about Israel's competence to arrest and prosecute Eichmann, or concerning Israel's right to represent world Jewry in this matter, were already divided between universalists and particularists.

However, the discussion during the first period, up to the Eichmann trial, had nothing to do with that which followed. Within this fifteen-year time frame, one should distinguish between segments of time and types of newspapers and journals. Until 1953, as in Israel, the public usually repressed the matter. From then on, a clear difference between the Yiddish-language and the English-language press is discernible.

Below we compare the three most important English-language Jewish periodicals – *Commentary*, of the American Jewish Committee, *Midstream*, of the Zionist movement, and *Jewish Frontier*, of the Labor Zionist Movement – and the main Yiddish-language daily, the famous *Forvets* (the *Jewish Daily Forward*), and the journal of the intellectual Yiddishists, *Di Zukunft*. The comparison shows that from the end of the war until 1953, the main concerns of all the journals, Zionist and non-Zionist alike – apart from internal problems of America and American Jewry – were the political struggle for the formation of a

Jewish state, the problem of the survivors in the displaced-persons camps in Germany, the War of Independence, and life in Israel, which was taking in mass immigration during those years. Even in the non-Zionist publications, the Jewish discourse underwent a practical Zionization of sorts during those years. It transcended mere political support for the demands of the Zionist movement and concern for the fate of the fledgling Jewish state; it reflected an active Zionist trend of thought that expressed an attitude toward the lesson of the Holocaust. I refer to three articles in *Commentary* that address our issue directly, on three personalities who engaged in anti-Nazi combat and uprisings: David Frankfurter, Ziviah Lubetkin, and Yitzhak (Antek) Zuckerman.[63] The *Forward* exhibited a similar trend.[64]

As stated, the turnabout in this general Jewish repression of public discussion of the Holocaust, in Israel and the United States, occurred in 1953, when the Yad Vashem law was passed. From then on, the difference between the English-language and the Yiddish-language press became perceptible in the United States. In the former, including *Jewish Frontier*, one of the first and the few publications during the war that pointed to the disaster that was befalling the Jewish people,[65] the lessons of the Holocaust were not discussed. The situation in the Yiddish-language press was quite different. The signal that indicated the change was an article by the poet H. Leyvik in *Di Zukunft*,[66] which cried out against the amnesia surrounding the Holocaust in Israel and, especially, in the United States. Leyvik also assailed the Jewish organizations and their leaders for their inability to agree on a date for a national memorial day for the victims of the Holocaust.

Starting in 1953, after that article appeared and after the date of the national memorial day was worked out, the two Yiddish-language journals carried remarks every April about the European Holocaust and its lessons in the context of the resurrection of Jewish statehood. *Di Zukunft*, as the organ of intellectuals, regularly marked the occasion with a special booklet and the daily *Forward* devoted at least one article to the subject.[67]

In their outlook and trend of thought, the articles in both publications resembled those published in the Israeli political press. The authors on both sides of the ocean, brought up in the Jewish national culture, be it the Zionist or the Bundist, lauded above all the Jewish heroism displayed in the Warsaw Ghetto uprising and elsewhere. They dwelled on the historical significance of the connection between the ghetto uprisings and the formation of the Jewish state, in that the uprisings marked the inception of the turnabout in Jewish history that led an exiled people to nationhood in its sovereign nation-state, a turn-about that changed the Jews' status in the community of nations.

Over the years, in the aftermath of the Eichmann trial, in the US as well in Israel, the ghetto leaders were also crowned in glory. Thus it was important to writers in both countries to defend the honor of the Eastern European Jewish folk heritage.[68]

As stated, the picture changed in the 1980s. The center of gravity shifted to English-language forums and the debate became a struggle for the future image of American Jewry – between those who tended to ascribe to the Jews as a collectivity a unique status in world history, and those of a universalistic-liberal worldview, who objected to this.

The two camps disagreed in several respects, three of which pertain directly to our discussion. The conservatives countered the liberals' traditional Jewish universalism, which originated mainly in the Reform Movement and the Jewish Left, by stressing the Jews' particularistic ethnic and national interest. Where liberals embraced the Western tenet of personal equality before the law, neo-conservatives underscored the crucial importance of political and economic power, whose job it was to protect both the culture and the social interests of the collective in a pluralistic society. In contradistinction to the liberals, who had become disenchanted with the Jewish state for various and sundry reasons, the conservatives supported the Jewish state loyally, foremost because Israel, by its very existence, embodied the revolution that the Jewish people had made from a politically unempowered to a politically empowered entity. Overall, one may say that the liberals continued to view society optimistically despite the historical events and that the conservatives had arrived at a pessimistic conclusion. Therefore, the conservatives became criers at the gates concerning antisemitic manifestations that liberals attempted to belittle. Therefore, too, the conservatives also sought to transform the Holocaust into a consciousness of vigilance, against which the liberals warned as a consciousness of emergency.

The most prominent representative of the neo-conservative stance toward the lesson of the Holocaust since the mid-1980s is Edward Alexander, a professor of comparative English and Hebrew literature. Alexander inveighes vehemently against those who opposed the dissemination of Holocaust studies in American universities on the grounds that the Holocaust as a historical phenomenon is utterly alien to American society. Alexander believes that there is a connection between forgetting the Holocaust and denying it. In his opinion, disregard of the antisemitic sources of the planners and perpetrators of the genocide of European Jewry, and of their antisemitic successors in the present time, creates a bizarre anti-Jewish alliance of sorts between antisemites and those who deny the Holocaust on the one hand and liberals who attempt to lend the Holocaust a universalistic meaning and status on the other. Both sides, he rules, are attempting to steal the Holocaust from the Jewish people.[69] Of greater concern to Alexander than the racist antisemites, however, are the universalistic liberals. For him, the meaning of transforming Auschwitz and its Jewish victims – and those of the other extermination camps – into a universalistic metaphor is not to exalt but to humiliate them and to help the enemies of all humankind, especially those who hate the Jews. Therefore Alexander concludes his article with an unusually caustic statement: 'Those who deprive the dead Jews of their deaths are of necessity in collusion with those who seek to deprive the living Jews of their lives.' In other words, a universalism that negates the special collective memory of the Jews, in reference to their disaster, is tantamount to an attempt to steal their Jewish identity. In this sense, Alexander considers it similar to the Nazi doctrine that denied the Jews the most basic human right – the right to live – and required, as a condition for continuing to live, that they prove they are not Jewish. Here, of course, the Jewish right to live, allegedly revoked, is not individual but collective. From this standpoint, Alexander's remarks are certainly justified if they refer to ultraliberals who rule out the existence of a Jewish nation. However, his terrifying comparison with Nazi ideology is out of place, not only in the moral respect, which Alexander certainly did not have in mind, but also from the ideational perspective, that of principle. Since the ultra-liberals consider universalism to be the defining characteristic of Judaism, their insistence on the universal message of the Holocaust is meant not to revoke the Jews' identity but to restore their true identity, in contrast to antisemitic historians and anti-Israel Arab propagandists who deny the Holocaust for political purposes. Today, more than ten years later, Alexander – who is also affiliated with the Israeli Right – has made Holocaust consciousness a political tool with which he attacks the ideology of the Israeli Left. We shall discuss this below in the context of the attitude toward this issue of rightist circles, especially Gush Emunim.

Earl Raab, director of the Jewish Federation of San Francisco and a prominent neo-conservative, took this policy of projecting from yesterday's lesson of the Holocaust onto today's antisemitic movements and manifestations to new lengths. Raab alleged a strand that directly links the Nazi attempt to annihilate the Jews to the political intent of the

PLO, the Khomeinist regime in Iran, and the followers of this regime in the Muslim world, to obliterate the State of Israel. Raab reproaches American Jews who protest a demonstration by a few dozen anti-semites in a Chicago neighborhood but respond with silence to overt slogans that urge the obliteration of Israel.[70] To Raab's mind, this intent – a continuation of the Nazi plot – is different from and more extreme than historical antisemitism.

The most lucid and unequivocal exponents of this view were the two leading personalities and trailblazers in the neo-conservative camp, the social thinker and pundit Irving Kristol and the editor of *Commentary*, Norman Podhoretz. In 1984, in the aftermath of the war in Lebanon, Podhoretz expressed his disapproval of the fierce criticism that various Jewish liberal circles leveled against Israeli government policies and noted with satisfaction that, despite this criticism, the Jews had emerged united from this political ordeal, which – to put it mildly – was not among the most successful. This occurred, he says, because, thanks to Israel, world Jewry is still a reality. Like Israel, world Jewry extricated itself from Lebanon slightly bruised but not overwhelmed by the crisis. By so doing, Podhoretz believes, the Jews proclaimed that threats and temptations would not banish their awareness that, at the present time, it is the Jews' prime imperative to deny Hitler post-humous victories, and above all it should be clear that, in the present generation, they must do nothing that might strengthen Israel's mortal enemies.[71] Four years later, Kristol proclaimed that after the Holocaust the State of Israel is the Jewish people's lifebuoy.[72]

Alongside radical neo-conservatives such as Alexander, Podhoretz, and Kristol, we find moderate neo-conservatives: Robert Alter, a professor of comparative literature and a regular contributor to *Commentary*, and the historian Henry Feingold, who researched American Jewry during World War II and dwelled on the attitude of its leaders toward the Holocaust in Europe.

Feingold explains what Alexander called the 'stealing of the Holocaust' in his own way and set it within a broader social back-ground. Whereas Alexander treats this theft as a continuation and articulation of the antisemitic ideology, Feingold lends the trend a political explanation. In his view, various deprived and victimized groups struggle to attain the status of victims of racism and genocide for reasons beyond the desire to obtain social or moral compensation for their suffering. What they want, he says, is political power. According to Feingold, all these groups learned that by controlling the past one can, to a certain extent, regulate or control the present and even the future. This makes history a battlefield in which the first casualty is truth. Therefore, Jewish historians of the Holocaust have been accused of fostering a sacred particularism that eternalizes the victim in order to obtain a special social status. Feingold includes the Jewish state in this struggle for history, because the state was established to compensate the victims of the Holocaust, even though, tragically and paradoxically, the overwhelming majority of them were no longer among the living upon its proclamation. Just the same, the state, which in his opinion has changed the progression of Jewish history by its very existence in a hostile region, continues to bear the fate of Jewish history. The menace of annihilation that threatens Israel is inextricably related to the global struggle between the Communist world and the free world, for example the American–Soviet crises during the 1973 Yom Kippur War. In other words, just as the German Nazis' lust to shed Jewish blood belonged to their global plan to dominate Europe and beyond, so the assault against Israel is part of the all-inclusive Communist scheme.

This reasoning makes Auschwitz a symbol of the fate of the Jewish people in the global struggle for world dominion. The Nazis considered the Jews their great enemies in their drive to attain their goals, and the Communists deem Israel to be an obstacle in their drive to dominate the Middle East. It is this that gives the concept of Auschwitz its special significance; it is this that distinguishes it from Musa Dagh, the mountain where the last of the Armenians holed up. The former is at the very heart of history; the latter remains on the fringes. In Feingold's words, 'the resonance of Auschwitz has a sustained world-wide implication. It remains linked in a chain of causation, rather than standing as an isolated event which occurred on the periphery of the historical canvas.'[73]

Beyond the lesson that emanates from the past, Feingold deems important the meaning of the change in the present. This, in his opinion, is symbolized by the transition from Auschwitz to Entebbe, from where Jews were murdered to where Jews were liberated by Israeli paratroopers. Therefore, just as 'Auschwitz symbolizes the end of the old universalistic Jewish dream, so Entebbe represents the new Jewish particularism'. Feingold, more than Alexander, is aware of and sensitive to the general significance of the Holocaust. Both, however, agree that its particularism is also its universalism. Feingold, adopting the viewpoint of historians and sociologists, argues that the Holocaust cannot be comprehended without its setting of modern society and the bureaucratic nation-state that loosed the technological and organizational forces of destruction. The Jews, he stresses, should be aware of this more than other peoples. Thus, they should sound the alarm whenever further danger looms, because their silence today may be a moral failure comparable to the Western leadership's insensitivity and inaction as the crematoria of Auschwitz released their smoke. It is clear from Feingold's standpoint, however, that the crier at the gate is the national or ethnic Jew, not the universalistic Jew as his sociologist colleagues believe. From this point of view, Feingold regards the Holocaust as a decisive event in Jewish history: the loss of European Jewry detached the rest of Jewry from its cultural origins; the establishment of the State of Israel transformed relations between Jews and other peoples; and the Jews, as a nation and not as individuals, became the agents that warn society against a further Holocaust.

A scholar with views much like Feingold's, although very critical of Alexander's, is Robert Alter. Alter's approach may be said to reside between that of the neo-conservatives and that of the liberals. He criticized both the conservative and the ultra-liberal perceptions pungently for having distorted the meaning of the Holocaust – the former in their power-centric nationalism and the latter in their universalistic altruism. With respect to the liberal Left, Alter argued that after millions of Jews had been annihilated so easily as the free world looked on, Jews must no longer treat their own strength with contempt. Although this strength is limited within the global political and military constellation: 'Jews cannot now contemplate divesting themselves of whatever modicum of power they can manage to wield. ... One hardly needs to be associated with the Zionist Right to reach this conclusion.'[74]

This is the only historical and existential lesson that Alter is willing to adduce from the Holocaust. In contrast to the views of theologians such as Fackenheim and Greenberg, and especially unlike the ultranational outlook of Alexander and even Feingold, he refuses to regard the establishment of the state as a direct outcome of the Holocaust. He believes the Jewish state would have arisen in any case, on the basis of the national community that Zionism had created in Palestine and its willingness to fight for statehood. Many historians of the Yishuv period agree. Alter rejects with special intensity the tendency to merge the lesson of the Holocaust with Israel's political and military struggle with the Arabs for Palestine and its impact on the attitude toward the Arabs in the territories that came under Israeli control in the Six-Day War. Tracing a line from the Nazi pathology to the Arab hostility, he explains, is both substantively and historically incorrect and, from the political standpoint, harmful to Jewish–Gentile relations.

It should be stressed, however, that even Alter does not build an impermeable wall between the lesson of the Holocaust and the Jewish state. Even if Israel was not established because of the Holocaust, its very existence as a sovereign Jewish state with a modicum of political and military power makes it a response, albeit limited, to the Jews' collective helplessness during the Holocaust. In this sense, Alter accepts the basic premise of the American neo-conservatives and, of course, of Zionists in the Diaspora and in Israel – that the establishment of Jewish statehood is a key development in Jewish history, one that has transformed relations between Jews and their surroundings, wherever they are, and predicates this relationship on a modicum of force. Exponents of this outlook disagree about the magnitude, scope, and validity of this force, ranging from the mystic approach of 'never again' to the *realpolitik* acknowledgment of the blessings and limits of force.

At the opposite pole of this spectrum of views are the liberal thinkers, of whom the most prominent are the Reform rabbi Arnold Jacob Wolf, a pundit and educator who has a personal relationship with the State of Israel; Leonard Fein, a public figure and editor of the monthly journal *Moment*; and Professor Ismar Schorsch, a historian and rector of the Jewish Theological Seminary in New York. The three of them sounded a powerful public warning against the coalescence of a Jewish-power myth and ethos that combines the lesson of the Holocaust, Israel's military strength, and the political influence of American Jewry into a national rite with religious ingredients. Wolf, the educator, links the Holocaust-and-state consciousness to the process of Jewish normalization. In his opinion, two novelties appeared on the Jewish public stage in this progression of historical and social development: a new Jewish type of the socially assimilated get-ahead technocrat and money man, and a State of Israel that has ceased to be Zion – the focus of the lofty yearnings and hopes of the Jew, whose true spiritual and moral identity may be fulfilled only there. Since then, this state has become an exemplar of something totally different: 'Israel now means power, particularly naked military power.'

This transformation from the particularistic to the normal has recurred with respect to the Holocaust. Instead of the traditional view that links the tragedy to Jewish martyrdom or martyrology, instead of vacillation over the question of theodicy in view of this horrific, problematic tragedy – the young in particular have assimilated the conviction that the Holocaust is above all a warning: 'If the Jews are powerless they will be killed, hence they must not be powerless again.'

Both types of Jewish normalization, that resting on economic power in the United States and that based on military power in Israel, are expressions of the process of Jewish assimilation. According to Wolf, however, it is not the same process that occurred in Europe a century earlier: 'In the Enlightenment period we were advised by Jewish thinkers to be Jews at home but human beings abroad. Now, apparently, the roles are to be reversed.' Outdoors, Jews demonstrate loyalty to their people and defend their collective interests; at home, a different climate devoid of all Jewish content prevails. This leads Wolf to an inverse apocalyptic state of mind. The Holocaust-and-power rite that corresponds to normalization in the Diaspora and in Israel – which many regard as a manifestation of the rebirth of the people after its disaster – spells the opposite of normalization: 'To me it is death of the Jewish spirit and the last assimilation of all.'

The paradox in Wolf's remarks is that this Holocaust rite, which leads to the power rite that expresses the destructive tendency of aspiring to a normalization that substantiates the assimilation process, also erects a buffer between the Jews and their surroundings by fostering a consciousness of constant siege and the conviction that they are at risk of annihilation. These emotions make the Jews potential victims in their own eyes and evoke estrangement from others' suffering – as American Jews reflect in their attitude toward African Americans and as Israel expresses in its attitude toward the Palestinians. In view of this pessimistic analysis and its attendant prophecy of devastation, all Wolf can do is ask the Jews to find a way to return to themselves, neither as victims nor as persecutors but as a people with 'a creative [and ancient] tradition in which we taught the world some of its greatest lessons'.[75]

Underlying Wolf's remarks was the idealistic Zionist viewpoint of some thinkers in the Reform Movement – rabbis and academics – who regarded the State of Israel as a phase in a spiritual and moral progression toward the 'yearned-for Zion'. They adhered to the uniqueness of Judaism as a moral and human faith by force of this religious and liberal utopianism, but there was a difference between them and their spiritual forebears who had founded the movement more than one hundred years earlier: they strongly associated the uniqueness, humanism, and universalism of Judaism with Jerusalem, not only as the celestial city but as the capital of Israel. Therefore, it was specifically from the Reform Movement, which in the distant past wished to normalize the status of Judaism as a religion and of the Jews as believers – an ideal to which much of the movement still aspires – that Wolf's vociferous protest against normalization emanated.

Six years later, in the midst of the debate concerning the United States Holocaust Memorial Museum in Washington and intentions to establish Holocaust memorials in other American cities, Leonard Fein wrote a caustic, derisive polemic about the Holocaust rite that was spreading among the Jews. In Fein's opinion, this ritual awakening and excitement originate in disenchantment and frustration on the part of secular Jews, who have despaired of utopian Messianism, and of believers, who have tired of waiting for the divinely appointed Messiah. Thus, the Holocaust rite has materialized as a surrogate of sorts, in which the tragic and satanic apocalypse usurps the place of the noble, exalted redemption. As the proponent of an approximation of the American version of the Zionist viewpoint, Fein reached a bitter conclusion: 'If Sinai is too far or too frightening – and for most of us it is both – look to Auschwitz, look to the one thing that absolutely sets us apart, that makes Jews special, look to the chimneys, O the chimneys.'[76]

For both Wolf and Fein, the 'smoking chimneys of the crematoria' – if one may use this horrible metaphor – are a surrogate for Mount Sinai. However, while Wolf regards this way of thinking as a dangerous signpost on the path to assimilationist normalization, Fein considers it a distorting tool with which to keep the Jews united and unique. Be this as it may, for both of them and for their opponents on the Right, the Holocaust and the State of Israel are tightly intertwined.

Alongside the liberal stance, a viewpoint developed at this time that sought indirectly and directly to untie the knot. A panel discussion held that year on the meaning of the Holocaust, in which most participants were academics of the younger generation, typified this approach.[77]

In his introductory remarks, the moderator of the panel, Professor Hillel Levine, dwelled on the change that was sweeping American Jewry with respect to Israel and the Holocaust. He noted that its positive attitude toward Israel – 'exaggerated flawlessness' – had been replaced by an equally exaggerated disillusionment with it. Increasingly, Israel was being portrayed as a political and financial burden on American Jews. Public preoccupation with the Holocaust provided a contrasting alternative focal point for Jews' collective identity and public activity. Notably, none of the participants addressed the problem presented in the introductory remarks, except in questions asked at the end on how to commemorate the Holocaust. Even the Israeli participants, Yehuda Bauer and the couple Sidra and Yaron Ezrahi, did not react to the moderator's assessments. All evinced an understanding of the popular need to sustain Holocaust remembrance in means and ways that spoke to the emotions, but they also expressed concern that this grass-roots Holocaust consciousness would become the central component of the Jewish identity of the American Jew. Their remarks reflected concern about the negative implications this might have for Jews' attitude toward their surroundings and their willingness to provide funding for Jewish education. In other words, while the moderator of the panel sought to underscore Holocaust consciousness as an alternative to the centrality-of-Israel mindset, the respondents stressed the negative alternative intrinsic to this consciousness, with respect both to good relations with non-Jews and to the development of Jewish education, as a result of the diversion of financial resources for the construction of expensive Holocaust memorials.

One cannot know for sure why the participants,[78] all of whom were personally connected with Israel, disregarded the moderator's introductory remarks. Perhaps they had not received the remarks in advance; they may have been written shortly before he published their responses to his questions. Even if this is so, however, the trend we noted remains valid and is manifested in a key article on this subject[79] by Professor Ismar Schorsch, rector of the Jewish Theological Seminary of the Conservative Movement in New York. The article, published three months before the symposium, presumably had considerable influence on the views of some of the participants, especially those from the United States.

Schorsch's article dwells first on the favorable aspect of the Jewish community's overall activity in commemoration of the Holocaust. This activity, sometimes performed with 'evangelic intensity', has had positive results in enhancing community cohesiveness and *rapprochement* among Jews affiliated with different currents. In this sense, it has done much to strengthen the Jewish collective identity and has aided in the struggle for Jewish continuity. The main theme of this book – the Israel–Holocaust relationship – is given one summarizing sentence only. Among the successes of the Holocaust rite, Schorsch notes that: 'It has easily replaced Israel, for the time being, as the dominant component of Jewish identity in America.' He makes this assertion without stating whether he approves or disapproves of the ease with which Israel has been shoved out of the center of American Jews' collective consciousness. However, one may adduce from the continuation of the article that Schorsch, whose Diasporist views were staunch and unchallenged at that time, wished thereby to stress the shallowness of Israel consciousness in the identity of American Jews. However, Schorsch refrains from accepting the Holocaust as a surrogate for the state and a factor that shapes and unifies Jewish identity.

Most of Schorsch's article is devoted to the impact of Holocaust consciousness on Jews and the public activity resulting from it, including Jewish–Gentile relations. He expresses concern that to foster a consciousness of Holocaust uniqueness, in disregard of mass-murder atrocities against other peoples, not only lifts the Holocaust out of its historical context but returns, so to speak, to the era of interfaith disputations. This is because the uncontrolled use of the Holocaust as an exceptional phenomenon returns the debate over Jewish–Christian relations to the period in which religious affiliation and devotion were primarily a matter of recognizing uniqueness. This tradition, Schorsch says, should vanish along with the religious polemics of that era. 'Unfortunately', however, 'our obsession with uniqueness of the Holocaust smacks of a distasteful secular version of chosenness. We are still special but only by virtue of Hitler's paranoia.'

In addition to causing a spiritual rift in interfaith relations, says Schorsch, the Holocaust-uniqueness viewpoint causes political damage by driving a wedge between Jews and potential allies among the other victims of organized human depravity. This, perhaps, leads to the most important conclusion in his view: that stressing the uniqueness of the Holocaust keeps it from also being an existential and political emblem of significance for non-Jews. Consequently, 'Moderating our rhetoric would advance our political interests.'

Schorsch's emphasis on the political utility that would accrue to the Jewish people from self-imposed moderation in stressing the uniqueness of the Holocaust is meant, *inter alia*, to distinguish between him, the Conservative, and thinkers in Reform Movement who laud the universal significance and mission of the Holocaust lesson. However, Schorsch is not only a man of thought; he is also and foremost a historian, and as such, his historical outlook is very similar to that of his mentor, Salo Baron. Schorsch identifies with Baron in criticizing what Baron called the 'lachrymose theory of Jewish existence'[80] – the panoply of suffering and devastation that entrenched itself in the Jewish historical tradition in the aftermath of the expulsion from Spain and the Chmielnicki agonies, and to which the greatest Jewish historians, from Graetz to Dinur, subscribed. In Schorsch's opinion, the very fact that the Holocaust greatly reinforced this attitude in the modern era makes it very dangerous, because it divides society into two clashing and hostile segments, Jews and antisemites. Were this the case, says Schorsch, Jewish history would have ended long ago. The truth is vastly different: throughout most of their tenure in exile, Jews have flourished economically and Judaism has flourished spiritually. Hostility toward Jews sometimes originates not in traditional and religious antisemitism but in jealousy of their success. Any other ethnic or religious minority that does well socially may encounter the same attitude.

Schorsch's remarks, following Baron, are correct in themselves but they disregard the fact that Jewish history since the beginning of exile – through the expulsion from Spain and up to the Holocaust – has undergone profound if not fateful changes because of the persecutions and destructions that the Jews have experienced. After all, as no one can ignore, exile means extraterritorial nationhood with everything this implies. The expulsion from Spain destroyed the great center of Sephardi Jewry, which, had it survived, would have been a counterweight to the Ashkenazi center in Eastern Europe, and the Holocaust put an end to the European era in Jewish history. Schorsch certainly did not evade this awareness but he found it very difficult to confront, because of his concern that the Holocaust might become a surrogate for Judaism and lead to the dangerous conclusion that attributes Jewish survival to antisemitism. This perspective is grave in that it transforms Jewish identity by positioning at its forefront not only faith, chosenness, and adherence to the national or ethnic heritage, but also others' hatred of and rejection by Jews.

If so, how does Schorsch propose to extricate Jewry from this thicket? The way out, in his opinion, lies in the awareness that Jews belong to humankind at large and that Diaspora history has made them different. Schorsch's solution is a renewal of the spirit and the faith that emanate from Lurianic Kabala, the teaching engendered by and pursuant to the destruction of Spanish Jewry. In his opinion, 'The Safed Kabalists brilliantly translated the Jewish faith of Galut into resoundingly universal terms.' In the worldview of the Safed Kabalists, the Jewish fate reflects the flaws and blemishes of cosmic and, of course, human existence. Accordingly, disruption and disharmony are a universal phenomenon. According to Schorsch's interpretation of Lurianic Kabala, 'the meaning of Jewish suffering lay not in its uniqueness, but on the contrary, in its typicality'. In this context, the term typicality carries a symbolic meaning, in contrast to uniqueness. While uniqueness aims to distinguish Jews from Gentiles, Lurianic Kabala, according to Schorsch, seeks to lend Jewish suffering a universal import. This leads Schorsch to the conclusion, so central for him and important in understanding his world, that Lurianic Kabala ascribes to the individual, and especially the Jew, a central role in obliterating the forces of chaos and evil that dominate the universe. Therefore, 'the exile existence of the Jew is not a punishment but a mission to raise the sparks of divine light helplessly trapped in the world of darkness.'

The aims of the universal mission which the Jews are assigned are identical for Schorsch, the Conservative, and for the secular ultra-liberals. What separates them is the source from which the Jews' destiny flows. For Schorsch, the source is a traditional Jew who has universal significance. For the ultra-liberals, the source is the opposite: a universality that has Jewish meaning. Accordingly, for Schorsch Jewish existence as a religious and ethnic entity is a basic rule; for them, it is secondary if not trivial. However, because he wishes to sustain the Jewish collectivity, Schorsch is highly concerned about relations between Jewry and other peoples. For this reason, he seeks vigorously to eradicate the consciousness of Jewish uniqueness, which may be construed as condescension toward others, and to replace it with the status of a metaphysical symbol, which would lend Jewish suffering a symbolic status. Therefore, he downplays the importance and uniqueness of the Jews' historical condition. For example, he believes that anti-Jewish hostility does not necessarily flow from traditional antisemitism; it is but an example of a universal phenomenon – jealousy of successful population groups. The argument is partly correct with respect to Western and Central Europe but is erroneous with respect to the large majority of Jews, who lived in Eastern Europe. However, Schorsch, unlike the ultra-liberals, is immersed in, not stationed outside, his people. As a historian of the Jewish people, a public figure, and a Conservative spiritual leader who currently heads the Jewish Theological Seminary, he gradually engineered a turnabout in his worldview on the uniqueness of the Jewish existential condition. In 1995, about fifteen years after his article on this matter was published, Schorsch wrote a document that set forth the seven principles of faith of the Conservative Movement:[81] the centrality of Israel; the overarching importance of the Hebrew language; devotion to *klal Yisrael*; the decisive role of the Torah in shaping the collective persona; study of Torah; guidance of Jewish life by *halakha*; and, the most basic precept, belief in God.

The first three tenets are pronouncedly national and are typical of particularistic Jewish life in an open modern society: the centrality of Israel for Diaspora Jews, the status of the Hebrew language as a unifying device for a nation dispersed among diverse languages and cultures, and the myth of *klal Yisrael*.

For Jews affiliated with the Conservative Movement, Schorsch argues, Israel's centrality is not a mere historical memory but also an ultimate goal. Therefore, most Conservative Jews maintain a regular personal relationship with Israel by means of philanthropy, visits, and sending children to summer camps. Their Israel connection is also evinced in pride concerning Israel's achievements and sorrow over its failures. Therefore,

> their life is a dialectic between homeland and exile. No matter how prosperous and assimilated, they betray an existential angst about anti-semitism that denies them a complete sense of at-homeness anywhere in the Diaspora, and their behaviour reflects the dominant thrust of Conservative Judaism not to denationalize Judaism.

The document does not mention the Holocaust. Although the omission is deliberate – Schorsch has always been a consistent opponent of the Holocaust rite – the implicit thrust of his remarks allows one to adduce his views on the Holocaust–Israel nexus. This flows from the different assessment he expresses toward antisemitism. It stands to reason that during the antisemitic eruptions around the world in the past decade, especially among African Americans, Schorsch began to wonder if it was at all possible for Jews to integrate fully into the free societies that they inhabit. Thus, the uniqueness of the existence of *klal Yisrael* is characterized largely by Diaspora Jews' national connection with the State of Israel and the antisemitism that prevents them from feeling fully at home in their lands of birth and residence. In other words, with respect to the historical essence of the Holocaust, if the Jews, despite their social success and integration, are still gripped with existential angst about antisemitism, then it and the suffering that caused it have never been mere symbols but rather a unique historical reality. Moreover, these feelings cannot be divorced from Jews' attitude toward the Jewish state. To put it differently, in a paraphrase of the title of Schorsch's book, *From Text to Context*, one may say that Schorsch transferred the problem from the Lurianic Kabalistic text to the Jewish historical context.

I have gone to lengths in analyzing Schorsch's two works not only because of their contents, which are important in themselves, and not because of his interesting turnabout in the period between the two, but because his public function adds considerable weight to his opinion in the public thought of Jews in America and elsewhere.

Therefore, one may presume that Schorsch, who in the early 1980s asserted that Holocaust consciousness had easily dislodged the centrality of Israel from the consciousness of American Jewry, attempted in the mid-1990s to restore the lost luster and underscore the centrality of Israel. He made this change because he fathomed the full significance of the centrality of the Holocaust for American Jewry, not necessarily in Jewish–Gentile relations but because of its significance for the contents of Judaism. Who was more aware than Schorsch, the head of an important American institution of Jewish studies, of the mammoth sums invested in building Holocaust memorial shrines at the expense of the development of Jewish studies? His very concern for the future of these studies makes his Israel connection important and decisive, and now, in a departure from the past, Israel's centrality became a prime tenet in the Conservative Jewish worldview. For this reason, Jewish existence, which Schorsch had formerly considered merely religious, is now perceived as national. Schorsch's intellectual writings deem the historian Heinrich Graetz, who taught at the Conservative seminary in Breslau, to be the author of the most celebrated Jewish national history, a work that influenced the Zionist thinking of Moses Hess. Therefore, Schorsch also lauds the immigration of more than one hundred Conservative rabbis to Israel in the past generation. Everything mentioned here is meant to predicate the Israel–Diaspora relationship on positive values and not on national disaster.

The second personality who has had a powerful effect on critical public thought concerning the over-encouragement of Holocaust consciousness is Professor Jacob Neusner, a historian and researcher of the Mishnaic and Talmudic periods. Neusner, also one of the important figures in the field of American Jewish public thought – his views enrich and sometimes enflame this thought – is the most extreme opponent of the integration of Holocaust consciousness into the American Jewish identity. An observant Jew, a student of Mordechai Kaplan, and a thinker whose views approximate those of the Conservative Movement, he developed his own pan-Jewish worldview that has shifted since the late 1960s from Brandeis-style American-Jewish Zionism to non-Zionism and even anti-Zionism – until he arrived at post-Zionism in terms of ruling out the existence of *klal Yisrael* in any sense other than the purely religious one.

Until the mid-1980s, Neusner's pan-Jewish perceptions could be summed up as resting on several complementary paradoxes. He was a

Zionist who affirmed the Diaspora. Although he considered Zion indispensable in the Jewish sense, he deemed the United States the most worthy place in which to live. He admitted that he was living in exile but depicted his exile as his home. He favored a preferential status for Israel in the overall Jewish interest but dwelled on the intrinsic value of the Diaspora. He acknowledged that Zionism is meaningless without the *aliya* (immigration) imperative but insisted on his principled right to refrain from obeying it personally. He regarded the State of Israel as the center of the total Jewish reality but rejected its pretension to guide Diaspora Jewry and shape its way of life.[82]

Since the mid-1980s, in the aftermath of his extremely critical attitude toward the State of Israel – the reasons for which cannot be discussed here – Neusner's thinking verged on non-Zionism if not anti-Zionism, until, as stated, it settled into a post-Zionist conviction that nullifies the concept of *klal Yisrael* as a national or ethnic phenomenon and preserves it only as a concept of religious faith, which he confines to believing Jews only. Thus he expressed his views in the mid-1990s:

> In the world viewed whole, Jews who are neither Judaists nor Zionists (and Israelis) do not form a social entity of any kind. But in diverse national contexts, Jews do form ethnic groups, that is, Jewish Americans, but not American Jews. They are not an American species of the genus Jew, but a Jewish species of the genus American.[83]

The shift of emphasis from American Jew to Jewish American is the gist of Neusner's existential Jewish outlook, which views the existence of collectivities primarily in social and cultural terms. In his view, the existence of *klal Yisrael* is hardly conceivable outside its two frameworks: the traditional (religious) and the recent (political). Consequently, 'I see no Jewish future for Jews outside the State of Israel, on the one side, or the synagogue on the other.' Those who reside anywhere else have either positioned themselves outside *klal Yisrael* or are about to do so. The proof is well known: the intermarriage rate and the estrangement of grandchildren from the Jewish community.

At first glance, this outlook does not contradict the current Zionist perspective. In practice, however, it contradicts it totally. Neusner, who emphasizes the concept Jewish American instead of American Jew, thoroughly undermines the perception of a worldwide, multinational

Jewish unity that transcends states and citizenships, as Zionism continues to profess. Hence, Holocaust consciousness as a historical phenomenon that expresses an exilic state of Jewish collective helplessness, an inseparable part of the Zionist perception, stands in utter contrast to Neusner's Jewish ethnic outlook. Therefore, he considers this consciousness an alien and artificial implant in the American Jewish reality.

In the late 1970s, Neusner was the first to note the difference between the unifying social function of the 'Holocaust and rebirth' myth in Israel and its insignificance and artificiality for American Jews. Jews in the United States, in his opinion, cannot proclaim that the United States has contributed a new chapter to Jewish history, at least not as Israelis do in their conviction that the establishment of the state marked the onset of a new era in Jewish history. Consequently, the Holocaust myth in Israel acts in the service of the main point, rebirth, whereas in the United States it stands independently as a marker of Jews' collective identity. It does so in two senses: in the negative sense, as expressed in the 'Hitler knew you were Jewish' formula; and in a sense even more serious, the identification of the Holocaust with the Jewish historical heritage – a sort of Holocaust = Roots equation, patterned after the famous television mini-series *Roots*, which retells the history of the African American community.

Neusner regards the similitude of the mentality in the two myths, Holocaust and Roots, as an attempt to predicate the collective Jewish identity in the United States mainly on a Holocaust consciousness that, it seems to me, one may term a 'defining myth' in this context since, in Neusner's opinion, it aimed to make the Jews singular by fostering the uniqueness of the Holocaust. Thus, 'Roots—Holocaust is the idea that being Jewish is an ethnic, not primarily a religious, category.' To Neusner's mind, this new perception represents a substantive historical change in understanding Jewish identity; it marks a transition in Jews' self-perception from a religious community with a unique faith to an ethnic group with a different and special historical experience. Paradoxically, since American Jews have not shared in the Jewish national resurrection in Israel, 'the "Holocaust" part of the myth tends to play a larger part in this country than it does in the State of Israel'.[84]

In other words, back in the late 1970s, Neusner pointed to a trend that would gather momentum in the next decade and that – as we shall see in the next chapter – may be defined as the Americanization of the Holocaust. He observed this trend with special concern because it was the kind of myth that offered neither reward nor compensation. In

Israel, the rebirth is the hope that offsets the despair that followed the devastation. American Jews have no such countervailing force. However, 'without Zionism "the Holocaust" is unbearable and to be avoided.' This is so because Neusner, in his immoderate fashion, lends Zionism an activist meaning that was once acceptable to the Zionist Labor Movement and especially its youth flank – *aliya*. Without *aliya*, the Zionism of American Jews is not true Zionism but hypocritical Zionism.

From this point of reference, Neusner locates a parallel and a similitude between American Jews' attitudes toward Zionism and toward the Holocaust. Just as their Zionism is hypocritical because they are not willing to fulfill it personally, so their Holocaust consciousness is artificial because they did not experience the Holocaust personally. 'We are spectators at someone else's drama', Neusner wrote a year later. 'But life is not for spectators. We pretended to be what we are not, not victims or survivors, not builders or Israelis.' Nor do American Jews intend to modify their historical condition and their status as Jews, because 'we chose without apology or guilt to make our lives here right now'.[85]

The overall social status that American Jews have attained leaves no room for Neusner's brand of Zionism. However he realizes that this Jewish community, most of which is not religious, finds it hard to exist without a unifying myth. Here, he rues with concern, the collective consciousness of the Holocaust steps in to fill the void.

He detects an explanation for this phenomenon in the collective psychology of a people that wallowed in pariah status and, after its great disaster, registered certain attainments in the community of peoples. Paradoxically, the Holocaust thinkers, Neusner alleges, did not relieve the Jews of the memories of their tragic past. On the contrary, it made them even more suspicious of their surroundings. Therefore, they are beset by the feeling, in view of the genocide, that *goyim* cannot be trusted, that the murders would not have attained such magnitude had a Jewish state existed before the Holocaust, and that as a consequence, one must support the State of Israel for the sake of the future of Jewry and its children.

Neusner utterly rejects this American Jewish psychology – a mentality pursued, in his opinion, by a spectator collectivity that does not play the game – for two reasons:[86] because it replaces the traditional Jewish religious identity and because it imposes on American Jews an ethnic status of American Jew instead of Jewish American, the status that corresponds naturally to, and fully reflects, their civic condition in terms of their social status.

Thus Neusner the ideologue, who advocates a divorce between the State of Israel and the Diaspora – especially the American Diaspora – has taken the place of Neusner the historian. After all, Neusner the historian should know, given his parable of players and spectators, that since the game is also something that the spectators need, they become participants in it. This is natural for a large proportion of American Jews – who regard the Holocaust and the Jewish state established in its wake as part of themselves, as a remembrance of the past, and as an expectation for the future, and who associate themselves with their national reality and have an influence on it. The very existence of this reality for more than two generations, in its popular and its intellectual forms, indicates that it has become a natural part of collective Jewishness.

In fact, Neusner understood this but refused to acquiesce in it. In the early 1990s, ten years after he published his series of articles on the Holocaust and its role in Jewish consciousness, he took up the matter again. In the introduction to a book he edited, containing a selection of articles on the Holocaust and American Jews, he admitted that the Holocaust consciousness had penetrated American Jewry, especially that of the third generation, in the aftermath of the spontaneous awakening that preceded and followed the Six-Day War. This war, coupled with the preceding dread and the subsequent eruption of joy, made American Jews active and fervent spectators in the drama of the transition from Holocaust to rebirth. Neusner also understood that the relationship of this war with the global struggle between Communism and the free world had endowed their feelings with general public legitimacy.

The view that the Holocaust is a unique phenomenon in world history, in Neusner's opinion, stems from this feeling and is meant to sustain it. Neusner opposed it vehemently because 'claims of uniqueness lead us into the heart of living religion'. From this point of view, the uniqueness of the Holocaust and the establishment of the state, given to the Jews by God to compensate them for their suffering, 'form the central mythic system of American Judaism'. Neusner found this outrageous, believing that historical situations are never absolutely unique but only relative. Only faith is unique: 'What is unique is the loving God Who, in love, has chosen and sanctified Israel, the Jewish people. That love, and not the Holocaust, forms what is unique to Israel and the Jewish people.'[87]

Here it is worth briefly comparing the views of Jacob Neusner, the traditional American Jew, and George Steiner, the secular European

Jew whom we discussed in the previous chapter. Both academics are renowned for their scholarly research and for the tempests that their views on Judaism, Israel, and the Holocaust; their eccentricity; and their Jewish anti-establishment approach have provoked from time to time in public thought. Additionally, the fact that both are so immersed in their respective cultural settings – Steiner is chiefly a European of Jewish origin, Neusner an American of Jewish origin – makes them similar in their public posture and spiritual world. As such, however, their attitudes toward the Holocaust and the state of the Jews are dissimilar. For Steiner, Holocaust consciousness is the existential expression of the European Jew; Neusner judges this traumatic experience to be utterly alien to American Jewry. Therefore, Steiner considers Israel the last possible refuge available to the Jews if, Heaven forfend, a new Holocaust befalls them, whereas Neusner cannot imagine so terrifying a possibility. Steiner regards the reality of the Jewish state as the diametrical opposite of the Holocaust; Neusner argues that the Holocaust and rebirth consciousness serves Israel in the crucial function of a unifying myth and explicates and compensates for the Jews' sufferings. Each of these thinkers, in his own way, is among Israel's harshest cultural, moral, and political critics. Paradoxically, however, the secular Steiner, who rejects Jewish nationalism more strenuously than the religious Neusner, is also more closely attached to the State of Israel because of the Holocaust trauma, from which he cannot and perhaps does not wish to extricate himself. Thus, in this sense Steiner accepts the Zionist fundamental that the Jewish state is the relative possible answer to the Jews' collective helplessness during the Holocaust, whereas Neusner, in his advocacy of untying the Holocaust–Israel nexus among Diaspora Jews, actually portends a trend that has recently gained a toehold in public thought – post-Zionism, which is gradually evolving into post-Israelism, as we shall see.

The post-Zionists are composed of several groups that, in their distinct worldviews and ways of life, share nothing but their rejection of Zionism. At the rightmost extreme are Orthodox fundamentalists who depict Zionism as devoid of Jewish values and therefore incapable of sustaining the Jewish state that it established. At the leftmost extreme are the ultra-liberals, many of them erstwhile Trotskyite Marxists, who reject Zionism as a national ideology and wish to see Israel become a binational state. In the middle are the moderate liberals, who reject Zionism because of the power-centric nationalist complexion it acquired in its years of struggle for the existence of the state; their program would replace today's Israel with a Jewish state predicated on universal Jewish ethical values. All groups – the Orthodox fundamentalists in both Israel and the Diaspora; the ultra-liberals, who concentrate in Israel; and the moral-liberals – have utopian aspirations that translate (with different degrees of intensity) into political attitudes, the Holocaust consciousness serving them as a motive and a justification in both the utopian and the political aspects.

This book, as noted in the chapter on the theological discourse, does not deal with the *haredi* philosophy of the Holocaust because this kind of thinking is alien to the central theme of this book: *Between Auschwitz and Jerusalem*. However, in the context of the post-Zionist attitude toward the Holocaust and the State of Israel, the *haredi* circles, especially those affiliated with Agudath Israel, deserve several remarks. It is not my intent to deal with their anti-Zionist attitude, let alone with the atrocity charges that they continue to level against Zionism for allegedly having forsaken the blood of the Jewish masses by deliberately refraining from rescue in the belief that their sacrifice and murder would justify the establishment of a Jewish state after the Holocaust.[88]

My only goals here are to explain why I have cast this approach, at least in part, into the post-Zionist rubric and to dwell on the paradox that flows from this approach in the *haredi* treatment of Zionism. Thus, on the assumption that the past generation's revision in Holocaust historiography concerning the Jews' behavior in ghettos and extermination camps criticizes the basic Zionist attitude – which, in their opinion, regards the murder victims as masses who went to their deaths 'like lambs to the slaughter' – it contains a post-Zionist element. At this point, it is worth noting that Agudath Israel publications in the 1970s expressed an argument that most Holocaust historians accept today: that Jews' heroism in the Holocaust should be judged primarily in view of their daily lives, adhering to their faith, keeping their families intact, and expressing concern for others in organized fashion despite their hellish living conditions. Obviously the pundit-rabbis of Agudath Israel place great emphasis on adherence to the faith and the Jewish way of life in the fullness of these terms. From the methodological standpoint, however, this approach is identical to that of the professional historians, most of whom are secular.[89]

The paradox in this approach, to which we alluded above, lies in the very highlighting of the victims' actions to sustain life as people and as Jews. This activism diverges from *kiddush Hashem* (traditional martyrdom) and is more similar to the activism that Zionism advocates. The difference is that martyrs forfeited their lives to protect their Jewishness, whereas in the Holocaust millions were murdered because of their Jewishness, given no opportunity to choose between a life of betrayal and a death of sanctity. The difference is that in their daily heroism the Jews demonstrated their wish to resist the objective fate that outside forces imposed on them. This trait, which some people adopt naturally in different situations, verges on the Zionist ethos of Jewish activism when made into a myth and a collective ethos. Furthermore, it is used today to attack Zionism, which, from a posture of ostensible estrangement and condescension, used the phrase 'like lambs to the slaughter' as a climactic expression of its 'negation of the Diaspora' doctrine. This is not the place to discuss the grim, painful, and misleading semantics of the 'lambs to the slaughter' concept or of the corresponding concept that was applied to the survivors, 'human dust'. However, since post-Zionist historiography invokes both in order to subject Zionism to defamatory criticism, it should be made clear that Zionism never rejected Diaspora Jews but rather the Diaspora condition. It is the Diaspora condition – the condition that gave shape to a Jewish person who should change in Eretz Israel, in the free Jewish society that would be built there – that they disparage. The same applies to the 'human dust', which connoted a situation where Jews as individuals have no sovereign entity of their own.

For those who accept the post-Zionist perspective in whatever hue – the Orthodox, the liberal, or the radical – the question of Jewish sovereignty in its broad, cultural sense and in its psychological sense is of little consequence. Therefore, they set out to revise the Israel–Holocaust relationship.

In 1987, the young historian David Biale published a book entitled *Power and Powerlessness in Jewish History*.[90] In this book, Biale – in contrast to Jewish tradition, the great historians, and, especially, Zionist ideology – attempts to prove that the Jews were never totally deprived of political power at any point in their history in the Diaspora. On the contrary, they evinced political resolve in organizing their internal lives and political sophistication in conducting their relations with rulers. Accordingly – as Salo Baron argued – they were better off as subjects in their countries of residence than lower classes such as the peasantry. The same year, Biale published an abstract of his historical hypotheses in the liberal quarterly *Tikkun*,[91] in what may be considered an attempt to transform historiography into public thought.

Biale was a leading spokesperson of the radical Jewish students in the late 1960s and the early 1970s who got caught up in the Jewish national cause and Zionism. Unlike many of his comrades, he neither settled in Israel nor attempted to become involved with it. Therefore, he is not among the disenchanted thinkers who became anti-Zionists; his personal ties with Israel remain strong.

His argument against historians such as Graetz and thinkers such as Hermann Cohen and Franz Rosenzweig, not to mention Zionist historians and thinkers, has several origins. One is the dilemma of the Jewish far Left in the 1970s, which developed a robust appreciation of both political and physical power as expressions of the new American Jewish identity.[92] The argument is associated with the new Diasporist ideology that dominates Jewish communities in the West, in which Jewish centers make political shows of force in order to protect their group interests in a society that is becoming ethnically more pluralistic. It flows from the urge to balance Zionist ideology with a Diasporist worldview by challenging several basic Zionist assumptions that distinguish between Jewish sovereignty in Israel and Jewish civic existence in Western countries. It also wishes to set the Holocaust within a broad Jewish historical context that rules out the claim that the Holocaust is typical of Jewish life in exile.

The post-Zionist approach of Biale and others of like mind rests primarily on the assumption that, paradoxically, the State of Israel, depicted in Zionist ideology and historiography as the diametrical opposite of Auschwitz, is itself a place where the Jews' immediate enemies threaten them with annihilation. Therefore, instead of the basic Zionist metaphor of the normal Jew, it offers the metaphor of the fighting Jew, the opposite of the victim-Jew. 'Yet, since the metaphor of the hero is tied indissolvably with the metaphor of the victim, Israel as the symbol of Jewish power remains tied to the Holocaust, the symbol of powerlessness.'

Biale is concerned that the lesson of the Holocaust, in which the Jewish people's pronounced helplessness became evident, would be applied as a retrospective historiographic judgment of all Jewish history in the Diaspora. Therefore, he strives to prove that Israel is more exile than redemption, to use the terminology of the political scientist Michael Walzer. This is so because of Israel's dependence on the superpower, the United States – a condition reminiscent of the Second Temple, when Greece and Rome alternated in control of the area. Although Israel is limited as a value and in its political worth, Biale admits that relations with and concern for the Jewish state reflect the political power of the American Diaspora and are pre-eminent in maintaining its unity. He also acknowledges the source of this: the Gordian knot between the beleaguered State of Israel and the Jews' historical disaster. This knot, based on the generalization of Jewish powerlessness as a historical phenomenon, is not only factually incorrect but may also disappear in the course of the Middle East peace process.

In view of this possibility, a favorable one in itself, Biale phrases a perception – which he did not invent, as we showed in previous chapters – concerning the universal, existential, and moral mission of the lesson of the Holocaust without obfuscating its particularistic nature as a Jewish catastrophe. Following Elie Wiesel, he argues that along with the general characteristics of this method of genocide, 'the total powerlessness of the Jews during the Holocaust also points to the fate of all humanity in the face of nuclear war'. In two respects, however, Biale carries this premise farther than Wiesel does. Wiesel regards the night that descended upon the Jews as an example or symbol of what may happen to other peoples; Biale likens the fate of the world in the shadow of the nuclear bomb to the fate of Jews who were incinerated in the crematoria of Auschwitz and the other extermination camps. Therefore, he concludes, there is no difference between power and powerlessness in the post-Holocaust world. In other words, in Biale's post-Zionist perspective the difference between Jewish state sovereignty and Jewish life in the Diaspora is null and void, and as long as political power is meaningful in Jewish life, it exists in its relative intensity and validity in both locations.

These principled post-Zionist arguments neither exhibit an anti-Israel political intent nor express a malicious intent to undermine and nullify Zionism as a liberation movement of the Jewish people. For this very reason, several remarks are in order on two major issues.

First, Biale does not seem to distinguish between politics and collective political power. All politics is based on a modicum of power. The economic utility that the Jews delivered to various medieval rulers attests to the extent of power that they possessed. In the corporative feudal society of the time, the Jews' condition relative to other corporative groups was not substantively different, and sometimes they had very convenient political arrangements with the rulers, as manifested in the privileges they received. This condition changed in the modern era, in which the feudal social structure was destroyed and replaced by the nation-state. During this era – from the French Revolution to the present – the Jews have been helpless as a collective, and their helplessness reached its tragic and visible peak, as even Biale admits, in the Holocaust. Zionism, in its stunning success in establishing the Jewish state despite its political and social limitations, wrought a turning point in the collective existential condition of the Jewish people among the nations. The reason is the sovereign power that it wields – a power possessed by no Diaspora community, not even American Jewry, a strong collective that has more political influence on the government than any Diaspora community in history since. Therefore, the state can provide any Jewish collective with a refuge from distress of any kind, whereas Diaspora Jewry is limited in its ability to admit Jewish immigrants to its countries of residence. Accordingly, the tendency to sever the tie between the lesson of the Holocaust – helplessness – and the possibilities created by the state's relative sovereignty is historically groundless and ideationally misleading.

The second remark pertains to Biale's substantive and metaphorical linkage of Auschwitz and the atomic bomb. The two are different in essence. Auschwitz symbolizes a malevolent and pathological attempt to exterminate a certain people, the Jews, whom members of another people, the Germans, perceived in their warped thinking as a menace to humankind. The nuclear menace, in contrast, threatens humanity because of power struggles involving politics and states; the destructive power has nothing to do with the delegitimization of the affected peoples. The regimes and rulers of human beings are delegitimized, not human beings as such. In the decade since Biale's article appeared, the revolutionary changes in the Russian empire and the disintegration of Communism have lessened the risk of nuclear devastation. However, antisemitism still exists; it erupts from various crevices, some of them surprising. Therefore, the historical meaning of Jewish sovereignty predicated on political power remains valid. It suffices to cite the aforementioned views of Ismar Schorsch, who considers anti-semitism a permanent factor in Diaspora Jewish existence.

It was Michael Lerner, editor of the quarterly *Tikkun*, who developed David Biale's observations, defined them in post-Zionist terms, and inserted the Holocaust–Israel nexus into his concept. Lerner made his journal available as a forum to post-Zionists in the United States, and especially in Israel. Lerner does not accept the post-Zionist prescription concerning the binational character of the State of Israel; as an observant Jew, he considers the existence of a Jewish state important. He also opposes repeal of the Law of Return as long as the menace of antisemitism exists in the world, even though the statute discriminates among members of different nations. The title of the book in which Lerner gathered his thoughts about Jewish affairs, the Holocaust, Zionism, Israel–Diaspora relations, and relations between Jews and Gentiles, especially African Americans – *Jewish Renewal: A*

Path to Healing and Transformation[93] – speaks for itself. *Jewish Renewal* is a liberal–ethical–religious utopia of sorts, which one may define as post-ideological relative to the set of social ideas that have guided Western society thus far. Thus, Lerner advocates a renewal of cooperative life between blacks and whites that transcends formal equality under law and even equality of social opportunity. He prescribes a renewal of community life that would partly dislodge the dominion of bureaucracy. This prompts him to demand the inauguration of a 'politics of meaning' that aims to steer and educate people toward moral values and not merely to keep them in line by means of rules and regulations.

This liberal–moral utopia should, in Lerner's opinion, inform the post-Zionist contours of Israel and its relations with the Diaspora. The principles of this post-Zionism are addressed first of all to relations between Jews and Arabs: the Palestinian people must be liberated from Israeli oppression and allowed to form an independent state, in a process that nevertheless assures Israel's security. As for Israel itself, post-Zionism demands the separation of religion and state, acknowledgment of the cultural pluralism of Israeli society, reinforcement of traditional and universal moral values, and sensitivity to problems of ecology.

From Lerner's standpoint, the entire doctrine boils down to the traditional religious concept of *tikkun 'olam* (reform or correction of the world), not only in its Jewish sense but at a level that embraces all of humankind. Thus, in contrast to the Jewish radicals who disseminated the slogan 'Never again' as a national message, he turns the same cliché into the declaration of a pan-human mission: 'never again' to racism, antisemitism, discrimination, and oppression, committed either by Jews or by anyone else, anywhere.

Basing himself on these premises, Lerner clashes swords with ideological approaches and political trends that seek to justify Israel's injustices on the basis of the Holocaust lesson. To foster this lesson in the manner of 'Never again', says Lerner, is to engage in Jewish paranoia.

Lerner does acknowledge the Jews' right to be paranoid, to some extent, in view of their experience in World War II – in the Holocaust and in their *de facto* abandonment by the Western governments. However, he considers such an attitude very dangerous because, outwardly, it turns friends or potential friends, for instance African Americans or those Palestinian Arabs who wish to make peace with Israel's existence and coexist with Israel in harmony and cooperation, into enemies. Inwardly, it stifles all criticism of Israel's mistaken and dangerous policies and of those Diaspora Jews who support Israel unreservedly. This attempt to invoke paranoiac fears that emanate from the Holocaust to gag uninhibited and candid public debate about Israel's relations with the Palestinians may ultimately trigger a general eruption of rage against the entire Jewish people for its ostensible support of the repression of the Palestinians.

In Lerner's opinion, the American Jewish neo-conservatives' power-centric perceptions and the Israeli government's power-centric policies are paradoxical. The neo-conservatives' views, he says, seek to deny the erstwhile and current weakness and vulnerability of the Jewish people and replace these traits with a largely imaginary sense of strength and might. The justification of the power doctrine by right-wing groups that deny the world the moral right to preach to Jews because it stood by silently as they were being led to the gas chambers, is also dangerous, because it leads to the Jews' isolation and is incorrect when applied to all non-Jews. Here, Lerner believes it worth distinguishing between grass-roots feelings and forms of governance that result from social and political developments. Thus, were it not for fascism, which rose to power for reasons other than antisemitism, the Holocaust would not have occurred.[94]

Those who read Michael Lerner's remarks cannot but reflect that his post-Zionism is nothing but the socialist–idealist liberal Zionism that the Zionist Movement espoused both before and after the establishment of the State of Israel. Everything he says contains fundamentals of the Zionism of Herzl and Weizmann, of Ha-shomer ha-Tsa'ir and Brit Shalom, and of Ha-po'el ha-Tsa'ir. Even in the Mapai activist camp, these ideas were not alien. Therefore, his post-Zionism relates not to the principles of the Zionist idea but to the foreign and domestic policies of Israeli governments over the past generation, especially since the Likud under Menachem Begin rose to power in 1977 and embarked on the Lebanon War in 1982. Into this vessel of Zionism as a humanistic national movement, which aspires to conclude a rational settlement with the Arab people that dwells in Eretz Israel and to establish a Jewish society there on the basis of the finest universal and Jewish principles of progress, Lerner has poured the utopian aspirations and yearnings of American ultra-liberalism in Conservative and Reform colors.

Summing up, one may say that this ideological debate was an extension of the principled and political dispute on the question of establishing the United States Holocaust Memorial Museum in Washington – a dispute that we discuss in the next chapter.

NOTES

1. See Anita Shapira, 'The Holocaust and the World War as Components of the Yishuv's Identity', *Ha-Tsiyyonut*, 20 [Hebrew], pp. 243–58.
2. Both aspects of the phenomenon are discussed at length by Yehiam Weitz, 'Shaping the Memory of the Holocaust in Israeli Society of the 1950s', in Yisrael Gutman (ed.), *Major Changes Within the Jewish People in the Wake of the Holocaust* (Jerusalem, 1996), p. 510*ff.*
3. Quoted ibid., p. 500.
4. Yizhak Gruenbaum, 'Ten Years Later', *Al Hamishmar,* 16 April 1993 [Hebrew].
5. Weitz, 'Shaping the Memory of the Holocaust in Israeli Society of the 1950s', p. 503.
6. *Al Hamishmar* (editorial), 13 April 1953 [Hebrew].
7. 'The Holocaust, the Betrayal, and Its Lesson', *Davar,* 16 April 1993 [Hebrew].
8. 'Memorial Days' (editorial), *Hatsofe,* 13 April 1953 [Hebrew].
9. Editorial, *Ha'aretz,* 13 April 1953 [Hebrew].
10. See especially 'The Screaming Mute' (editorial), *Herut,* 27 April 1963 [Hebrew].
11. 'Holocaust and Heroism' (editorial), *Ha'aretz,* 27 April 1963 [Hebrew].
12. 'On This Day, in This Country' (editorial), *Davar,* 27 April 1963 [Hebrew].
13. 'Holocaust and Heroism' (editorial), *Lamerhav,* 27 April 1963, p. 2; Y. Ben-Leah, 'The Bridge Between Holocaust and Rebirth', *Lamerhav,* 28 April 1958, p. 3; 'The Jewish Rebellion Is Not Over' (editorial), *Lamerhav,* 28 April 1957, p. 2; Yitzhak Bezalel, 'The Holocaust, the Uprising, and the War of Independence – Two Peas in One Pod', *Lamerhav,* 15 April 1969, p. 3 [all in Hebrew].
14. 'Remembrance and Reminder' (editorial), *Lamerhav,* 15 April 1969, p. 2 [Hebrew].
15. See, for example, Tom Segev, *The Seventh Million: The Israelis and the Holocaust,* tr. Haim Watzman (New York: Hill & Wang, 1991).
16. Eliezer Livne, 'Reflections on the Holocaust', *Yedioth Ahronoth,* 16 April 1963 [Hebrew].
17. See Dinah Porat and Tuvia Friling, at Chapter 1, Note 19, p. 49, in this volume.
18. 'On Holocaust Day', *Al Hamishmar,* 24 April 1979 [Hebrew].
19. 'To Cope With the Holocaust', *Davar,* 24 April 1979 [Hebrew].
20. 'The Holocaust Should Not Recur' (editorial), *Ha'aretz,* 24 April 1979 [Hebrew].
21. Israel Eldad, 'It's Not the Same Thing', *Yedioth Ahronoth,* 27 April 1984 [Hebrew].
22. 'A Dual Imperative' (editorial), *Ha'aretz,* 27 April 1984 [Hebrew].
23. 'Indeed, Let Us Remember' (editorial), *Hatsofe,* 27 April 1984 [Hebrew].
24. 'Remembrance Day' (editorial), *Maariv,* 24 April 1979 [Hebrew].
25. 'Holocaust and Heroism Day' (editorial), *Hatsofe,* 24 April 1979 [Hebrew].
26. Israel Eldad, see note 19.
27. 'On Holocaust Day' (editorial), *Al Hamishmar,* 24 April 1979 [Hebrew].
28. See 'On Holocaust Day' (editorial), *Al Hamishmar,* 24 April 1979; 'To Cope With the Holocaust' (editorial), *Davar,* 24 April 1979; and 'The Holocaust Should Not Recur', *Ha'aretz,* 24 April 1979 [all in Hebrew].
29. Goetz Aly, *Endlösung* (Frankfurt: Fischer Verlag, 1995).
30. Boaz Evron, 'The Holocaust as a Boomerang', *Politika,* June–July 1986, pp. 8–9 [Hebrew].
31. Ibid., pp. 20–3.
32. Ibid., pp. 6–7. Ten years later, Idit Zertal, editor of *Politika* in the 1990s, repeated

Wasserman's arguments and definitions – without citing their source – concerning the deliberate dissociation of Holocaust remembrance from the other tragedies in Jewish history and repeated the concept of 'nationalizing the Holocaust'. However, she carried this line of reasoning to greater lengths. To be charitable, she is willing to assume that 'it may have been necessary to appropriate the memory of the Holocaust as an asset for the immense political enterprise of establishing the state'. However, 'this destroyed genuine remembrance by conditioning its meaning on the results of the Zionist victory'. This happened, in her opinion, because the nationalization of the Holocaust and its victims' memory 'blurred the meaning of the historical event of the murder of millions of Jews by the Germans – millions of people at the hands of other people – and blurred the portrayal of the persons murdered and the specific circumstances of their lives and death'. See Idit Zertal, 'The Memory Mill', *Ha'aretz*, 12 April 1996 [Hebrew].

33. *Ha'aretz*, 2 March 1988 [Hebrew].
34. 'The Two Sins of Education', *Yedioth Ahronoth*, 7 April 1994 [Hebrew].
35. 'To Learn a Universal Lesson, Too' (an interview by Uri Kashti with Dr Moshe Zuckerman), *Ha'aretz*, 28 November 1995. Zuckerman expanded on his assertion concerning the political 'instrumentalization' of the Holocaust by the Israeli leadership and the 'Holocaust code' that has a powerful influence on Jewish public opinion in his book, *Holocaust in a Sealed Room – The 'Holocaust' in the Israeli Press During the Gulf War* (Tel Aviv; 1993) [Hebrew].
36. Remarks based on my conversation with Steiner in his home in England.
37. In the monthly journal *Nekuda* between 1980 and 1995, we found only twelve articles on Holocaust-related themes – less than one per year. The quarterly *Nativ*, published by intellectual circles on the far Right, carried more articles: thirty pieces between 1988 and 1985 on subjects related to the Holocaust, antisemitism, and Germany (an average of three per year).
38. Ariel Fisch, *Zionism of Zion* (Tel Aviv, 1982), p. 108 [Hebrew].
39. Meir Seidler, 'The Arabs Are Worse Than the Nazis', *Nekuda*, July 1991 [Hebrew]. Notably, the *Nekuda* editorial board also allotted space for a different articulation of the lesson of the Holocaust: an article by the psychologist Zvi Mozes, a resident of Karnei Shomron and director of the Center for Treatment of Stress Situations in Kedumim. Mozes finds a connection between the collective traumatic residue of the Holocaust among the Jews and political extremism on the Left *and* the Right.
40. Zvi Mozes, 'We All Need a Psychological Rebirth', *Nekuda*, October 1991 [Hebrew].
41. Arye Stav, 'Germany – The Sin and Its Reward', *Nativ*, May 1993, p. 9 [Hebrew].
42. Arye Stav, 'The Reward of Terror', in Yona Hadari-Ramage, *Let's Think It Over* (Tel Aviv, 1994), p. 388 [Hebrew].
43. Eliav Schuchtman, 'Then and Now – The Eve of the Holocaust and Its Lessons', *Nativ*, May 1994, p. 20 [Hebrew].
44. *Iton 77*, May 1997 [Hebrew].
45. See my book, *The State of Israel in Jewish Public Thought: The Quest for Collective Identity*, Chapter 1.
46. Dan Diner, 'Cumulative Contingency: History and Self-Justification in the Israeli Discourse', *Alpayim*, 1996 [Hebrew].
47. Yigal Elam, 'The Past Is But a Piece of the Present That Used to Be and Is No More', in Yona Hadari-Ramage (ed.), *Let's Think It Over* (Tel Aviv, 1994), pp. 427–8.

48. Saul Friedlander, *Memory, History, and the Extermination of the Jews in Europe* (USA, 1992), p. xi.
49. Saul Friedlander, *When Memory Come* (Jerusalem, 1980), pp. 170–1 [Hebrew].
50. See David Vital, *The Future of the Jews – A People at a Crossroads?* (USA: Harvard University Press, 1990).
51. David Vital, 'Power, Powerlessness, and the Jews', *Commentary*, January 1990.
52. Gershon Shaked, 'Anyone Who Argues That Jewish and Israeli Identity Can Be Defined without the Component of Dread Is an Ostrich', in Yona Hadari-Ramage (ed.), *Let's Think It Over*, p. 657.
53. Ibid., pp. 644–55.
54. Ibid., p. 658.
55. Ibid.
56. Gershon Shaked, 'Alexandria', in *Nowhere Else* (Tel Aviv, 1988), p. 184 [Hebrew].
57. A. B. Yehoshua, *Yes to Normality* (Tel Aviv, 1980), pp. 20–2 [Hebrew].
58. A. B. Yehoshua, 'To Cure the Hermaphrodite', in Yona Hadari-Ramage (ed.), *Let's Think It Over*, p. 270.
59. Haim Guri, *Facing the Glass Booth: The Eichmann Trial*, pp. 285–6, [Hebrew].
60. Amos Oz, *From the Slopes of Lebanon* (Tel Aviv, 1987), p. 25 [Hebrew].
61. Ibid., p. 156.
62. Hanoch Bartov, *I'm Not the Mythological Sabra* (Tel Aviv: Am Oved, 1995), p. 47 [Hebrew].
63. See Ziviah Lubetkin, 'The Last Days of the Warsaw Ghetto: A Survivor's Account of a Heroic Chapter in Jewish History', *Commentary*, May 1947; David Frankfurter, 'I Killed a Nazi Gauleiter!', *Commentary*, February 1950; Zelda Popkin, 'A Warsaw Fighter in Israel', *Commentary*, January 1951.
64. See, for example, Feigle Miendzizhetski (Vlodke), 'Der Vidershtand in der Varshaver Geto', *Forvets*, April 1953.
65. See articles in *Jewish Frontier*, May 1942, November 1942, July 1943 and January 1944.
66. H. Leyvik, 'Ekhsht tsen yar un mir nemen shoin fargesn', *Di Zukunft*, April 1952.
67. See articles by Vlodke, *Forvets*, April 1958; A. Menes, *Forvets*, 21 April 1962 and 2 April 1963; A. Menes, *Di Zukunft*, April 1952. See also editorial *Di Zukunft*, April 1963.
68. In 1961, in a special supplement on the uprisings, *Forvets* began to publish a list of the persons murdered, itemized by place of residence, in the manner of the subsequent Israeli campaign to note the name of each Holocaust victim. In 1964 the newspaper published lists of destroyed communities.
69. Edward Alexander, 'Stealing the Holocaust', *Midstream*, November 1980.
70. Earl Raab, in 'The Meaning and Demeaning of the Holocaust – A Symposium', *Moment*, March 1981.
71. Norman Podhoretz, *Commentary*, July 1983.
72. Irving Kristol, Symposium, *Commentary*, February 1988.
73. Henry L. Feingold, 'Determining the Uniqueness of the Holocaust: The Factor of Historical Valence', *Shoah*, Vol. 2, No. 2 Spring 1981.
74. Robert Alter, 'Deformations of the Holocaust', *Commentary*, February 1984.
75. Arnold Jacob Wolf, 'The New Assimilationists', *Conservative Judaism*, Summer 1980. See also A. J. Wolf, 'The Centrality of the Holocaust is a Mistake', *National Jewish Monthly*, October 1980.

76. Leonard Fein, 'Informed Uninformed', *Moment*, October 1986.
77. 'The Meaning and Demeaning of the Holocaust – A Symposium', *Moment*, March 1981.
78. The participants, in alphabetical order, were Yehuda Bauer (Hebrew University), Arnold Eisen (Columbia University), Sidra and Yaron Ezrahi (Hebrew University), Geoffrey Hartman (Yale University), Paula Hyman (Columbia University), Michael Meyer (Hebrew Union College), and Earl Raab (San Francisco).
79. Ismar Schorsch, 'The Holocaust and Jewish Survival', *Midstream*, January 1981.
80. Ismar Schorsch, 'The Lachrymose Conception of Jewish History', in *From Text to Context – The Turn to History in Modern Judaism* (USA, 1994), pp. 376–88.
81. Ismar Schorsch, 'The Sacred Cluster: The Core Values of Conservative Judaism', 1995.
82. See my book, *The State of Israel in Jewish Public Thought: The Quest for Collective Identity*, pp. 215–19.
83. Jacob Neusner, 'Is There a Future for the Jewish People?', *Jewish Quarterly*, No. 150 Summer 1993.
84. Jacob Neusner, 1979, 'How the Extermination of Jewry Became the Holocaust', in *Stranger at Home* (USA, 1981), pp. 88–91.
85. Jacob Neusner, 1980, 'Beyond Catastrophe, Before Redemption', in *The Jewish War against the Jews* (New York, 1984).
86. Jacob Neusner, 1980, 'Other Times, Other Places, Us', ibid., pp. 71, 76.
87. Jacob Neusner (ed.), *In the Aftermath of the Holocaust* (New York/London, 1993), pp. vii–x.
88. See Dinah Porat, at Chapter 2, Note 51, p. 82, in this volume.
89. On this matter, see the following articles published over the past thirty years in the English-language journal of Agudath Israel, the *Jewish Observer* (New York): (1) Joseph Friedson, 'Why Didn't They Fight Back', September 1973; (2) 'The Holocaust' (editorial), September 1973; (3) Mordechai Gifter, 'A Path through the Ashes', June 1974; (4) M. Scherman, 'An Understanding of the Holocaust', June 1974; (5) Rabbi Yaakov Weinberg, 'A Churban of Singular Dimension', June 1975; (6) Rabbi Yitzhak Hunter, 'Holocaust,' October 1977; (7) A. Scheinman, 'The Six Million Kedoshim', September 1980; (8) Shlomo Berger, 'Reflections on Remembering the Holocaust', May–June 1983; (9) Rabbi Avrohom Hakohan, 'After Churban, the Groundswell of Love', February 1985; and (10) Rab Yosseif Friedson, 'Heroes of the Warsaw Ghetto', March 1993.
90. David Biale, *Power and Powerlessness in Jewish History* (New York, 1987).
91. David Biale, 'Power, Passivity, and the Legacy of the Holocaust', *Tikkun*, January–March 1987.
92. See Chapter 6 of my book, *The State of Israel in Jewish Public Thought: The Quest for Collective Identity*.
93. Michael Lerner, *Jewish Renewal: A Path to Healing and Transformation* (New York, 1994), pp. 261–4.
94. 'The Holocaust' (editorial), *Tikkun*, May–June 1995.

5

The Pundits' Discourse:
The Holocaust as an Ethnic Mission

The issue that catapulted the internal discourse about the role of the Holocaust in the Jewish collective consciousness from its intimate setting to American Jewry at large was the dispute over the establishment of the United States Holocaust Memorial Museum in Washington. Here again, however, an ostensibly internal discussion among American Jews on an issue pertaining to them alone acquired a substantive and symbolic Israel connection. This is said mainly in reference to President Carter's motives in taking the initiative in 1977–78 that led to the establishment of this museum, and the dispute concerning whether or not to give the President of Israel, Chaim Herzog, a role at the opening ceremony of the museum some fifteen years later, in April 1993. The two accounts, described at the beginning and the end of Edward Linenthal's book,[1] deserve a brief retelling here.

In 1977, tension erupted between President Carter and the American Jewish leadership because of the former's statements on the Palestinians' right to self-determination. The tension mounted later that year upon the accession of Menachem Begin to the Israeli premiership. In October 1977, the United States and the Soviet Union issued a joint statement in favor of recognizing the legitimate rights of the Palestinian people. Then came an American arms sale to Saudi Arabia, including sophisticated F-15 aircraft. Amidst this tension, several academics and political functionaries in the President's circle came up with the idea of suggesting that Carter take the initiative to establish a central Holocaust memorial in the United States. The memorial, they said, would be a gesture honoring Israel on the occasion of its thirtieth anniversary and would symbolize America's support for Israel's establishment and continued existence. The idea was presented to Carter by Stuart Eizenstadt, his advisor on Jewish affairs, and the president accepted it. In May 1978, when Menachem Begin visited Washington and both houses of Congress debated the arms sale, Carter proclaimed, in the presence of Begin and some 1,000 rabbis from all over the

United States, the formation of a federal commission to commemorate the Holocaust in the US.

About fifteen years later, shortly before the museum held its inaugural ceremony, the matter came full circle in an incident of totally different significance. As the list of speakers at the ceremony was being elaborated, the question of including President Herzog among them came up. The chairman of the museum's executive committee and one of the main benefactors in its construction, the millionaire Harvey Meyerhoff, opposed inviting Herzog on the grounds that this would link the museum to Israel too closely. Other members of the commission concurred, and Herzog was not invited to speak. Only after vigorous intervention by President Clinton – who in this sense was honoring Carter's intention to have the museum symbolize American support for Israel – was the decision reversed and Herzog invited to speak on Israel's behalf.

The progression of this affair pinpoints and symbolizes the change that occurred during the fifteen years between the intention and its outcome. The tension between the two is the subject of this chapter.

The commission was officially established by presidential order on 1 October 1978. The chairman was Elie Wiesel; Irving Greenberg was named its secretary or academic director, and a young academic named Michael Berenbaum was appointed as his aide. The commission had thirty-four members – historians, clerics, public figures, and politicians from both houses of Congress, Jews and non-Jews alike, as well as Holocaust survivors. It began its work in January 1979 and issued its report in December of that year. Several historians on the panel, such as Lucy Dawidowicz and Raul Hilberg, were already famous Holocaust scholars. The tenor of the report, however, was dictated by Wiesel, already renowned as a bearer of the Holocaust message, and Greenberg, well known as an original and controversial Orthodox thinker in the field of theology and the Holocaust. The youngest member of the group, Michael Berenbaum, played an appreciable role and would eventually become the exponent of the ideological policy that the museum has represented and symbolized since it opened.

The introduction to the report,[2] which sets out to explain the historical and philosophical conception on which its recommendations are based, states that two determining assumptions informed the commission in all of its discussions: the Holocaust is unique and its remembrance is a moral imperative. However, as a commission that was established for pronouncedly political motives and that functioned amidst a reality of political pressure from other ethnic groups that sought inclusion in the 'club' of victims of mass annihilation (the Armenians for example), it had to choose its words carefully in maneuvering between the universalistic and the particularistic perceptions of the Holocaust. Thus, with laudable public resolve, the commission dwelled on the uniqueness of the Jewish Holocaust but, to keep its conclusions and the historical picture in balance, did not build an impermeable buffer between the genocide perpetrated against the Jews and mass killings of members of other peoples. Following Elie Wiesel's approach, the commission distinguished between the scheme to annihilate the entire Jewish people and the defeats and oppression that other peoples have faced. It stressed that the genocide at issue was devoid of economic and territorial logic, as in the purge of most of the population from a given territory. The Holocaust also lacked an evident political or military rationale, since the Jewish people was not a belligerent in World War II. The Holocaust is unique in terms of its plan for the utter annihilation of the Jewish people. The killing of Gypsies, in contrast, was not planned, and the thousands of Polish children who were torn from their families were sent to Germany for adoption, not to extermination facilities like Jewish children. However, the commission also believed it correct to assume that had the war lasted longer than it did, or had Nazism been the victor, the Jews might not have been the only victims of the exterminationist intent.

For the same reason, and to avoid a polemic with the Christian world and disputes among its own members, the commission downplayed the importance of traditional Christian antisemitism as a psychological and ideological background factor in the genocide of the Jews. Instead, it stressed that the Holocaust is in fact related to the secularization of society and the disappearance of religious values, which diminished the value of human beings as born in the image of God. An ironic paradox was also emphasized: although traditional religious antisemitism contributed to modern antisemitism, antisemitism led to mass murder – generally and in the specific context of the all-out annihilation of the Jews – in modern secular society. The report reinforced its critique of modernism, in favor of religious values, by arguing that all historians and sociologists who discuss the Holocaust agree that only in a modern state, with its efficient bureaucracies that orchestrate a sophisticated technological system and are obsessively devoted to whatever task they are given, can the idea of genocide be fulfilled.

So far, the report did not depart from the accepted view of the causes of the Holocaust, except in its emphasis on modern society's abandonment of religious values. In one respect, however, the report deviated from the conventional wisdom: by assigning some of the guilt for the demise of millions of Jews to US government policies during the war. It is quite out of the ordinary for an official federal commission to rule publicly that 'our failure to provide adequate refuge or rescue until 1944 proved disastrous to millions of Jews'.[3] Farther on, the report accuses the US Department of State and the British Foreign Office of not only having failed to rescue but of having prevented it deliberately – a grave charge indeed. The report also dealt critically with the question of why Auschwitz was not bombarded, although this discussion lacked the intensity of the treatment of the Jewish refugee problem.

The commission's accusations concerning the omissions and aims of US government policies during the war provide unchangeable evidence of the special status of the American Diaspora, not only in its economic and political power but also in its feeling of normality. After all, the charges are leveled not at a collaborationist government such as that of Vichy but at the fortress of democracy, the country that eventually defeated Nazi Germany. Therefore, the criticism pertains to citizens who have an equal status and feeling in a democracy – a phenomenon that Jews have seldom experienced in modern society, even in countries where the emancipation succeeded.

The commission regarded this criticism as part of the collective memory that should be fostered and preserved to prevent a recurrence of the Holocaust or anything like it in the future – even with respect to a country like the United States, which not only fought the Nazis but prosecuted its leaders for their war crimes. However, the reader of these bold words cannot but suspect the presence of an additional and covert intent: when some of the guilt for the deaths of millions of Jews is assigned to the United States government, the Holocaust becomes an American problem, not only because of its universal significance but because of America's particularistic liability. Thus the first step was taken – albeit by negation – to what Michael Berenbaum would later call 'the Americanization of the Holocaust'. Therefore, intentionally or inadvertently, the Jews became part of the American ethnic minorities' 'culture of grievance' against the Anglo-Saxon majority that had deprived or harmed them at various points in time – African Americans for having been enslaved, Native Americans for having been massacred, Hispanics for having been exploited, and Jews for having been forsaken.

One doubts whether Elie Wiesel, who was personally responsible for the report as the chairman of the commission, had this trend of Americanizing the Holocaust in mind. In fact, as we have seen in previous chapters, Wiesel rejected this way of thinking. However, it definitely reflected the intentions of dynamic, young Michael Berenbaum. This difference in approaches strained their relations, even though Wiesel was Berenbaum's mentor. At a certain point it prompted Berenbaum to resign from the commission; eventually, Wiesel stepped down from the commission presidium and Berenbaum returned to play a major role as the museum's academic director.

From this perspective, the Wiesel–Berenbaum dispute is emblematic of an intergenerational and intercultural difference in attitudes. Elie Wiesel is an untitled Jew. He lives in the United States but writes in French. He belongs concurrently to the Diaspora and to Israel, in its function as the Jewish nation-state. Berenbaum, in contrast, is a hyphenated Jew – 'American-Jewish'. The pivotal public experience in his life was not the Holocaust, as in Wiesel's case, but the 1967 Six-Day War, which prompted him – like many of his contemporaries – to feel and to fulfill the status of normality in American society. As this feeling gathers strength, it leads gradually and at different velocities from American Jew to Jewish American. This, as previously explained, signifies a shift of emphasis and center of gravity from Jewish ethnicity or even nationality to the American civic entity. The Americanization of the Holocaust not only reflects this trend but has stimulated and hastened it.

Since Berenbaum is the most salient representative of this trend of thinking among his cogenerationists – in his prolific journalistic writing, his many public appearances, and his political and academic role in commemorating the Holocaust – it is proper to trace the development of his thought.

Berenbaum is a post-Zionist in terms of his Jewish worldview, but not in the manner of Michael Lerner, editor of *Tikkun*. Lerner's post-Zionism denotes an ambition to reorder Jewish society in Israel. Berenbaum's, in contrast, means staying out of Israeli affairs and erecting a fence between it and American Jewish society. From this standpoint, Berenbaum's views closely resemble those of Jacob Neusner, whom he esteems as one of the most important Jewish scholars of our time, and are very far from those of his mentor, Elie Wiesel, whom he calls one of the greatest Jewish intellectuals of our time.

In his references to Israel, Berenbaum seems at first to be an objective observer. He cites the prodigious achievements of the Zionist Movement – establishing a Jewish society and a sovereign state in

Eretz Israel – and of Israel itself in absorbing vast numbers of immigrants and developing a modern economy. In his opinion, however,
these achievements are incomplete in that they have not revolution-
ized, that is to say normalized, the lives of Jews as Zionism wanted.
Politically, despite its sovereign status, Israel depends on American aid
and American Jewish support, as shown in the Six-Day War and, *a
fortiori*, in the Yom Kippur War. Economically dependent, it needs
constant outside assistance. Its new Hebrew culture, too, is heavily
influenced by Western culture and especially that of the United States,
which most of Israeli society regards with enthusiastic approval if not
admiration. As evidence, Berenbaum cites the hundreds of thousands
of Israelis who have emigrated to the United States. He concludes that
the exile against which Zionism rebelled in hopes of creating an alternative Jewish reality also exists in Israel. Not only are parts of Israel
exilic, but the entire Israeli national reality is merely another version of
the Diaspora reality that Zionism had criticized.

Paradoxically, Israel's dependency from its formation to the great
victory in 1967 placed it in the center of American Jewry's collective
reality for nearly two generations. Israel's centrality in Diaspora
Jewish life peaked at the time of this war, as manifested in the lavish
assistance it was given. However, this Israeli domination of mainstream Jewish life lasted into the mid-1980s, when the Lebanon war
and the ascendancy of aggressive national trends in Israel began to
undermine its centrality among American Jews. Therefore 'This
Israel-centered chapter in American Jewish life is drawing to a close.
Israel will continue to enjoy strong political support from American
Jews, but will no longer dominate American Jewish consciousness.'[4]
This denotes the liberation of American Jewry from Israeli custodianship. From now on, American Jewry will be assertive and
non-apologetic about its own decisions and priorities.

To this point, there is nothing novel about Berenbaum's analysis
and views. Berenbaum loyally reiterates Jacob Neusner's approach.
However, his remarks are but a preface to the main tenets of his worldview, which distances itself from Neusner's.

According to Berenbaum, the process of integrating American
Jewry into American society has picked up more and more speed in the
economic, academic, and political realms. Normalization in this sense
has already reached a stage where Jewish intellectuals whose concerns
focus on Judaism, such as Wiesel and Neusner, are recognized and
esteemed by society at large. Berenbaum augments this assessment,
which most American Jewish intellectuals share, with his own opinion:

'The United States Holocaust Memorial Museum is yet another example of American Jewry's movement toward the center of national life.' Then, to lend his remarks greater emphasis, he writes, 'The Museum will take what could have been the painful and parochial memories of a bereaved ethnic community and apply them to the most basic of American values. ... The museum will emerge as an American institution that will speak to the national saga.'[5]

We quote Berenbaum verbatim because only thus can the full significance of his intent be expressed. Only thus, too, can the reader appreciate the extent to which Berenbaum, in trumpeting American Jews' achievements in their march toward integration and in striving to introduce something Jewish in the pantheon of American social values, failed to notice that he has transformed his coreligionists' disaster and the sufferings of millions of murdered Jews into a tool for the attainment of total and perfect acceptance in American society. Thus, he argues, in a gradual, kind, and loving process toward all human beings, American Jewry is fashioning its own collective identity in America's pluralistic society. In this progression from parochial misfortune to what Berenbaum, as in the title of his article, calls 'the nativization of the Holocaust', the uniqueness of American Jewry – the collectivity which, as stated, is using other Jews' suffering to better its own position – will find expression. Berenbaum realizes that Holocaust consciousness has a utilitarian function in both the US and Israel but believes that the two countries exhibit a basic difference in the conclusions they draw from it. In Israel, the Holocaust is cited to prove the world's hostility to the Jewish people, whereas in the United States it prompts Jews to strengthen their commitment to society's pluralistic values – a divergence that further elevates the partition between Israel and American Jewry. In the late 1980s, when the article was written, Holocaust remembrance still united the two large Jewish centers, and the suffering was a shared national saga. Today, however, as the differences between the two communities are widening, the factor that once united them threatens to become a separating factor since the nativization or 'Americanization' denotes the liberation of the Holocaust from its particularistic Jewish ghetto. This makes it the legacy of humankind, in contrast to accepted thinking in Israel.

Berenbaum knows that Holocaust consciousness must pay a price for its having come 'out of the ghetto', to use Jacob Katz's famous term, by being de-Judaized. The price, however, is worth paying because of the dialectical return that it elicits. 'For the Jews to solidify the place of the Holocaust within Jewish consciousness, they must establish its importance for the American people as a whole.' In other words, the internal Jewish wish to remember no longer suffices under today's new and irreversible circumstances; instead, exogenous recognition by non-Jews is needed. To put this differently, the Jews can reinforce their Jewish convictions only by achieving the sympathies of non-Jews. 'By sharing a private and painful experience with the world', Berenbaum explains, 'the Jews have transformed it, and in turn, it has changed us.'

Notably, Berenbaum, for reasons not of interest here, attempts in subsequent articles to tone down his views on both Israel and the uniqueness of the Holocaust.[6] He dissociates himself from his previous advocacy of universalist normalization of Jewish life and admits that Jewish existence is still very vulnerable. He revokes the divorce between Israel and the Diaspora and acknowledges that the establishment of the Jewish state and the Holocaust are the two mainstays of the overall Jewish entity. He also distances himself the concept of de-Judaizing the Holocaust, explaining that the very comparison of the Holocaust with other peoples' disasters underscores its Jewish uniqueness.

Be this as it may, even though he has softened his stance, he has hurled concepts such as 'nativization', 'Americanization', and 'de-Judaization' of the Holocaust into the void of the public debate, where they resonated directly and indirectly in the debate concerning the establishment of the Holocaust Memorial Museum in Washington. Arguably, the exhibition at the museum and the response it has attracted confirm the ideational perception that underlies these concepts. Although the panoply of suffering retells the Jews' disaster, the public response, especially at the popular level, stresses the pan-human lesson, foremost with respect to American society. Thus, it has made the Holocaust part of the American cultural heritage and transformed its lessons into moral imperatives that should guide this society's development.

When the museum opened, the popular press from coast to coast greeted it with a sense of warm identification. Importantly, many writers for these newspapers are African American. Thus, a journalist from Cleveland writes: 'I walked in, a black man shaped by his own history: obligated to remember that the blood of millions of his ancestors – degraded, captive and destroyed – courses in him.' After touring the exhibit, however, 'I walked out a black man unashamed to be shaped' – and *shaped* is the key word – 'by something else', the Jews' disaster. In the wake of the Holocaust comes its lesson: 'I walked out with this obligation: to remember that if the blood lost by my own is to be truly honored, the blood lost by the others must be treasured and felt.'[7]

Another black journalist, this one from Chicago, expresses his amazement at the willpower of the Jewish leaders who acted in various ways to found the museum. This is especially important, he says, because 'the Holocaust Memorial Museum is not just about Jews, not about the "eternal Jew" as victim'. The museum urges its visitors to probe the thinking of the victims and the victimizers, the objects and perpetrators of the genocide, the recipients and inflicters of suffering. Therefore, 'I hope the Museum's sponsors are not deterred by their fellow Jews who are embarrassed when reminded that their antecedents were so degraded just 50 years ago.' Then comes the recurrent comparison:

> I recall when blacks preferred not to sing Negro spirituals because it reminded them of slavery. But I firmly believe that Hitler would have been less palatable if, before his arrival, there had been established several national museums in which the world could see, in meticulous detail, the sick, sick horrors of slavery and the lynch eve that followed.[8]

These remarks by two black intellectuals who possess a strong and painful ethnic consciousness show that the intention in Americanizing the Holocaust – to lift it out of its historical context – is correct. Even if we define one of the origins of whites' attitudes toward blacks and those of the Nazis toward Jews as racism, the cases are substantively different in terms of their results. Slavery, however inhuman in its symptoms and consequences, aspired to economic exploitation of the blacks; the Nazis intended to *exterminate* the Jews. They succeeded to a certain extent: when all is said and done, blacks are an important part of American society while Jews, as a nation, have ceased to be part of European society. Hence, the absolute comparison of exploitation, humiliation, and abuse to mass murder, including that of children, is incorrect not only historically but morally. Obviously, however, this objection does not apply to the grass-roots feeling that the Americanization of the Holocaust intends to stimulate.

Indeed, Philip Gourevitch, an editor with the *Jewish Daily Forward*, the English-language edition of the *Forverts*, dwelled on this phenomenon in his account of his visit to the museum, which was printed in the *New York Times*. Although Gourevitch criticized the idea behind the museum, the impressions he culled from speaking with visitors are undoubtedly accurate reflections of their emotions. He met Protestant women from the Midwest, who likened supporters of the abortion law to Nazis who murdered Jewish children. He heard a devout Christian teacher explain to her pupils that the Jews were murdered because they did not believe in Jesus. Gourevitch admits, however, that all his interlocutors told him they had found the place very interesting. He also notes that they spoke more about the present than about the past. Finally, their responses were influenced no less by their pre-existing opinions than by the exhibit they had just seen.[9]

One should not infer from this that the favorable response to the museum stems from popular emotions only. The national newspapers on the East Coast, such as the *Washington Post*, also ran favorable articles by top journalists. Thus, George Will, one of the most important conservative commentators in the print and electronic media, asks why it was necessary to establish this museum on the main thoroughfare of Washington, DC, of all places – the boulevard that, with its buildings and monuments, represents the success of American society. His reply: 'Because one message of the museum is that there is no permanent safety in social arrangements.'[10] Therefore, the museum, stationed on the thoroughfare that represents the victory of the American way of life and political system, reminds everyone that the only sure thing in contemporary society is doubt – 'so far so good'.

Charles Krauthammer, another senior commentator – of Jewish origin – initially opposed the museum idea because he did not wish the Jews to be identified as history's eternal victims. He changed his mind after visiting the exhibit, concluding that the United States is the safest place in the world to remember the Holocaust as a general lesson. Although Poland, where the Jews were murdered, is one vast memorial site, one cannot be sure that this memory will survive forever in the country and among the people that collaborated with the Germans in annihilating the Jews. Krauthammer then acknowledges that Israel has a memorial institution – Yad Vashem – and may itself be termed a remembrance, but 'there will be those in generations to come who will not trust the testimony of Jews'. Therefore, America will do for the Jews what the Jews could not do for themselves during the Holocaust and, perhaps, will not be able to do in the future, even in Israel. 'With this building, America bears witness. The liberators have returned to finish the job. First rescue, then remembrance. Bless them.' Handsome remarks indeed for a skeptic who 'repented'.

Stuart Eizenstadt, one of the most important patrons of the idea of the museum during the Carter Administration, shares this view. 'The

Holocaust Museum is an American museum about a distinctively
Jewish event with a universal message.'" This message, according to
Eizenstadt, is threefold: fraternity among people of all races and faiths,
peaceful resolution of all conflicts between peoples, and the obligation
of the community of nations to avert the menace of mass destruction.
Eizenstadt begins his article by recounting the circumstances that led
to the idea of establishing the museum. Although they were related to
US–Israel relations, as we recall, his remarks on the significance of the
museum make no reference to this nexus. The universal human
mission has become not the main thing but the only thing.[12]

Do the foregoing quotations reflect the views of the American press
in this matter at the time they were written? The answer is yes. A
review of articles and writings in a hundred daily newspapers, from
coast to coast, leaves the impression that this was indeed the attitude.
Most of the very few objections to the museum appeared in letters to
the editor.

Did the attitude of the press affect public opinion and create a mass
movement of visitors? Yes and no. In the museum's first three years, it
was visited by nearly six million people. According to a census of visitors in 1993 and 1994, 31 per cent were Jewish, 31 per cent Protestant,
and 22 per cent Catholic. Fifty-three per cent of visitors in 1993 and 63
per cent in 1994 were under the age of 45. The upturn is traceable to
an increase in visits by schoolchildren with their teachers. The
numbers, the relative youth, and the large majority of non-Jews indicate how much interest and sympathy the museum evoked. For
example, 59 per cent of visitors were 'very impressed' and 38 per cent
were 'impressed' with what they saw. Thirty-four per cent said they
intended to visit again. Other figures, however, circumscribe the
impression. First, 91 per cent of visitors belonged to groups defined in
the United States as white; only 9 per cent were black, Hispanic, or
Asian, as against an average representation of 16 per cent among visitors to other museums. Thus, the intention of speaking to the hearts of
groups that have experienced racial and social discrimination has not
yet been fulfilled. The authors of the survey believe that teams of
educators and historians representing the museum should take systematic educational action to correct this. Moreover, the Holocaust
museum attracts a more highly educated visitorship than any other
national museum in the capital: 74 per cent of visitors have university
degrees as against 61 per cent of visitors to the other museums.
Countrywide, 26 per cent of the population are university graduates at
some level. In other words, the proportion of the highly educated

among visitors to the Holocaust museum is almost three times the national average. Although 60 per cent of respondents stated that they had visited at the recommendation of friends or because of word of mouth, only 17 per cent came to Washington for this purpose only. These data on the visitors' ethnic makeup, education, and intentions indicate that the museum has stimulated massive interest among members of a special population group: whites and the well educated, groups in which Jews are well represented – 33 per cent as against 2–2.5 per cent in the population at large.[13]

Nevertheless, the phenomenal sympathy with which the daily press greeted the museum,[14] along with the throngs of visitors, commands our attention. Admittedly, the more exotic an exhibit is, the stronger its allure is to the public. However, the drawing power of the Holocaust Memorial Museum undoubtedly reflects emotional identification more than it does a rational conclusion. This emotional identification originates less in universal values of human dignity and freedom than in the internal problems of American society which, in its public culture, is highly sensitive to human suffering. Even if this sensitivity is external only, it serves as an accepted criterion in public. Therefore, identification with people's suffering and outrage against injustices inflicted on them is an inseparable part of the culture of this white majority, even though this population group does not count among the erstwhile or current sufferers.

Accordingly, in a society still struggling to assure equal rights and vanquish racism; in a society still plagued by past and current injustices and wrongdoing toward minority groups, especially the African Americans; in a society in which the more progress is made toward formal equality in all senses, the clearer is the extent to which racial prejudice is entrenched in people, irrespective of their skin color – in such a society, commensurate with progress toward equality, the emotional gap among the races is steadily widening in all respects: in schools, in housing, in the economy and, especially, in the sense of irreparable polarity.

Thus, the Holocaust museum, the greatest show of human suffering in American history, piques the emotions of two types of people: the racially deprived and those whose consciences are uneasy with respect to interracial relations. For both types of people the Holocaust that befell European Jewry, the coreligionists or conationalists of Jewish Americans, expresses a personal warning and forewarning. In this sense, the popular feeling overlooks the unique historical conditions that evolved in interwar Europe and takes no interest in the

special status of European Jewry in the past century. All it sees is the
embedded potential of satanic evil in human society and the relationship between this evil and racist ideology. In view of these feelings, the
lesson of the Holocaust has acquired a universal, pan-human significance and has been applied to American society. Thus, even if a few
articles took exception to the Holocaust museum in Washington – due
to its cost and its Jewish particularism – they are a drop in the ocean of
favorable attitudes of non-Jews toward the idea of preserving the
memory of this horrible evil.

While public thought at the grass-roots level was powered by
emotions that corresponded to the feelings of a great many visitors to
the museum, public thought at the intellectual level focused on the
question of American Jews' ethnic identity and the status of this
community in the array of American ethnicities. This question, which
lurks behind the entire discourse explored in this book, became palpable in the context of the establishment of the Holocaust Memorial
Museum in Washington. This is because – in contrast to the academic
questions (of theology, history, and ideology) discussed in the previous
chapters – the issue here is a symbol meant to substantiate the uniqueness of the Jewish fate on the one hand and the Jews' integration into
American society on the other. The museum was intended to point
both to the Jews' tragic past and to their contribution to American
society – a contribution that reflects the Jews' attainments in this
society and a covert statement of gratitude to it, as it had done so well
for its Jewish citizens.

The museum's manifest symbolism touched off a pro-and-con
debate among intellectuals. This taxonomy of opponents and proponents is overly schematic because it does not reflect the full range of
views and attitudes expressed. The debate did, however, elicit one clear
and explicit message: all the discussants, despite their disagreements,
shared the conviction that American Jews, including themselves, are
natural ideational and cultural members of the American civic society.
In 1990, three years before the museum opened, Professor Howard
Husock of Harvard University unveiled the argument that the
museum symbolizes the Jews' separation from the American 'common
civic culture of tolerance', which remains the best protector of religiously or politically exceptional individuals and groups. From now on,
through the establishment of the museum, the Jews are placing their
trust more in having been persecuted than on the general principles
that gave American society its contours. This, he believes, will grant
the Jews less security, not more, because it accentuates their specialness

and undermines the fragile constellation that the various ethnic groups in American society share.[15] Husock's views resemble those of Jacob Neusner, the greatest opponent of the museum and everything it stands for, whom we already know as consistently averse to making Holocaust remembrance part of the collective consciousness of American Jewry. In utter disregard of the universalistic trends embodied in the idea of the museum and the goal of Americanizing the Holocaust, Neusner stubbornly continued to point to the danger that Judaism – not American Jewry – faces from its preoccupation with the Holocaust rite. Neusner regards the museum as the symbol of a process that began with the 1967 war and peaked when the museum was established – an infusion of new content into Jewish ethnicism, 'a Jewishness of Holocaust and Redemption'. This Jewishness, he says, espouses total distrust of the Gentiles and reliance on power – political in the case of American Jewry, military in the case of Israel. Moreover, this is occurring amidst the abandonment of traditional Jewish faith and adherence to a new faith – faith in power that will save the Jewish people from total assimilation. Neusner takes issue with this perception, stating that the doctrine of nurturing the Holocaust-and-redemption awareness has failed totally. Therefore, from Neusner's point of view, the *kaddish* that would be said in the memory of the Holocaust victims when the museum opened would also be a requiem for the Jewish people. He realized that the recitation of the Yizkor prayer there would generate excitement and cause tears to flow. 'But some wonder whether on high above the Mall the angels weep too for that other word by Judaism, the religion set forth by the Torah, Oral and Written, that for American Jews is now mostly faded memory.'[16] These remarks place Neusner, an ordained Conservative rabbi, on the brink of an Orthodox stance, especially that of Agudath Israel.[17] Like the Orthodox, he is dismayed at the thought of losing traditional Judaism, that rooted in religious faith, and its social framework – the Torah. However, while the Orthodox regard this loss as the path to total assimilation, Neusner is fearful of Jews with a secular, power-centric consciousness that would erect a barrier of suspicion and hostility between themselves and the society surrounding them.

Melvin Bukiet, literary editor of the liberal journal *Tikkun* – and the son of a Holocaust survivor who gave a large donation to the museum – also considers the museum an expression of the new Jewish fixation with power. 'I see the existence of the museum as a statement of raw power, and that's the only thing I like about it. A blatant kowtowing to the survivors' attainments in contemporary society.' Lamentably, however, the museum will not meet the expectations of donors such as Bukiet's father; instead, paradoxically, it will help American society to forget. The reason: 'It is the melting pot announcing "you belong to us".' In his opinion, the American melting pot has not only annexed the Jews' suffering but has appropriated symbolic concepts that, from the historical standpoint, were typical of Jews alone. Thus America has transformed the concept of ghetto into a metaphor for urban slums because 'there is an iconography to Jewish history that encourages others who are covetous of its passion to try to appropriate its imagery'. Although he appreciates Jewish power, like Neusner he considers it anything but a source of leverage for Jewish survival. Both agree that the museum, more than it symbolizes the Jews' disaster in Gentiles' eyes, expresses their strength in American society. Both realize that this position of strength will not stanch the Jews' assimilation and may even hasten it. Both concur that American Jewry's secure and respected status in society makes this show of force unnecessary. Both also believe that only in Israel is the nexus of Holocaust and rebirth, or of disaster and power, meaningful for Jews. Bukiet, who diverges from Neusner in his emotional attitude toward Israel, states in so many words: 'I believe that Yad Vashem, on the hill west of Jerusalem, is the sole legitimate repository of this particular history.' Beyond this, because Bukiet, like Neusner, realizes that the Jews' social assimilation in America is building up momentum, he is convinced that 'authentic memory of the Holocaust will live or die with the Jewish state, which is as it should be, there in the state of the martyrs and commemorated on Yom Ha-Shoa'.[18]

One doubts that Bukiet's opinion derives from Zionist convictions, but it is undoubtedly related to his Jewish and humanistic outlook. In this sense, Holocaust remembrance is very important to him. Furthermore, as an aware intellectual who harbors no self-delusions, he understands that in one location only, Israel, will this remembrance will be assured for posterity. Elsewhere – in the free Diaspora communities – it will dissolve as the Jews assimilate, and the museum is a way station very close to this destination.

David Frum of Toronto composed his own cerebral variation on the theme of power. He notes that the anti-racist, universalist moral ideology underlying the idea of the museum may acquire an anti-Israel interpretation and intent, depicting Israel as a Jewish state that represses the Arab masses. He also regards the museum as a striking reflection of the attractive and fashionable ideology of victimhood that all sorts of deprived groups have heartily adopted. This ideology, he believes, has turned into political power: 'Victimhood is now power.' However, it is not a power of which one should beware; 'it is ... an especially debilitating and corrupting form of power: one that Jews – who throughout their history have rejected power for the sake of truth – must find strength to abjure'.[19] However, he considers Israel, the Jewish state surrounded by lethal enemies, another case altogether. Israel has a genuine need for power and not only because Jews were once real victims of powerlessness, as against metaphors for general human suffering such as the conceivers of the museum wish to depict them. Thus Frum, an evident conservative who backs Israel's tough political policies, connects the attempt to reconstruct the Holocaust as a metaphor for human suffering and the ideology of victimhood.

Jonathan Rosen, one of the editors of the *Jewish Daily Forward*, the English-language edition of the *Forverts*, is also offended by the museum as a symbol of the Jew as an eternal victim who makes his suffering into a metaphor for all of humanity. Rosen, however, shifts the Jew-as-victim issue from the ethnic-political plane to the level of Jewish–Christian relations: 'Christian culture had assigned Jews the role of suffering witnesses hundreds of years ago. Were Jews to voluntarily offer themselves up to play the role once more?' This question is typical of second- and third-generation American Jews, who consider themselves a normal part of a society different from that which existed in Europe, where the Holocaust took place. Underlying it is a furtive concern about implanting the European anti-Jewish tradition in American society. Indeed, Rosen fears that just as Jesus lent the tenets of the Jewish faith a universal interpretation, thereby isolating the Jews from their surroundings, so the universal interpretation given to their suffering in American society, which played no role in this suffering, will re-isolate them within it. In other words, Rosen reiterates in cultural terms what Frum states in political rhetoric: universalization of the Holocaust as a metaphor may ultimately become the Jews' undoing.

Rosen's colleague on the editorial board of the *Forward*, Philip Gourevitch, continues in the same vein. In a passionate essay describing his visit to the museum, he also takes up the matter of the Jew as a metaphor of the victim. Here he draws an important distinction between the Holocaust Memorial Museum and plans to build additional ethnic museums on the history of Native Americans and African Americans. Gourevitch notes, correctly, that these museums will retell the history of the respective groups on American soil, whereas the Holocaust museum describes a segment of Jewish history that has nothing to do with an American setting. Therefore, the museum causes Jews to be identified as a people or sect composed of victims of perse- cution and murder. Were it not for this, it would not have been built.

> This fact points to the centrality of victimology in contemporary American identity politics. At a time when Americans seem to lack the confidence to build national monuments to their ideas of good, the Holocaust has been served as an opportunity to build instead a monument against absolute evil.[20]

Herein, in Gourevitch's judgment, lies a mistake. One cannot learn lessons from absolutes. The absolute belongs to God, and it is like Him: unique.

It is noteworthy that neither of these young English-language editors of the *Forward*, neither Rosen nor Gourevitch, connected Israel with the museum issue. Perhaps it is because their Jewish newspaper symbolizes the Americanization of American Jewry in its transition from Yiddish to English. That transition, however, is a different version of the trend illuminated at the museum and is undoubtedly an organic development that belongs to American society. This is why the Israel issue does not perturb them when they discuss the museum. One may even say that the contrast juxtaposes their Americanization to that advocated by their contemporary, Michael Berenbaum, whom they mention in their article. In an interesting and noteworthy twist, Melvin Bukiet, of all people – an editor of an ultra-liberal journal and a critic of Israel – stresses his ideational and emotional connection with Israel as a Jewish national center, while Rosen and Gourevitch, editors of a newspaper defined as Jewish, do nothing of the sort. In this respect, in contrast to *Tikkun*'s critical attitude toward Israel and Zionism – indicative of a disposition toward and involvement in both of them – Rosen and Gourevitch seemingly perpetuate the historical tradition of the Yiddish-language *Forward*, whose editor, the socialist and universalist Abraham Kahan, urged the Jews to integrate into American society. This may point to one of the reasons for their extreme criticism of the museum: concern that its message will dash their employers' historical vision[21] just as it is coming to pass, all by itself as it were, with no need for a special effort on the Jews' part.

Another critic of the trend of Americanizing the Holocaust through the concept of victim is Alvin Rosenfeld, professor of literature at Indiana University, who lacks the liberal credentials of the editors of *Tikkun* and the *Forward*. Rosenfeld transfers the discussion from the political and cultural planes to the social level. He warns of the attempt to generalize, within the Holocaust framework, the murder of European Jewry and the suffering of various minority groups in America and elsewhere. To commingle the victims of these historical situations 'is to metamorphose the Nazi Holocaust into the empty and all but meaningless abstraction, "man's inhumanity to man"'.

According to Rosenfeld, this propensity in understanding the Holocaust has been evident since the 1950s. Today, however, it has taken on a political complexion and become an ideological tool in the struggle against social oppression. Thus, American culture has spawned collective identities predicated on victimhood. The rhetoric of oppression, he says, has become fashionable in American politics, academia, and the arts, and its exponents frequently employ the signs and symbols of the Nazi Holocaust to describe what they consider their own victimization within American society.

Rosenfeld links this phenomenon to the escalating tendency to transform the suffering of victims and the noble self-sacrifice of the handful of rescuers into a universal moral metaphor. This is a departure from the truth: just as the sufferings or privations of various American groups should not be likened to the Holocaust, so the actions of the few rescuers do not attest to the rule. What happened in Europe is primarily a story of genocide, not of rescue, and this genocide targeted members of a certain people because of and under certain historical circumstances. To ensure accuracy in remembrance of the Holocaust, this perspective should be preserved. Then, addressing himself to the disciples of Americanization of the Holocaust, Rosenfeld adds: 'A similar sense of perspective is required in considering the other contemporary distortions introduced by the relentless Americanization of the Nazi destruction of European Jewry.'[22]

Thus far, we have presented the views of those who oppose or take exception to the idea of the museum, and have set forth the range of their views and the differences in their underlying outlooks. Notably, it took a modicum of public courage to express the minority view amidst the passion, enthusiasm, and identification with the museum that gripped the overwhelming majority of pundits and respondents to their critiques. Intellectuals who defended the conceivers and administrators of the museum had a much easier mission: to add a little depth to remarks already made by passionate supporters.

The debate between proponents and opponents revolved around two themes: the role of the Holocaust in the American ethnic consciousness and the attempt to make it a metaphor for evil and human suffering. These two human themes, although distinct, overlap because the Holocaust as a metaphor may become a universal symbol and emblem of the historical deprivation of various American ethnic groups. In both cases, an evident attempt is made to deprive the Jews of something that, they feel, is particular to them alone. The essayist Anne Roiphe acknowledges and, in part, justifies this feeling, but she is convinced that for the very reason of the intensity of the horror that came to light in the Holocaust, its pan-human metaphorization – of evil and of suffering – cannot be thwarted in the long run. 'This process offends some', she admits, 'but the tides of time would do the same thing, anyway.'[23] Therefore, all people should be given an opportunity to identify with the Holocaust as they see fit, and every public method of perceiving the Holocaust, in both the present and the future, should be treated with understanding.

Roiphe's logical and acceptable argument, that the Holocaust cannot be prevented from becoming a pan-human metaphor, nevertheless fails to explain American Jewry's extraordinary effort to create institutional symbols – Holocaust museums – to formalize this metaphor.

This issue was taken up by the essayist Leon Wieseltier, the literary editor of the *New Republic*, a monthly that expresses the intellectual mainstream between the ultra-liberal *Tikkun* and the neo-conservative *Commentary.*

Roiphe's attitude toward the problem is typified by an emotional post-modern existentialism of sorts that upholds all manner of subjective perceptions. Wieseltier's approach, in contrast, is driven by a pronounced ideology that defines ethnicity as a building block of American society. There is no unhyphenated Americanism; every type of Americanism carries an adjective corresponding to the place and culture of its origin. Therefore, the grand and tragic past of European Jewry also belongs organically to America, because 'The past of America is elsewhere (here the past is a foreign country). The collective memory of this country will always include names and dates foreign and far away.' Wieseltier not only justifies the Holocaust museum by citing the pluralistic ethnic nature of American society but also defends its location on the main boulevard of Washington, which presumably represents the accomplishments of the American culture and system of government. He believes it symbolic that the exit from the Holocaust museum opens onto a view of the monument to the founder of American democracy, Thomas Jefferson, the architect of the world's only regime that, according to Wieseltier, has made people free while remaining skeptical about their value. Therefore, after exploring the Holocaust museum, 'you think in the light of what you have just seen, that it was no small achievement to found a democracy upon a pessimistic view of human nature. And you think in the light of what you have just seen, that it was just as well.'[24]

Wieseltier actually creates two juxtaposed metaphors: 'the Holocaust', which represents human foulness, and 'American democracy', which proves that libertarian governance can be maintained without illusions about human morality and sagacity. Thus, a dialectical relationship has come into being on the lawns of Washington, along the banks of the Potomac, and in the river's placidly flowing waters, between the absolute human evil and the relative possible good, between the hope for humankind that wells from the grand boulevard and the awareness that the atrocity perpetrated in Europe may not be the last of its ilk.

Wieseltier is not a utopist in the sense of Berenbaum, who preaches Americanization of the Holocaust as a Jewish moral mission vis-à-vis American society. However, he believes in the real America, a 'tolerant country but ... not an innocent country'. However, even when it is not innocent of wrongdoing, America should understand that 'a home to all the peoples of the world is also a home to all the scars of the world'.

Thus, it is clear that every ethnic group may present its disaster in any way it chooses. All the scars of these groups, coupled with democratic governance and human freedom, add up to the wholeness of America. Within this collectivity of scarred people, the Holocaust of European Jewry loses its national uniqueness. Wieseltier lauds the presentation in the museum as a pedagogical gem because it 'illustrates the sufferings of all who suffered' and stands in contrast to the presentation at Yad Vashem in Israel: 'It resists the rhetoric about Shoa v'Gvurah, Holocaust and Heroism, as if there was as much heroism as there was Holocaust.'

This explains why Wieseltier's article does not mention Israel in the context of the meaning of the Holocaust. Generally speaking, it says nothing about the Jewish national significance of the Holocaust, concerning itself solely with the Jewish-human significance, which has become pan-human. In so stating, Wieseltier undoubtedly wishes to erect another partition between the State of Israel and the American Diaspora.

This stance definitely stems from his general view of relations between Israel and American Jewry. About ten years earlier, Wieseltier had concluded that American Jewry and Israel are two different and mutually independent Jewish realities. As a person culturally and socially associated with Israel, he acknowledged that Israel commands a special place in the American Jewish reality, especially with respect to Hebrew culture and, in particular, the Hebrew language, without which Jewish culture is inconceivable – and the existence of Jewry as a collectivity depends on Jewish culture. However, the important matter for him in relations between the two Jewish entities is the conviction among most American Jews that America is not just another place of exile. This, in his opinion, is the paradoxical American contribution to what Zionists call the normalization of the Jewish people. Thus, the essential idea of classical Zionism, 'negation of the Diaspora', is dying or is already dead.

The death of classical Zionism inaugurated the post-Zionist era, in which classical nationhood gives way to ethnicity, of which the United States provides a pronounced cultural, ideational, and political example. Therefore, instead of the Jews as a minority integrating into the Anglo-Saxon American culture, as the previous generations believed, the American culture is in every sense a culture of minorities.[25]

This is the worldview underlying Wieseltier's remarks on the Holocaust and the way the museum portrays it. In his realistic fashion, he considers the Holocaust an important and substantive dimension of the American-Jewish ethnic identity – but in the pan-human sense, not in the Jewish national sense. Although Wieseltier is not a universalist with a moral mission, he is a practical American pluralist. From this standpoint, he joins those who regard American society as the most universalistic in the world, both in the diversity of its integrated cultures and in the proliferation of its converged ethnic historical traditions. Thus, the museum symbolizes the dialectical unity of American society or the fertile tension between the particular and the general, between the ethnic and the pan-American.

Has Wieseltier, in his post-Zionist perceptions and in his attempt to integrate the Holocaust ethos into American culture, made peace with the dissolution of the Jewish people? I think not. In an anguished, angry article written after the assassination of Israeli Prime Minister Yitzhak Rabin, in which he demands the banishment from *klal Yisrael* of those who justified the murder, he employs the concept of 'us' and takes pains to stress that 'by us I mean the Jews, and not only the Jews in Israel'.[26]

'Us' is more than a word; it is a concept laden with traditional values and historical experience. In this case, it is a spark from the flame that engulfed the Jews and Wieseltier's cogenerationists in 1967, before and after the Six-Day War. If a spark remains, the embers must still be glowing. However, the times have changed since then and the winds have shifted.

The change in trend is summarized tellingly by Edward Norden (who is writing a book on the future of American Jewry) in an article entitled 'Yes and No to the Holocaust Museums' – with reference to the institute in Los Angeles and the new museum in Washington. According to Norden, things have changed since the 1950s, when most Jews considered the State of Israel the only response to the Holocaust. If Israel were again to be in distress, Heaven forfend, American Jewry would take its side and offer assistance. In the meantime, however, a small but highly influential Jewish minority, such as the radical intellectuals and Jewish liberals, has come to regard Israel as a burden, an obstacle to overcome. This also casts doubt upon the centrality of Israel, especially as reports from Israel, since the war in Lebanon and the Intifada, have become increasingly embarrassing. In the Diaspora, in contrast, a generation has grown up that refuses to succumb to the concept of Israel as the sole center of world Jewry. Members of this generation are coming around to the belief that anything done in Israel can be done more effectively in the United States. Thus, the museum in Washington is more than a monument to the memories of the dead millions and a modicum of compensation to the survivors who have made the United States their treasured home. It is also a 'declaration of independence'.[27]

The remarkable paradox here is that this declaration of independence enumerates among its adherents some who reject the idea of the museum and some who affirm it. For both, the Holocaust-and-rebirth nexus, in the sense of the fate, destiny, and function of *klal Yisrael*, has been broken. Even those who acknowledge the significance of the pairing consider it valid or relevant only in Israel and not in the Diaspora. For most of them, then, the Holocaust-and-rebirth combination has been replaced by a Holocaust-and-humanism nexus, a pairing of concepts that are not mutually exclusive, since one may say that rebirth, too, retains an exalted human significance. However, in the current historical context, for a variety of commingling reasons, Israel and Diaspora Jewry are becoming estranged, their relations occasionally marked by tension in view of political background factors – religious (government policy concerning the status of heterodox movements in Israel) or social (the use of philanthropic money for Israel's needs or for the Diaspora's). At such a time, these two pairs of concepts symbolize the contrasts between the two Jewish perspectives, one focused on Israel and other on the world.

The tension between these two worldviews is the theme of the concluding chapter of this study.

NOTES

1. Edward T. Linenthal, *Preserving Memory: The Struggle to Create America's Holocaust Museum* (USA, 1995), pp. 17–20, 257–60.
2. *Report to the President: President's Commission on the Holocaust*, Elie Wiesel, Chairman, 27 September 1979, pp. 1–9.
3. Ibid., p. 6.
4. Michael Berenbaum, *After Tragedy and Triumph* (New York, 1990), pp. 157–63.
5. Michael Berenbaum, 1986, 'The Nativization of the Holocaust', *After Tragedy and Triumph*, pp. 3–16.
6. See Berenbaum, 1987, 'The Uniqueness and Universality of the Holocaust', *After Tragedy and Triumph*, pp. 18–32; 1989, 'Is the Centrality of the Holocaust Overemphasized?', *After Tragedy and Triumph*, pp. 47–52.
7. Robert Brown, 'Done to One, So Done to All', *Cleveland OH Daily*, 10 May 1993.
8. Vernon Jarret, 'Memory Must Not Fade', *Chicago Sun-Times*, 22 April 1993.
9. Philip Gourevitch, 'What They Saw at the Holocaust Museum', *New York Times Magazine*, February 1995. The Israeli journalist Nira Rousseau reported similar impressions from her visit to the museum: 'To Be Passive, To Be Guilty', *Ha'aretz Supplement*, 12 April 1996. According to information cited in Rousseau's article, approximately two million people visit the museum each year, more than one-third of whom are not Jewish.
10. George F. Will, 'Telling Their Truth', *Washington Post*, 22 April 1993.
11. Charles Krauthammer, 'Holocaust', *Washington Post*, 23 April 1993.
12. Stuart E. Eizenstadt, 'Holocaust Memorial Deserves Capital Place', *Christian Science Monitor*, 28 April 1993.
13. US Holocaust Memorial Museum, *August–September Telephone and On-Site Surveys*, September 1994.
14. This opinion is based on a survey of articles, pieces, and letters to the editor in more than one hundred daily newspapers across the United States.
15. Howard Husock, 'Red, White and Jew: Holocaust Museum on the Mall', *Tikkun*, July–August 1990. Notably, five years later, Jon Wiener, a university lecturer in California, urged an end to the emphasis on the uniqueness of the suffering of European Jewry because such an emphasis blurs the universal meaning of the Holocaust. See John Wiener, 'The Other Holocaust Museum', *Tikkun*, May–June 1995.
16. Jacob Neusner, 'A Judaism of Memory Alone', *Baltimore Sun*, 21 April 1993.
17. Esther Jungreis, 'Memorials and the Silent Holocaust', and Shmuel Rieder, 'Of Dedications and Reflections', *Jewish Observer*, June 1993.
18. Melvin Jules Bukiet, 'The Museum vs. Memory: The Timing of the Holocaust', *Washington Post*, 18 April 1993.
19. David Frum, 'Holocaust Wasn't Made in America', *Toronto Saturday*, 1 May 1993.

20. Philip Gourevitch, 'Behold Now Behemoth', *Harper's Magazine*, July 1993. Interestingly, a non-Jewish conservative monthly of pronounced religious leanings, *First Things*, devoted a special column in October 1993 to responses to Gourevitch's article. Although the editor did not express an unequivocal attitude toward the article or toward the need for the museum, he explicitly opposed the spread of 'victimhood culture' in American society.

21. Rosen's article attracted dissenting responses from readers, e.g., in the *New York Times*, 30 April 1993. In the same context, Gourevitch's harsh critique of the film *Schindler's List*, which he likened to the museum in the sense that both aim more to be showy than to illuminate the historical truth, was censured by many readers and defended by few. See P. Gourevitch, 'A Dissent on *Schindler's List*', *Commentary*, February 1994; Letters from Readers – *Schindler's List*, *Commentary*, June 1994.

22. Alvin H. Rosenfeld, 'The Americanization of the Holocaust', *Commentary*, June 1995.

23. Anne Roiphe, 'A Holocaust Museum? Yes, and Open to All', *New York Observer*, 17 May 1993.

24. Leon Wieseltier, 'After Memory', *New Republic*, 3 May 1993.

25. See my book, *The State of Israel in Jewish Public Thought: The Quest for Collective Identity*, pp. 293–4.

26. Leon Wieseltier, 'Israelity', *New Republic*, 27 November 1995.

27. Edward Norden, 'Yes and No to the Holocaust Museums', *Commentary*, August 1993.

Summary: The Mythic Ethos
of Holocaust and State

The polarized public discourse, which this book calls *Between Auschwitz and Jerusalem* – with its theological, ideological, academic, and political aspects – reached its symbolic and, perhaps, its substantive terminus when the Holocaust Memorial Museum in Washington opened its doors. The cumulative impression is that all bones of contention in the past generation concerning the Holocaust and rebirth issue have been played out. The historical, spiritual, and ethical *meaning* of these disputes has been fully elucidated; from now on, their interrelations will be determined by the *substance* of the dynamic of social life. Therefore, in this context, as in others even more substantive and important, the Jewish people seems to have reached a fork in the road: one path heading toward the universal destination in its particularistic American garb, the other leading back to the particularistic Jewish origin in its universalistic sense.

In other words, the public discourse is polarized not only in the tragic, dialectical contrast between Auschwitz and Jerusalem but also in the tension that reigns between them – a tension that threatens to snap the rope. This is so even though this between Auschwitz and Jerusalem relationship still carries a sense of existential mystery. Thus, it has acquired a layer of myth and ethos that magnifies its historical importance in shaping the collective identity.

By so stating, I do not imply that *only* these two recent phenomena in the history of our people – the nadir of tragedy and the apogee of achievement – have shaped the collective Jewish image in the past two generations. On the contrary: other effects and processes that are wholly unrelated to them, directly or indirectly, have been influential, such as the growing trend toward cultural integration in the Diaspora countries, not only as consumers but also as creative players. Our view of intermarriage, a development that has eroded various Diaspora Jewish communities, should take this trend into account. Other events of this kind are the absorption of mass immigration in Israel and the

Jewish–Arab conflict, for each has contributed to the collective Jewish persona. All these factors have combined over the past two centuries to transform the Jewish people from an inward-facing religious community into a multifaceted society that other cultures permeate freely; from an isolated community, deliberately segregated from its surroundings, into a collective immersed in its surroundings; from a nation of coexisting ethnicities into a sovereign people in its own nation-state, where these ethnicities are forced to coexist; and from a nation whose fate was affected by others to a nation that affects the fate of another people, the Palestinian people.

Nevertheless, the Holocaust and the state are crucially important because they have inaugurated a new era in Jewish history. Both denote and symbolize the existential catastrophe and the national watershed that not only transformed the Jews' destiny but also affected their image as a people by furnishing them with a fundamental myth (*Gründungsmythos*) that explains their collective existence.

The Holocaust brought the millennia-old European chapter of Jewish history to a close. Although Western Europe has an active Jewish community and although efforts (which may eventually succeed to a small extent) to revive Jewish community life in Russia are being made, the Jews ceased being a 'European people' after the core of Eastern European Jewry was destroyed.

Pursuant to this, the historic episode of the existence of Jewish centers in Muslim societies also reached its end within a few years after the Holocaust and immediately after the establishment of Israel. The uprooting and replanting in Israel of Iraqi and North African Jewry wrought a substantial change in Jewish history. For two centuries up to that time, various historical processes had relegated Oriental/Sephardi Jewry to the fringes of Jewish social activity. After this collective settled in Israel, however, it moved from the periphery to the center of national and cultural activity. It influences the fate of the State of Israel and, therefore, the image of Jews everywhere.

Hence the historic significance of the Jewish state lies not only in its establishment but also in its existence, for it has changed the image of our people from a non-territorial nation to a territorial one. In this context, I quote below a terse passage from Emmanuel Ringelblum's moving and edifying diary, published by Yad Vashem.

In an entry dated May 1942, Ringelblum writes: 'The [Jews] enjoy speaking Polish. Very little Yiddish is heard in the streets.' Ringelblum notes that this has been attributed to various psychological factors. 'However', he adds, 'I consider it evidence of a large-scale linguistic assimilation that was evident before the war and is now even more conspicuous among the Polish-speaking masses.' His conclusion: 'This teaches us that without territorial ingathering, we are doomed to total assimilation.'[1]

The territorial aspect of the issue has a sidebar: the aspect of Jewish sovereignty. The sovereignty at issue here is not that of the State of Israel with respect to its subjects – itself a radical novelty in Jewish history since the nation was dispersed – but mainly to sovereignty with respect to the Jewish people that resides outside Israel, a sovereignty reflected in the Law of Return and in the resources and efforts that Israel pledges to its implementation. We have observed this in the case of Jews from the former Soviet Union and from Ethiopia. It is this ability to fulfill the Jewish collective political will that distinguishes this period from its predecessor; it is also the watershed that separates the tragedy of the Holocaust from the achievement of rebirth.

It is multidisciplinary research on the Holocaust in the past generation, of all things, that has illuminated the contrast between the two. The more this research attains greater breadth and depth, the more specific it becomes. It teaches us about daily life in the ghettos, the nightmarishness of the labor and death camps, the valor of temporary life, the leadership, the underground, and so on. The more detail we add, the more we appreciate the natural heroism of the individuals involved: the heroism of children who smuggled food, of women who struggled to feed their families, of teachers and intellectuals who industriously pursued their studies, of political activists who worked for the public good, and of so many others. Paradoxically, however, as our view of the heroism of the individual improves, the impotence and failures of the collective become blurred. We must not disregard the fact that in those wretched years, the Jewish people lacked the inner collective ability to unite on behalf of its brethren and failed to muster the political clout to persuade the Allied forces to do more to stop the Germans from carrying out their malevolent plan.[2] In this context, one cannot but ask the following question: Had the Jewish people had a state during those terrible years, if only a mini-state with a million or a million and a half Jews, and had this state made 100,000–150,000 soldiers available to the Allies on this vital Mediterranean front, would the Western leaders not have viewed the Jewish catastrophe in a different light?[3]

The point of these remarks is not to repeat the superficial view, which sometimes prevails among great and small minds, that Israel can or could defend the lives of Jews everywhere. Instead, I refer to Israel's capacity – relative but important if not decisive – in the international political constellation, in contrast to the helplessness of all Jewish organizations in the Holocaust era, a weakness originating, among other factors, in internal disunity and discord in the face of the national disaster. This relative capacity symbolizes the historical watershed that the Jewish people has crossed in the present era.

This change, this turning point in Jewish history, has an additional facet. As a result of the calamity of the Holocaust and the change effected by the State of Israel, we have become, on the one hand, a nation with a historical memory, including the ethoses, myths, traumas, and true and false messages that are intrinsic thereto. On the other hand, we have become a nation without an existential cultural continuity of language, patterns, and ways of life. I speak not only of the State of Israel, where a far-reaching and, therefore, a painful change was set in motion deliberately and very abruptly, but also of Diaspora Jewry. Here I refer specifically to American and former Soviet Jewry, for in both of these cases the Jews' culture was transformed beyond recognition – in the former through freedom of choice, and in the latter due to the totalitarian regime. In this respect, we Jews are different from other nations, although upon the establishment of the state, with everything this implies, our nation acquired a more diversified image and regained several characteristics of normal nationhood.

This normalcy, despite the restrictions and limits that apply to it, should not be disregarded among the factors that gives the contemporary Jewish image its contours. I discuss this below. For the present, I wish only to remark that, tragically and paradoxically, it was not only the State of Israel that contributed to this normalcy but the Holocaust, too, because with it the Jewry of Eastern and Central Europe, a unique example of a national entity with its own language, culture, and economic structure, despite the lack of a majority in any territory where it dwelled, disappeared. The eradication of this center also obliterated the most conspicuous sign of the ostensibly anomalous Jewish nationhood. It follows that the uniqueness of Jewish existence today is more a matter of collective consciousness and feeling than of a shared reality.

The existential fracture and the national watershed, the antitheses of gradual evolution, make one ask whether it will be possible in the future to write a history of the Jews as a world people, a nation that remained intact despite its dispersion. The classical Jewish historians tackled this problem over a century ago by seeking some central idea that unifies Jewish history in all periods and places of exile.

Heinrich Graetz pointed to religious faith. Simon Dubnow stressed the national ideal and the Jews' role in it. Benzion Dinur illuminated the messianic yearning for resurrection. These historians, and others such as Salo Baron and Raphael Mahler, in their attempts to demonstrate the oneness of the Jewish people despite its territorial dispersion and cultural disunity, found a reality that, despite the changes that had swept it, exhibited sociocultural continuity. Graetz observed how the Enlightenment slowly but steadily transformed the Western Jewish ways of life. Dubnow lived amid a Jewish collective whose community structure, the *kehilla*, evolved from a religious into a national institution as a logical and natural product of the Eastern European national milieu in the twentieth century up to World War I. Dinur traced the evolution of the messianic fervors and yearnings into a national, ideological and political movement that aspired to re-establish the territorial center in Palestine. Even Mahler, with his Marxist–Borochovist worldview, was able to envisage in the 1930s the normalization of the Jews through their integration into the modern economy and society, particularly in the Soviet Union.

For this reason, each asserted the correctness of his outlook and waxed optimistic about the united future of Jewry. Graetz regarded Jewish history as evidence of the primacy of the idea in history. Dubnow considered non-territorial nationhood the pinnacle of national and cultural consciousness. Dinur foresaw a protracted process of national ingathering in the historic territorial base. Mahler, invoking the dialectical paradox, believed that the anticipated national normalization would be driven by the modernization of Jewish society in the socialist regime that would surely come.

Observation of the Jewish national image today shows that such views no longer have any place in Jewish life. Jewry is no longer a nation that revolves around the religious idea. Even if Diaspora Jewish life without synagogues and religious symbols is hardly imaginable, there is a vast difference between this and a dominant religious idea. Neither does the aggregate of Jewish organizations in Western countries add up to the national and cultural autonomy that Dubnow envisioned. Finally, the wellsprings of territorial messianic fervor have dried up, at least to some extent. For Israel's new immigrants, Zion is more a place of refuge than a utopian goal.

Thus, in the future, the historian who contemplates the overall Jewish experience will confront not a wholeness but rather a collection of fragments unified by dialectical tension. In the public realm, this tension is manifested in two fields: the ideational and normative, and the political and organizational. Two clashing processes shape the visage of Jewry today. The first is centrifugal, leading the Jewish people toward a situation that is conventionally termed normal; the second is centripetal, maintaining it in its abnormality.

The concept of normalization, discussed at length in my book, *The State of Israel in Jewish Public Thought: The Quest for Collective Identity*, needs further clarification when the Holocaust–State nexus is discussed. This is because these two historical phenomena, at first glance, have clashing properties in this respect. The Holocaust revealed the uniqueness of Jewish existence tragically; the state seemingly transformed this situation by renormalizing the Jewish people.

The Jewish normalization process had three phases: first the political phase – the Emancipation, the struggle for equality in civil rights, beginning in the West during the French Revolution and ending more than a century later in Russia after the 1917 revolution; then came the sociological phase – deghettoization, to use Jacob Katz's telling expression – with all of its social, economic, and spiritual implications; and finally the political phase, the awakening of the Jewish national movement, which aspired to self-determination to various extents – from national autonomy through national territory to a nation-state in Palestine.

The three phases represent three processes. The first two moved from West to East; the third flowed from East to West. Consequently, two intentions converged in the Jewish normalization: the general or universal, aspiring to equalize Jews' civil rights, and the particularistic, striving for self-determination on a national basis. Therefore, from the personal–civil or the national–collective perspective, the question of normalization evoked the problem of common Jewish identity. It ignited a principled debate in the assembly of representatives at the beginning of the French Revolution. It was presented bluntly by Napoleon to the assembly of Jewish dignitaries that he convened in Paris. It rested at the forefront of the struggle of the *maskilim* for equal civil status. It was part and parcel of the religious *Weltanschauung* of the Reform movement. It became a focal point of Jewish national thought, especially in its Zionist incarnation. And it inspired Jews in the free Diaspora countries to vacillate about their collective identity after the establishment of the Jewish state. In the past generation, the Holocaust–State nexus has become part of the protracted debate over Jewish normalization, in which the historical tension between the particularistic and the universalistic perspectives also exists. Thus, the three-dimensional paradigm that I have used to compartmentalize and explain the trends in Jewish public thought on normalization after the Holocaust and the establishment of Israel is also suitable for understanding the diverse approaches in the issue at hand.

In my aforementioned book, *The State of Israel in Jewish Public Thought: The Quest for Collective Identity,* I distinguished among three ways of thinking in which the normalization issue served as an emblem or a point of departure: general normalization, singular normalization, and Jewish normalization.

General normalization is the simplest and, perhaps, the most simplistic: it perceives the Jews as a religious community, not a nation. This worldview is rooted in a universalistic perception of the rights of individuals as persons and citizens in a liberal democratic society. Thus, it is essentially anti-Zionist; it opposes the formation of a special relationship between Diaspora communities and the State of Israel.

The second approach, which I call singular normalization, underscores everything that is positive in Diaspora Jewish existence. It accepts Israel as a historical center but not as the sole center on which Diaspora Jewry hinges. The examples given are the Alexandria–Jerusalem relationship in the Second Temple period and the Babylon–Palestine relationship after the destruction of the Second Temple. These relationships, predicated on bilateral equilibrium and reciprocity, were correct and are worthy of emulation in the new situation that has arisen since Israeli statehood was ordained. For those who so believe, this situation seems normal with respect to the cultural and social reality in the United States, where every ethnic group maintains relations with its country of origin at some level and degree of intensity. In their opinion, the singularity of this connection for the Jews lies in its scale and intensity, the likes of which are unknown among other communities. From this perspective, the complexion of the Jewish entity is merely religious and cultural. Arguably, a majority of members of leading Diaspora elites, especially in the United States – Zionist and non-Zionist alike – espouse this outlook.

The third approach may be called, paradoxically, Jewish normalization. It stresses the singular and aberrant elements of Jewish existence so strongly as to make them normal. Its exponents include Israeli leaders, a majority of Israeli intellectuals, and a minority of Zionist intellectuals in the Diaspora. From their standpoint, the exile, in its ideational, symbolic, and psychological senses, is here to stay as a component of the Jewish identity. They regard the Diaspora consciousness and the aspiration for redemption as being intertwined. For them, world Jewry is above all a nationality connected to its national center, the State of Israel. Without this connection, the Jewish collective, embracing Israel and the Diaspora, has no future.

However, although discussion of the Holocaust–State relationship is a link in the historical chain of 'normalization vacillations' – as I define it – it differs from its precursors in two senses. First, most of the segment of the Jewish people that dwelled in Europe and confronted this question has been murdered; the surviving remnant has struggled to retain its particularistic identity. Second, the Jews again have a history, in which they are a majority and on the basis of which they maintain political sovereignty. Paradoxically, this revolutionary achievement of the perception that we have defined as Jewish normalization has imbued the two other forms of normalization, the general and the singular, with momentum and thrust. This thrust is manifested in reinforcement of the ethnic, cultural, and territorial consciousness that leads directly to a Diaspora ideology typical of singular normalization. The very fact that the Jews have established their own state in a defined territory, where they constitute a majority and possess a reasonable degree of national sovereignty, has created a normal situation in the universal Jewish sense. From now on, the Jewish people with its Diaspora will resemble other peoples that have diasporas, such as the Italians, the Irish, and the Armenians, to name only three. Moreover, in the past generation, as millions of people have migrated rapidly from impoverished countries of origin to developed countries that promise better living conditions, the term diaspora has broadened to embrace them, too, and is becoming an increasingly universal phenomenon. In many respects, particularly internal organization and relations with the homeland, one may say that these diasporas have adopted 'Jewish characteristics'.[4] In other words, the most distinctive indicator of the Jewish image is becoming a universal one, or so it would seem. In this sense, apparently, Jewishness is gradually losing some of its distinctiveness, as territory has become the basis of the crux of Jewish nationhood. From this territorialist perspective, it follows that a form of collective existence that exceeds the limits of the territorial state is possible, with the relations between the nation-state and the diaspora being mainly religious, cultural, and familial.

This 'diasporism' is coupled with another universal phenomenon: ethnic consciousness. American society has changed radically over the last generation, its culture progressing from the 'melting pot' ideal to recognition of the ethnocultural diversity of its constituent groups. This transition has created an important symbolic change in the national definition of American citizens. Americans are no longer

simply American; their Americanism is preceded by an ethnic designation. Thus, alongside the historical Jewish American, we now have
the Italian American, the Chinese American, the African American,
and the Native American (formerly the Indian), among others, across
the entire spectrum of nationalities represented in this society. Once
again, it would seem, Jews have ceased to be unique.

In view of this effect of diaspora and ethnic ideology, one of the
most obvious signs of the normalization of Jews is the deletion of the
term exile from their collective consciousness and its replacement by
the term diaspora. This obliterates the negative connotation associated
with Jewish life outside the homeland and replaces it with a favorable
attitude.

More than eighty years ago, in a debate with Simon Dubnow, Ahad
Ha'Am spoke of two ways in which Jews may relate to their state of
exile:[5] subjective repudiation and objective repudiation. The former
originates in the individual's value system or psychological complexion; the latter is based on general indicators beyond the individual's
personality. Ahad Ha'am explains:

> When we speak of 'negating exile,' we must remember first of all
> that, in the subjective sense, all Jews are 'negators of exile' – all,
> that is, but for a minority that considers the Diaspora a blessing
> and a mission for Jews.

As against the subjective repudiation of exile, which Ahad Ha'am
recognizes and even endorses, he sees no justification for the repudiation of exile as preached by Herzlian Zionism, a denial of the Jews'
ability to survive in the Diaspora and develop their national liberty
there, permanently rather than temporarily.

Ahad Ha'Am's assertion is no longer valid in our time. Most Jews
do not negate exile in the subjective sense, let alone the objective one.
Not only do Jews consider themselves secure in the Diaspora but,
paradoxically, the existence of the State of Israel helps reinforce this
feeling, because Israel affords Jews the freedom of choice between
their countries of birth and their homeland. This option diversifies the
freedom and range of choice of Jews everywhere. It also purges exilic
life of its coercive element. Even the Jews of the former Soviet Union,
who until a few years ago were deemed to be living in exile because of
the totalitarian regime that enveloped them, have quit their exile in this
sense. This is the true ideological background of the efforts made by
groups of Jewish politicians and intellectuals in Russia, with extensive

American support, to revive religious, communal, and national Jewish life in the former Soviet Union.

Alongside the aforementioned territorialist perspective, which recasts the national image while attempting to preserve some unity among its dispersed fragments in other countries, a personal-existential territorialist outlook is evolving. The intent of this mindset is to shatter the unifying national framework espoused both by Zionism and by the ethnicist-Diaspora perspective. This approach, which may be defined as an essentially anti-Zionist, post-Zionist liberalism, is popular among certain circles in the Diaspora and in Israel. According to this attitude, it is territory – including the political regime and the culture of territory – that determines the identity of the people who inhabit it. Therefore, Jews living in the United States are primarily American in all respects, and Jews who live in Israel are principally Israeli in the same way. The only distinctive bond of substance that can exist between them is their religion and, to a certain extent, their culture. The normalist gist of this outlook, with its liberal and territorial fundamentals, manifests itself in urgings to repeal the Law of Return. This demand, espoused by Jewish intellectuals in the United States and Israel, originates not only in the recognition that the law is an anti-democratic and anti-liberal statute that prescribes different rights for different categories of human beings, but also in their belief that the Law of Return symbolizes, more than anything else, the wish to maintain and foster, artificially and even arbitrarily, the abnormality of Jewish existence.

The intention to normalize the existence of the Jewish people as a nation in its own territory, and of individual Jews as free and equally empowered citizens in the democracies, directly affects the way those who espouse this view understand the Holocaust. Exponents of this perspective also tend to downplay the Jewish exclusivity of the Holocaust and endow this event with universal significance. Not satisfied with the view that the Holocaust itself sounds a warning to humankind, they argue that the Jews' catastrophe is merely part of the cataclysm that befell much of humankind. The more aware we become of its pan-human dimension, they say, the more its national peculiarity will be lost. Below I discuss the importance of this trend with respect to the image of the Jewish people.

The dialectical opposite of the centrifugal normalization tendency is the particularistic centripetal one. The two are linked by the same historical events and share the same time frame. They also switch positions at the focus of Jewish communal consciousness and solidarity, depending on political events and cultural processes. In terms of their influence on the image of the Jewish people, however, they differ not only in fundamentals but in structure. The normalization attitude is totally ideational, its setting wholly intellectual. The centripetal approach is political and ideological; it pertains to the way Israel is organized and concerns itself with Jewish institutions in the Diaspora. In this respect, it overtly expresses the existential and political interest of the Jewish establishment on a global scale, emphasizing the attitude that the national-unity idea can be realized only through the institutional system. For this reason, the distinction between ideational principles or an ideological doctrine and institutional interests is not always clear; in most cases the two even correspond and overlap. Therefore, the advocates of normalization are individual intellectuals or transient groups, while the upholders of the exclusivity outlook belong to the public, political, and intellectual elite of Jewish society. Both categories influence the image of the nation – the former by stimulating objective processes by bringing them to public consciousness in their intellectual commentary, the latter by strengthening existing attitudes and impeding and counteracting revisionist processes. Consequently, the *Weltanschauung* of the exclusivity-seekers focuses on practical issues in socio-educational affairs and the security of the state. The centripetal approach coalesced incrementally over more than thirty years, from the end of World War II to the 1980s. It advanced from stage to stage: from the struggle of the majority of Jews to establish the Jewish state, to support of the mammoth enterprise of absorbing mass immigration, to the heady days of the Six-Day War, and thence to the agony and trepidation of the Yom Kippur War. In the United States, this centripetality resulted in the Americanization of Zionism, in the 'we're all Zionists' sense.

The trend embraced Zionists by awareness and Zionists at heart: young radicals who seceded from the general radical movement because of its antisemitic manifestations and its leaders' indifference to the mortal danger that Israel faced on the eve of the Six-Day War, along with neo-conservative intellectuals who overtly identified the Jewish ethnic and national interest with the national, social, and political interests of the United States.

From the standpoint of those who think this way, the Holocaust carries primarily a particularistic Jewish meaning and teaches the Jewish collective a lesson in how to confront its existential dangers. Therefore, the slogan 'Never Again' in its power-centric sense, shared by the Zionist far Left and, in the main, the neo-conservative national

Right, created a linkage between the lesson of the Holocaust and the value of the State. The act of combining the two components cast them into a dialectic relationship.

In this period of time, starting in 1967 – as Israel was so entrenched in Jewish public consciousness as to have become a civil religion – the alternative to Israel consciousness, Holocaust consciousness, had already began to emerge. At first, the trend was relegated to the fringes of public consciousness amid the anxiety and suspense of the Six-Day and Yom Kippur Wars, especially during the latter, in which, unlike its precursor, the anxiety did not give way to the joy of victory. The concern about Israel's possible defeat was compounded by criticism of and disbelief in the Israeli leadership, as manifested in the protest movements that arose after the war.

Paradoxically, this dispiritedness did not prompt American Jews to evade the problem by stressing the difference between their status and that of yesteryear's European Jews and contemporary Israeli Jews. The opposite occurred. Four years after the Yom Kippur War, the Americanization of the Holocaust began – not in traditional mourning over the devastation that had visited the Jews but in identification with the individuals' suffering and as a moral lesson for humankind. The moral lesson and the psychological emotion that arose from the Holocaust corresponded to the American folk ethos and, over the years, became an ideational platform of sorts: the Americanization of the Holocaust.

In Israel, in contrast, a politicization of the Holocaust took place at this time. In this process, the lesson of the Holocaust is integrated into the political struggle between moderates and radicals on how to solve the Jewish–Arab struggle for Palestine. In its radical version, this politicization leads to the Israelization of the Holocaust, for this dispute touches primarily, and mainly, on the Jews who dwell in Israel.

This book has described the tension between the two trends, the centrifugal and the centripetal, in terms of the three approaches discussed above. To continue the summarizing discussion, let us summarize them.

The first approach attempts to ascribe absolute universal significance to the Jewish Holocaust. According to this view, the Jews' sufferings and catastrophe are no different from the genocide of the Armenians during World War I, the slaughter of the Biafrans, the devastation caused by the atomic bomb in Japan, and even the massacres of Indians by European settlers in various periods of time in South America. This approach may be defined as markedly centrifugal; its ideational and political significance is expressed in the concept of Americanization of the Holocaust in the US and in a neo-Canaanism of sorts in Israel.

At the opposite extreme is a clearly centripetal approach, which deliberately attempts to transform the Holocaust into a collective experience that unites the Jewish people and a worldview that consolidates it as a national entity. Some attempt to endow the Holocaust with religious significance. This mindset, typical of Israeli and American right-wing groups, fosters a mentality of national siege in a world that, from its standpoint, is socioculturally open. It believes, for example, that the impending holocaust will emanate not only from the Arabs who encircle Israel but also from the Western world, which is as willing today as it was in the past to abandon the Jews to their fate. The practical inference arising from this is to seek power. This, a cornerstone in the Jewish normalization perception, takes on two forms: military power in Israel and political power for Jews in the United States and elsewhere in the Diaspora.

The third approach, which lies between the first two, is favored by moderate liberals and conservatives and by Zionists who espouse liberal and social-democratic values in Israel. Both camps note the inherent historical error that the radical liberals make by attempting to cast the Holocaust in a purely universal light, but they warn against the opposite approach, the ultranationalist attitude that tries, theoretically and practically, to erect a barrier of consciousness between Jews and their surrounding society. As stated, they disregard neither the Jewish uniqueness of the Holocaust nor several of its implications, such as the need for a politically and militarily strong Jewish state, but they express concern about the growing tendency to replace the drive to foster Jewish intellectual endeavor with an effort, which is also growing, to put the Jews' suffering and fate on public display. They have a further concern: that the Jewish collective persona may be transformed from People of the Book to People of the Crematorium. This attitude corresponds to what we have defined as singular normalization.

Be this as it may, each of the three approaches strives to attain a different kind of normalization by means of the Holocaust. The first: normalization through integration; the second: normalization through strength; and the third: normalization of Diasporism.

The contemporary historian, although accustomed to tracing the social and spiritual changes in Jewish history of the past century, some caused by exogenous factors and others endogenous, cannot but marvel at the speed of the Jewish transformations in recent generations. The most important change in the past decade has been the shift in the focus of national identification from the State to the Holocaust. Therefore, this transformation deserves an explanation, albeit a partial one.

The fact that the Holocaust focus has become a common denominator among Diaspora and Israeli Jewry – and even more characteristically and interestingly, as a recent study shows, between Israelis of European and of Asian/African origin[6]– points to the different ways in which the State and the Holocaust are perceived in the Jewish collective consciousness. One may say that it is ideationally, politically, and psychologically more convenient and expedient to identify with the Holocaust than with Israel. Now that the controversy over the expression 'like sheep to the slaughter' has ended, and now that the dust has settled from two internecine battles – that between historians and community leaders over the Jewish leadership's attitude during the war, and that concerning evaluations of the activities of the Judenrate on the one hand and the underground and resistance on the other – a kind of equilibrium has been established. Because this development includes a balancing or a reconciliation of the terms 'Holocaust' and 'heroism', all of Jewry is able to unite around its catastrophe.

This is how the myth of the Jewish masses' silent valor vis-à-vis their tragic fate is generated. This myth leaves no room for speculators and profiteers, for those who frequented nightclubs and parties in the Warsaw Ghetto – even if they constituted a tiny minority. This myth has no room for Judenrat members who played favorites in meting out suffering and death, nor for the Jewish ghetto police who aided the Germans' genocide, nor for the *kapos* in the death camps who helped the Nazis impose their reign of terror, whether for personal interest or because their impulses had got the better of them. Folk-level mortification and rage also figure in the new mythology. Thus the expressions 'like lambs to the slaughter' and 'human dust' have become weapons to use in castigating the Zionist leadership, the institutionalized Yishuv, and, in particular, the Labor movement. No one has the interest or the patience to consider the origin of these terms: they were coined not by those who dwelled safely in Palestine but by Abba Kovner and Emmanuel Ringelblum in the ghettos. Nor is anyone inclined to understand that the term 'human dust', irrespective of its bad taste at the time, was meant not to disparage the few survivors but to describe the Jews' state of exile and its lack of sovereignty. Ben-Gurion thought this definition was also valid with respect to American Jewry.

These are some of the symbols of the civil religion: fostering and identifying with the memory of the catastrophe, pilgrimage to murder sites, assiduous study of books and sources that describe what took place, and the adducing of historio-philosophical and even theological lessons.

How did the Holocaust dislodge the State of Israel as the focus of centrality? It happened not only because of the natural and sincere intensity of popular emotion that accompanies the Holocaust consciousness, but also because of the inevitable difficulties that the State of Israel has encountered on the path that it has taken. Political life amidst history is a continuous process of shattering myths and disillusionment with utopias. This makes the idealization of daily affairs unsustainable, unlike the potency of idealization by mytholo- gizing a past that does not extend into the present.

The statehood consciousness, unlike the Holocaust consciousness, sows controversy and tension among Jews. The question of Israel's security and image has divided and continues to divide the Jewish people, both in Israel and in the Diaspora, into 'hawks' and 'doves'. By its very definition, the Jewish state has aggravated the schisms among the Jewish religious streams – Orthodox, Conservative, and Reform – in the interpretation and validation of religious law and in questions of equality of status in the Jewish state.

Paradoxically, it was the success of Zionism and the state that created the internal tensions that beset Israel today. The masses of Jews from Muslim countries have not yet completely integrated into a society whose cultural die had largely been cast before they arrived. They find it hard to blend into the Eastern European Zionist tradition, with all this implies: the Diaspora past, the Palestinian Yishuv, the path to statehood, and the shaping of a sovereign society. Motivated by the desire to integrate, they find it easier to identify with Jewish tradition and the memory of the Holocaust as a pan-Jewish tragedy than with a modern Zionist ideology rooted in countries and cultures that are not theirs. Even the youth, alienated, rightly or wrongly, from Israel's democratic manifestations and ways of life, find it easier to accept the message of the significance of nationhood through the genuine emotion and profound experience that the death-camp visits afford them. This phenomenon is likely to recur with the former Soviet immigrants, for whom the realities of Israel are wholly alien.

In the myth-shattering atmosphere that hovers over Israel and presses against its confines, one finds a considerable degree of rejoicing over others' woes, a fashionable cynicism, personal frustration, and wrongdoing for its own sake. Such an atmosphere no longer leaves room for an even-handed assessment of Israel's historical achievements and situation. There is no place for the view that Israel's suffering originates not in its failures but rather in its relative achievements, as manifested in an ingathering of exiles that has yet to result in their fusion, the maintenance of democracy even where a liberal atmosphere is as yet lacking, and a sane attitude of the majority toward the Arab minority even if war shows its cruel face time and again. Despite the internal and external problems that buffet this society, which has been living in a state of emergency since the 1930s in its national struggle and the absorption of immigrants on a scale unprecedented in human history – despite all these, a culture of sanity is taking shape. All in all, in comparison with the other radical movements that surfaced in nineteenth-century Europe, and in comparison with other nations embroiled in existential national struggles with other nations, the Jewish state need not cringe in humiliation.

Consequently, of the two myths that affect the Jewish people's image today – the State of Israel and the Holocaust – the disaster, by revealing a general national impotence, has triumphed over the manifestations of collective audacity and achievement. The consciousness of national rebirth seems to have lost more in this reckoning than the consciousness of the Holocaust has gained. In the long term, this may present a threat to Jewish unity, a unity that will not amount to much unless Israel commands centrality in national consciousness and is recognized as the most reliable representative, among all other Jewish collectivities, of the people's collective interest. Failing this, despite the Holocaust commemoration that ostensibly unites the Jewish people, a process of national disintegration will ensue and gather momentum, as Ahad Ha'Am warned almost a century ago.

It is memory that fashions the image of a people. Recollection of the Exodus, the destruction of the Temple, martyrdom, the expulsion from Spain, the Chmielnicki pogroms – all of these, coupled with yearnings for redemption and the messianic-utopian perspective, have furnished the underlying rationale for Jewish nationhood with its ethos. These, however, have never progressed from symbols to the focal point of public and educational activity. The Jewish people, as a collective, has existed with them but not by virtue of them. It has survived because it knew how to learn, because it summoned the wisdom to build a communal organizational system, and because it founded a national movement that had the strength, even after the devastating blow dealt to it, to rise up, struggle for its political independence, and build a

Jewish society in Palestine. Without this constructive action, no commemoration of martyred victims and no educational memorial marches will sustain Jewry as a national collective.

We may sum up, I believe, by saying that the historian who writes the history of the Jews from the Holocaust to the establishment of the State will not find any dominant theme that characterizes Jewry as a national body. On the contrary, he or she will find clashing trends that, although visible in the past, have strengthened their grip in the wake of the Holocaust and the establishment of Israel. Historians will stress the pluralism of a collective that lives and functions creatively amid five major cultures: the Anglo-Saxon, the Hebrew, the Russian, the French, and the Spanish. They will describe a religious society with four main streams: ultra-Orthodox, modern Orthodox, Conservative, and Reform, a web that has created a 'Jewish Protestantism', so to speak. They will have to ponder the different ways in which the general Jewish collective is perceived – a difference that originates in the differences in the political status of Jews who dwell in their own sovereign state and those who settle for civil liberties in their countries of residence.

One should add to this pluralism the contradictions, or the increasingly powerful contrasts, between the interest of Jews and the Jewish interest. For example, it is in the interest of Jews as individuals that society be more receptive and accommodating toward them. This has the effect of accelerating the process of assimilation into the host society, as is occurring today. The Jewish interest, however, is to sustain the collective, to drive a wedge of some kind between individual Jews and the society that envelops them. The conflict between the needs of the national collective and the individual's rights also comes up in this context. One need but recall the vitriolic polemics in the 1980s between Israel and American Jewish organizations concerning the freedom of choice of Jews leaving the Soviet Union. One cannot ignore the fact that the attitude of the American Jewish leadership was informed by a residual sense of guilt for the Holocaust. For this reason, the leaders marshaled their political forces, over the objections of Israel and the Zionist movement, to grant refugee status to emigrants from the USSR who had received and were carrying Israeli passports. The conflict in this incident was so intense that Jewish leaders and intellectuals failed to realize that after the Jewish people had set up its own state to solve the problem of Jewish refugeeship once and for all, it was again demanding refugee status for free Jews who had been invited to take up residence in their own state.

However, there is another and perhaps contrasting aspect of the Jewish national image that points to the will and the action needed to keep this divided nation united. Its motives are historical heritage, religious tradition, and tribal feeling. These are nourished on a reality that embraces not only public welfare but substantial national concern. In the Diaspora it manifests itself in concern for the Jewish demographic contraction, caused by intermarriage, assimilation, and a plummeting birth rate. In Israel, it is reflected in concern for immigrant absorption, the cultural quality of Jewish society, and Israel's moral reflection in the state of war in which it is immersed.

Thus, to sum up, one may point to three mythical ethoses that fashion the image of the Jewish people in our times. The first, that of religion, is typical of the Diaspora. The second, that of statehood, is valid in the State of Israel. The third, that of the Holocaust, is evident in both places. Unity and disunity coexist within and among each of them. Because the religious dimension is not within the purview of this chapter, we merely note that the believers are beset with tension among not only between the various streams but also within them – tension between the Orthodox and ultra-Orthodox, and between conservative and liberal attitudes within the Conservative and Reform camps concerning the right of women to serve as rabbis, intermarriage, and so on. As stated, however, this is not our main concern in the present forum.

What concerns us here is the Holocaust and the State. As we conclude, we would do well to pause briefly and contemplate their ambivalent relationship. The tension between them originates in the difference between them as historical phenomena. The former embodies the impotence of the Jewish collective will; the latter demonstrates the strength of this will. It is the Holocaust that symbolizes the Jews' pariah status during World War II in the ethical consciousness of the nations and in the political calculus and military strategies of the leaders of the free world. The State of Israel, in contrast, was established with the consent and assistance of most of the enlightened world, not only for reasons of politics and self-interest but also because of the wish and pressure to compensate the Jews for their collective suffering. Today, in view of the changes that are sweeping the globe, Israel needs more than ever to integrate into the universal process in which new political superstructures will take shape. It follows that the extremist perspectives of the two myths lead to opposite conclusions. Emphasizing the uniqueness of the Holocaust drives an unmistakable wedge between Jews and other nations, whereas it is the concept of statehood, by underscoring the normal fundamentals of sovereign life, that induces a *rapprochement* between Jews, in both Israel and the Diaspora, and the non-Jewish peoples.

However, the two myths also have common aims that produce opposing results. One may say, on the one hand, that the mythic ethos of the Holocaust reinforces the mythic ethos of the state and strengthens Israel's relations with the Diaspora. On the other hand, the amplification of the Holocaust myth in the Diaspora detracts from the centrality of Israel in the Jewish collective consciousness, in two ways: by creating a facile, contradiction-free folk mythology and by creating an intellectual acknowledgment of the universal nature of the Holocaust. The universalization and Americanization of the Holocaust provide ultra-liberal Jews with the most convenient way to integrate themselves into the society to which they belong without repudiating their Jewish origins. They relieve these Jews of the collective stigma of belonging to a collectivity of persons who have been persecuted and murdered for being exceptional. The normalization of the Jews' suffering and the de-singularization of their tragedy, in view of the disappearance of Eastern European Jewry – which represented the special existential problem – turn the Holocaust, tragically and paradoxically, into a medium that liberates the universal Jew from his personal exile. It is the exile that, from each historical period to the next, singled out the universal Jew as an alien in society's midst, be it traditional antisemitism as in the past or racism today, be it a Communist regime or the protest movement of the American blacks. It is the great success of the universalization of the Holocaust consciousness, notwithstanding denial arguments, that invalidated, temporarily or permanently, the delegitimization of the Jew as an inseparable part of the society in which he lives. From this standpoint, to carry the paradox further, this success is hastening the dwindling of the Jewish people and exacerbating its disintegration.

At the opposite pole of universalism is particularism – national, religious, statist, and power-centric. Particularism is another reflection, and a servant, of the Jews' normalization. The paradox here is that the Jewish state, which by its own lights is the opposite of the Holocaust, still serves the purposes of those who attempt to inflict a new Holocaust on the Jewish people. The response warranted by this posture is to buttress the state by dint of its armed forces, even if by depriving a neighboring people of its rights or severely restricting them – an action that stimulates profound discord in Jewish society.

These two clashing perceptions, one open to general society and one that flinches from it, point to two cultural and ideational trends in Jewish society: the centripetal and the centrifugal. Strangely, both trends, despite their clashing intentions, are fomenting schism among the Jews. The former is doing so because of its neo-Canaanite universalism; the latter has the same effect because of neo-Zionist particularism. Each, in its own way, undermines the foundations of the common denominator of *klal Yisrael* (the congregation of Israel).

Thus, as the twentieth century drew to its close – after having witnessed the decisive watershed in Jewish history, the Holocaust disaster and the establishment of the State of Israel – and as the twenty-first century begins, the Jewish people faces its greatest historical paradox. Its greatest disaster in history and its greatest national victory in history, which kept it united and cohesive for fifty years, are now hastening its disintegration. All the fateful questions in Jewish affairs converge in this collision between the universal and the particular: who is a Jew as a *halakhic* issue, relations between religion and state as a problem of state, Israel–Diaspora relations as a national issue, and Holocaust consciousness in Jewish–Gentile relations.

In this sense, the tension between Holocaust consciousness and State consciousness, like their erstwhile harmony, is primarily the result of socio-cultural developments and ideational and political changes among the Jews. Therefore, the quest to restore their equilibrium, as one of the mythic ethoses that are shaping the collective persona of the Jewish people, should begin with an exploration of these basic questions.

Thus, in fact, the circle with which we began the first book – the quest for national identity – has closed. However, it is also open, because Jewish existence, posited between the tension of normalization and non-normalization, is still in the midst of its quest. The more the tension among its elements rises, so Jews become more aware of the need to find an interim path between them.

The discussion in this book, first published between the centenary of the First Zionist Congress and Israel's jubilee, fits into the discourse of the past few years concerning the doctrine known publicly as post-Zionism. The development of thought that may eventually untie the historical Gordian knot between Holocaust and the State, whether it is steered by a subjective *Weltanschauung* or by objective processes, is one of the indicators of the post-Zionist phenomenon in both of its forms: negative post-Zionism, a fundamentally anti-Zionist outlook in its universalist and anti-national worldview, and positive post-Zionism, which accepts Zionism as a normal historical phenomenon but claims that its very achievements as a national movement are steering it to the end of its path.[7] In both senses, although they are mutually exclusive, untying the Zionist Gordian knot between the State and the Holocaust, which in its various forms has given individuals and the collectivity another dimension in the historical and spiritual significance of the resurrection of Jewish sovereignty in Palestine – is a post-Zionist phenomenon. From this standpoint, there is a symbolism in the forty-year historical path that the discourse in this book has followed, from the cornerstone-laying for Yad Vashem in Jerusalem to the opening of the Holocaust Memorial Museum in Washington. Termination of the state of war between the Jewish people and the Arab nation and others makes one inquire about the fate of Zionism and the status of the State of Israel among the Jewish people in the century to come.

Historians are not futurists who float conjectures about what to expect; they are not statespeople who cast their eyes on distant horizons; and they are not prophets of retribution or consolation. They know the past, are conscious of the present, and are not sure about the future. They are sure of only one thing: that there is no surety, that historical developments have many surprises in store. Thus, historical development is replete with existential paradoxes and is often controlled by dialectical processes. Therefore, anyone who explores Jewish history, not as an observer on the outside but as a human being on the inside, also hopes that the clash between the centrifugal and the centripetal trends discussed here is also part of a dialectical process, and that the balanced synthesis that can unite and unify the myth and the ethoses of Holocaust and State will be found.

NOTES

1. Emmanuel Ringelblum, *Diary and Notes from the Warsaw Ghetto, September 1939–December 1942* (Jerusalem, 1992) [Hebrew].
2. See David S. Wyman, *The Abandonment of the Jews: America and the Holocaust, 1941–1945* (New York, 1984).
3. When I asked this question of George Steiner, famous for his criticism of the State of Israel and its pernicious effect on the Jewish spirit, he agreed with me, albeit reluctantly, that things might have been different.
4. See George Pre've'lakis (ed.), *The Networks of Diasporas* (Cyprus: KYKEM, 1996).
5. See Ahad Ha'Am, 'The Negation of the Exile', *The Complete Works of Ahad Ha'Am* (Jerusalem and Tel Aviv, 1949), p. 399 [Hebrew].
6. See Yair Auron, 'The Holocaust and Me', Chapter 3 of *Jewish-Israeli Identity*, a study on the attitudes of education students from all Israeli school systems toward

contemporary Judaism and Zionism (Tel Aviv: Sifriat Poalim and the Kibbutz Seminary, 1993), pp. 90–103 [Hebrew].

7. See Yosef Gorny, 'From Post-Zionism to the Renewal of Zionism', in Pinhas Ginossar and Avi Barelli (eds), *Zionism: A Contemporary Polemic* (Ben-Gurion University of the Negev, 1996), pp. 514–30 [Hebrew].

Index

academic discourse, 15, 83–124, 125
activism (Jewish identity), 58
affiliation, limited or marginal, 100
African Americans, 203–4, 211
'age of violence', 89
Ahad Ha'am, 87, 156, 228
ahavat Yisrael, 36
AJC *see* American Jewish Committee
Alexander, Edward, 166–7, 168, 169, 170
Alexandria–Jerusalem relationship, 226
Al Hamishmar (publication), 129, 131, 134, 137
aliya (immigration), 180
Alter, Robert, 168, 170–1
Aly, Goetz, 140
Ambiguous Relations (Shlomo Shaffir), 14
American Council for Judaism, 21, 22, 23, 24, 26, 55
American Jewish Committee (AJC), 18–19, 20, 21, 22; Joseph Proskauer head of (1940s), 20, 21, 29
American Jewry: and academic discourse, 88; Americanization, 212; Ben-Gurion on, 233; Diaspora, special status of, 199, 210; and Eichmann trial, 26, 27; and ethnic designation, 75, 228; and Holocaust consciousness, 6, 7, 8; ideological discourse, 164–91; Israel contrasted, 215–16; and theology, 74, 75; uniqueness, 202
'Americanization' of the Holocaust: academic discourse, 95, 96; ideological discourse, 181; Israel–Diaspora relationship, 5–6; and moral lesson, 231; public consciousness, 5; pundits' discourse, 199, 200, 202, 203, 204, 209, 212, 213
annihilation: of Armenians, 92, 94, 95, 96, 169, 231; genocide distinguished, 95; of Israel, threatening, 113; Israeli athletes, murder of (1972), 148; of Jews, 30–2, 85–8, 92, 105, 167–8, 198, 204; of Native Americans, 78
Anti-Defamation League, 48n.3
antisemitism: and Arendt, 38; and atom bomb, 189; black, 11; and Diaspora Jewry, 178; and genocide, 103; and Holocaust commission,

198; Holocaust, roots of, 88, 101, 104; press coverage, lack of, 19; and total state, 86; uniqueness of, 115; Western civilization, not accepted in, 38
Arab violence, 149
Arafat, Yasser, 161
Arbeit Macht Frei, 150
Arendt, Hannah: Ben-Gurion, attitude towards, 37, 47; on Eichmann Syndrome, 7–8, 15, 17–18, 35–48; Jewish army, support for, 147; and Jewish historical memory, 36; and Palestinian problem, 78; paradoxes concerning, 35–8, 44–5, 47, 48; secular perspective, 43, 45, 47; on totalitarianism, 19, 36, 86; on Zionism, 14, 37–8, 41–2, 46; *see also Eichmann in Jerusalem: A Report on the Banality of Evil* (Hannah Arendt)
Armenians, annihilation by Turks, 92, 94, 95, 96, 169, 231
assimilation process, 43, 45, 93, 112, 209, 210, 238; and normalization, 172, 173
atomic bomb, 65, 189
Aufbau (German-Jewish publication), 37, 38
Auschwitz: Arab policy, moral justification for, 77; and atom bomb, 189; symbol of fate of Jews, 169; and theology, 53; *see also* extermination camps
'Auschwitz borders', 152
awareness, consciousness distinguished, 125–6

Babylon–Palestine relationship, 226
Baeck, Leo, 36, 38
Baer, Yitzhak, 90
Balfour Declaration (1917), 24
Bar-Ilan University, 148, 150
Baron, Salo, 87, 94, 175, 176, 186, 224
Bartov, Hanoch, 163
Bauer, Yehuda: and American Jewry, 173–4; on genocide, 83, 102; on Holocaust Museum, 97; particularist/universalist debate, 93–4; uniqueness doctrine, 95–6; Yad Vashem, founding member of, 92
Bauman, Zygmunt, 104–8, 113, 116

Begin, Menachem, 9, 12, 135, 141, 161, 196
Bell, Daniel, 45–6
Ben-Gurion, David: and American Jewry, 233; and Arendt, 37, 47; Blaustein, meeting with (1951), 19, 21; and Diaspora Jewry mentality, 39; on Eichmann trial, 29, 32–3, 34, 35, 142; and Goldmann, 29; on Jewish identity, 30, 31; and Proskauer, 20, 25, 30; and Scholem, 34
Berenbaum, Michael, 197, 199, 200–3, 212, 215
Berger, Rabbi Elmer, 24–5
Berkovits, Rabbi Eliezer: ideological discourse, 128; theology, 53–4, 58, 64, 70, 71
Bettelheim, Bruno, 39
Biafrans, slaughter of, 231
Biale, David, 47, 186–9
biblical era, 59
blacks: and American society, 203–4; antisemitic attitudes, 11; enslavement of, 78; whites, cooperation with, 190
Blaustein, Jacob, 19, 21
Blumenfeld, Kurt, 37
Bolshevik regime, 111
Boltstein, Leon, 47
Borowitz, Eugene, 72, 74–5
Brit Shalom, 37, 191
Brocke, Edna, 50n.52
Bukiet, Melvin, 209–10
Bund intellectuals, 106, 151
Burke, Edmund, 116

Canaanite Zionists, 55, 139, 140, 144, 154
Cargas, Harry, 68
Carter, President Jimmy, 94, 196–7; Administration of, 205–6
Célan, Paul, 114
Chmielnicki pogroms, 235
Chomsky, Noam, 78
Christianity, 1, 7, 26, 76
Churban, 71, 73
'civil religion', 52, 231, 234
CLAL (National Jewish Center for Learning and Leadership), 59, 74
Clinton, President Bill, 197
'cognitive dissonance', 17
Cohen, Arthur, 63
Cohen, Geula, 41
Cohen, Hermann, 187
Colombus, Christopher, 78
commandments, 118–19
Commentary (periodical), 164, 165, 214
commission, Holocaust, 24, 197–200
Communist Party, 140
Communists: German abuse of, 96; Israel, attitude to, 169
concentration camps, 99
consciousness of Holocaust: awareness distinguished, 125–6; and Begin, 135; Eichmann

trial, 132; historical phases, 6–10; in Israel, 6, 8–10; Jewish society, effect on, 4; remembrance, 5, 8, 118; in United States, 6–8, 10
Conservative Judaism: and American Jewry, 7; and Fackenheim, 54; and Schorsh, 177, 178; and Wiesel, 70, 71
conservatives, Jewish, 166
'crimes against humanity', 21
culture, 126, 127

Daily Forward (periodical), 164, 165, 204, 211, 212
Davar (publication), 129, 131, 132, 134
Dawidowicz, Lucy, 90, 94, 95, 102, 197
'deabsolutation', 77
Declaration of the Establishment of the State of Israel and the Nazi and Nazi Collaborators (1950), 32
dialectical Zionism, 139–40, 163
Diaspora Jewry: American, special status of, 199; annihilation of, 85; and antisemitism, 178; Ben-Gurion on, 39; Berkovits on, 64; Elam on, 154, 160; and exile, 61; and heroism, 130; Israel, relationship with, 5–6, 7, 11, 13, 20, 74, 177, 179, 203, 217; moral dilemmas affecting, 101; and Neusner, 179–80; non-Jews, leaders' attitudes towards, 38; and other Diasporas, 227; political responsibility, existence of Israel, 61; Rubenstein on, 62; separation of Jewish people, 21; Vital on, 156, 160; Yehoshua on, 159–60; *see also* 'negation of Diaspora' doctrine
Diner, Dan: and Eastern and Western European traditions, 151–2; and 'Jewish historical memory', 36; and Shaked, 161; and State of Israel, 160; on Zionism, 141–2, 152, 153, 162
Dinur, Benzion: and Bauer, 94; and Gutman, 90; on Holocaust, roots of, 88; and particularism, 84–7, 89; and remembrance, 8; resurrection, yearning for, 224; and Schweid, 112; and Steiner, 121
dissonance, cognitive/existential, 17
Divine mission, 61
Divine providence, 54, 55
Di Zukunft (periodical), 164, 165
Dreyfus, Alfred, trial of, 24
'dual loyalty', 8, 24
Dubnow, Simon: and Arendt, 37, 40, 43; and Dawidowicz, 90; and Dinur, 85; and Horowitz, 100–1; on Jewish nationhood, 47, 224

Each Had Six Wings (Hanoch Bartov), 163
Eastern European tradition, 152
Eastern Jewry, value system, 23
Eban, Abba, 150, 152

Egyptian–Soviet arms deal, 134
Eichmann, Adolf: abduction, 7, 18, 19, 20, 39, 52; capture, 26, 164; execution, 18; internment, 29; public opinion, 18–19; statist discourse, 8, 15, 17–51; trial *see* trial of Eichmann
Eichmann in Jerusalem: A Report on the Banality of Evil (Hannah Arendt), 7, 17, 35, 41–2, 45
Eizenstadt, Stuart, 196, 205–6
El Alamein, defeat of Rommel's forces at, 140
Elam, Yigal, 153–4, 160, 162
Eldad, Israel, 135, 137
Elkana, Yehuda, 143–5
Ellis, Marc, 72, 76–9, 80, 120, 121
Emancipation, 93, 225
Enlightenment, 172, 224
Eretz Israel Labour Party (Mapai), 9, 128
Ethiopia, Jews from, 222
ethnic cleansing, 143
ethnic mission, Holocaust as, 16, 196–219
Ettinger, Shmuel, 89–90
European Jewry, 31–2, 41, 162, 207–8; mass annihilation of, 22, 85, 88
Evron, Boaz, 94, 140–1, 142, 143, 151
exile, Jewish people in, 61, 85, 130, 157, 162, 176; 'negation of exile', 68, 130, 131, 228
'existential dissonance', 17
Exodus, 235
extermination camps, 11, 67, 99, 150, 188; *see also* Auschwitz
Ezrahi, Sidra and Yaron, 173–4

F-15 aircraft, 196
Fackenheim, Emil: Greenberg's ideas contrasted, 61; Horowitz, criticism by, 101, 102; ideological debate, 128; on Israeli politics, 70; Katz, influence on, 93; military force, justification, 64; and Orthodox culture, 71; Petuchowski, criticism by, 76; on statehood, 67; theological discourse, 54–9, 61, 64, 66, 67, 70, 71, 76, 79; Wiesel, criticism by, 66
fascism, 157
Fein, Helen, 103–4, 108
Fein, Leonard, 171, 173
Feingold, Henry, 47, 168–70
Feldman, Ron, 47
Final Solution, 25
Finkelstein, Norman, 14–15
Fisch, Ariel, 148
force, justification for use, 64–5
Forvets (periodical), 164
Frankfurter, David, 38, 165
French Revolution (1789), 116, 225
Friedlander, Saul: beliefs, 92, 154–5; and Shaked, 161; and State of Israel, 160; and Vital, 156, 157; and Zionism, 155, 162
From Text to Context (Ismar Schorsch), 178
Fromm, Erich, 39, 150

Frondizi, Arturo (Argentinian President), 29
Fruchter, Norm, 46
Frum, David, 210–11
fundamentalism, 107, 184, 185

'Galut Judaism', 61, 176
genocide: annihilation distinguished, 95; bureaucracy, 99; and Dinur, ideas of, 85; and Holocaust commission, 198; holocaust distinguished, 102; justification by Nazis, 94; Lemkin on, 108; Levene on, 109; universalization, 91
Germany: Polish people, abuse of, 96; reparations agreement signed with (1952), 9; ghettos, 7–8, 27, 86, 210; leaders of, 166
God: belief in, 177; chosen by His people, 60–1; role in history, 53, 54, 58, 62, 63, 65; Wiesel on, 66–7
Goldmann, Nahum, 29, 35, 49n.26
Gotthalf, Yehuda, 129
Gourevitch, Philip, 204–5, 211, 212
goyim (non-Jews), 38, 182
Graetz, Heinrich, 179, 187, 224
Greenberg, Irving: and CLAL (educational enterprise), 74; force, justification of use, 64–5; and Holocaust commission, 197; on Holocaust–rebirth nexus, 59–60; and Kant, 93; on statehood, 67; and theological meaning, 79; and Wiesel, 70, 71, 72
Gruenbaum, Yizhak, 129
Grynszpan, Herschel, 38
Gulf War (1991), 64
Guri, Haim, 9, 17, 160
Gush Emunim, 62, 147, 148, 167
Gutman, Yisrael, 83, 90, 91–2
Gypsies, annihilation of, 92, 94, 198

Ha'aretz (publication), 127, 130, 131, 132, 134, 135
Hadari-Ramage, Yona, 150
Hakibbutz Hameuhad, 132
halakha, 59, 177, 239
Halpern, Ben, 26–7, 28, 35, 40
halutsic aliya (Zionist pioneering), 21
Haman, 87
Handlin, Oscar, 21–4, 25, 26, 39
Ha-po'el ha-Tsa'ir, 191
haredi (ultraorthodox) theologists *see* Ultraorthodox Judaism
Ha-shomer ha-Tsa'ir, 92, 191
Haskalah, 93
Hatsofe (Religious Zionist paper), 130, 132, 136, 137
Hausner, Gideon, 36, 40–1
Havurah movement, 47
Hebrew language, 126, 177–8
Heine, Heinrich, 110
Hellenistic period, 88
Herberg, Will, 7, 10

heroism, 130, 131
Herut (publication), 131, 132
Herzl, Theodor, 3, 37, 191
Herzog, President Chaim, 196, 197
Hiddush ha-shem, 118
Hilberg, Raul, 197
Histadrut (General Federation of Labor), 128
history, God's role in, 53, 54, 58
Hitler, Adolf, 55, 91, 93, 94
Hitlerjugend, 145
Holocaust: 'absolutation' of, 77–8;
    'Americanization' *see* 'Americanization' of
    the Holocaust; and annihilation, 95;
    commemoration in US, 94; commission to
    commemorate, 24, 197–200; consciousness
    of, 4–10; definition by elimination, 93;
    dehumanization of, 143; ethnic mission, as,
    16, 196–219; and genocide, 95, 102; God,
    role in, 53, 54, 58; helplessness of Jews, 58;
    historiography, 86–7; nationalization of,
    146; 'nativization', 203; particularist
    approach *see* particularism; 'politicization'
    of, 76, 145, 231; and rebirth, 56, 57, 59, 69,
    133, 181–2, 184; religious significance, 232;
    roots of, 88, 101; 'singularity', 87, 91, 92,
    106, 108, 111; and State of Israel, 4, 14, 64,
    66; 'stealing of', 168; theological meaning,
    52; uniqueness of *see* uniqueness doctrine;
    universalist approach *see* universalism;
    vulgar theory of, 118–19; and Zionism,
    162; *see also* lessons of the Holocaust
Holocaust in American Life (Peter Novick), 14–15
Holocaust commission, 94, 197–200
Holocaust Industry (Norman Finkelstein), 14–15
Holocaust Memorial Museum, Washington:
    Berenbaum on, 202; 'declaration of inde-
    pendence', as, 217; emotional identification,
    207; establishment, 74, 90–1, 97, 196, 203,
    208, *see also* Holocaust commission;
    Gourevitch on, 204–5, 211; Holocaust
    consciousness, 12; ideology, 13–14; opening
    of, 220; public debate, 74; and victimiza-
    tion, 204; visitors, 1–3, 206–7
Holocaust Remembrance Day, 111–12, 135,
    136
Holocaust (television series 1976), 12
Holocaust–State nexus: ideological discourse,
    125, 127, 128, 132, 136, 139, 141, 147, 149,
    178; Israel, 128, 132, 134, 136, 139, 141,
    147, 149; and normalization, 225; origins, 4;
    theology, 58, 62, 70–1, 73–4; United States,
    178; *see also* Israel–Holocaust nexus
Horkheimer, Max, 152, 153
Horowitz, Irving, 99–103, 108
'humanistic Judaism', 95
Husock, Howard, 208, 209
Hussein, Saddam, 144

identity problem, 125

ideological discourse, 15–16, 125–95; Israel,
    127–63; United States, 164–91
Im bo ha-zikaron (When memory comes), 154
Indians, massacres of, 92, 231
Intifada, 74, 138
Iran, Khomeinist regime in, 168
Irgun fighters, 130
Isaac, Jeffrey, 47
Isaiah, 163
Israel: American Jewry contrasted, 215–16;
    Diaspora Jewry, relationship with, 5–6, 7,
    11, 13, 20, 74, 177, 179, 203, 217; Holocaust
    consciousness, 6, 8–10; Horowitz on, 100;
    ideological discourse, 127–63; Iraqi Jewry
    in, 221; mass immigration in, 220; North
    African Jewry in, 221; repression stage,
    9–10; *see also* State of Israel; Zionism
Israel Defense Forces, 3, 8
'Israel and the Trauma of Genocide' (Dan
    Diner), 141
Israel–Holocaust nexus *see* Holocaust–State
    nexus

Jacobs, Paul, 27–8
Jakobovits, Immanuel (former Chief Rabbi of
    British Jewry), 72, 73–4
Jaspers, Karl, 40, 43, 44
Jefferson, Thomas, 214
Jerusalem: and theology, 59, 69, 71, 79; Yad
    Vashem, 3, 8, 9, 13
Jewish condition, 27, 177
Jewish Daily Forward (periodical), 164, 165,
    204, 211, 212
Jewish Frontier (periodical), 164, 165
Jewish liberals, 63, 166, 185
Jewish people: ambivalence of, 105;
    'Americanization' of, 6, 7, 8, *see also*
    'Americanization' of the Holocaust; annihi-
    lations, 30–2, 85–8, 92, 105, 167–8, 198,
    204; blacks, conflict with (1968), 10, 11;
    collective identity, 3–4, 6, 28, 30, 58–9, 73,
    100, 147, 155, 221; as 'coreligionist'
    community, 22, 88, 116–17; dual loyalty
    among, 8, 24; exile, in *see* exile, Jewish
    people in; fragmentation of society, 4;
    haredi Jewry, 14, 30–1, 80, 85, 185; help-
    lessness of, 58, 142, 188; history, phases of,
    59; institutions, sensitivity to American
    public opinion, 18; life, right to, 167;
    Middle Ages, destruction in, 87; military
    force, justification for, 64–5; and moder-
    nity, 59, 71, 105–6; Nazis' perceptions of,
    25, 94–5, 96, 102; non-Jewish attitudes to
    138; passivity of, 56; as POWs, 41; prosper-
    ity, postwar generation, 6–7; psyche of,
    Arendt on, 42; and rebirth, 56, 57, 59, 69,
    133; resurrection consciousness, 4, 8;
    Spain, expulsion from, 176; status in
    modern society, 105; suffering inflicted on,

2–3, 67, 76, 97; survival of, 69, 72, 112–13; as victims, 157, 204; well-being, 23–4; 'Zionization' of world society, 11; *see also* American Jewry; antisemitism; Diaspora Jewry; Eastern Jewry; European Jewry; Iraqi Jewry; Judaism; North African Jewry; Palestinian Jewry; Polish people, Jewry; Sephardi Jewry; Western Jewry
Jewish Quarterly, 109
Jewish Renewal: A Path to Healing and Transformation (Michael Lerner), 189–90
Jewish Theological Seminary, New York, 171, 174, 177
Jewish–Arab conflict, 149, 152, 156, 161–2
Jewish–Gentile relations, 4, 38–9, 99, 170
journals *see* periodicals
Judaism: and Christianity, 1, 7, 26; 'humanistic', 95; intermarriage, rejection of, 36; moral values of, 22; non-secular, Wiesel on, 70; uniqueness doctrine, 172; *see also* Conservative Movement; 'Galut Judaism'; Jewish people; normalization, Jewish existence; Orthodox Judaism; Reform Movement
Judea-Samaria, settlement enterprise in, 139, 149
Judenrat, role of, 63, 233

Kabala, Lurianic, 176, 177
kaddish, 209
Kahan, Abraham, 212
Kaplan, Mordechai, 179
Karnei Shomron, 149
Kasztner, Rudolf (Israel), 9
Katz, Jacob, 202, 225
Katz, Steven, 92–3, 96
Ka-Tzetnik (author), 9
kiddush Hashem (traditional martyrdom), 185
King, Martin Luther, 7
Kishinev pogrom, 24
klal Yisrael (congregation of Israel), 177, 178, 179, 180, 217, 239
Knesset, 8, 9
Kook, Hillel, 38
Kovner, Abba, 233
Krauthammer, Charles, 205
Kristol, Irving, 168
Kushner, Tony, 109–10

Labor movement, 233
Lamerhav (publication), 132
Land of Israel, 59
Lanzmann, Claude, 161
'Lavon affair', 37
Law of Return, 59, 222, 229
Lebanon war (1982), 6, 74, 138, 168, 191
Lebensraum, 140
Left, national, 136, 137
Leibowitz, Yeshayahu, 145

Lemkin, Raphael, 108
Lerner, Michael, 189–91, 200
lessons of the Holocaust: Alter on, 170, 171; Americanization of the Holocaust, 231; Bauman on, 107; Biale on, 187; and consciousness, 12; and Holocaust Memorial Museum, 1, 3–4, 203, 205; and Jewish collective problem, 147; Oz on, 163; and post-Zionism/neo-Zionism, 138; theology, 63, 73; Vital on, 156
Levene, Mark, 109
Levine, Hillel, 173
Leyvik, H. (poet), 165
liberal tradition, 109–10
liberals, Jewish, 63, 166, 185
life, right to, 167
Likud government, 12, 74, 137, 139, 191
limited affiliation doctrine, 100
Linenthal, Edward, 196
litterateurs, 111, 157
Livne, Eliezer, 133–4
Lubetkin, Ziviah, 165

Maariv (Jewish publication), 41, 127, 136–7
McCarthy, Mary, 42
Madagascar plan, 142
Magnes, Judah, 37, 78
Mahler, Raphael, 224
Mapai (Eretz Israel Labour Party), 9, 128, 133; Central Committee, 32
Mapam (United Workers' Party), 128
'March of the Living', 11
marginal affiliation doctrine, 100
Marrus, Michael, 99
martyrdom, 72, 118, 171, 185, 235
maskilim, 225
mass killing *see* annihilation; genocide; Holocaust
Matzpen group, 140
Mazover, Mark, 108
Medina ke-hilkhata (Boaz Evron), 151
Mein Kampf, 137
Meretz party, 139
Messiah, 54
metahistory, 110
Meyerhoff, Harvey, 197
Michman, Dan, 80
Middle Ages, destruction of Jews in, 87
mission (Jewish identity), 58, 71
modernism/modernity, 59, 71, 105–6, 116, 198
Moment (journal), 171
Montgomery, Bernard Law (1st Viscount), 140
Mortera affair, 24
motives, 5, 11–12
Mozes, Zvi, 149
Munich, murder of Israeli athletes (1972), 148
Musa Dagh, 169
Museum, Memorial *see* Holocaust Memorial Museum, Washington

Nahshon (son of Amminadav), 58, 64, 67
National Religious Party, 136, 139
National Socialism, 91
nationalism, 107–8, 112, 115, 146, 147, 229
'Nationalizing Remembrance of the Six
    Million' (Henry Wasserman), 142
Nativ (journal), 139, 149
Native Americans: annihilation, 78; museum
    proposal, 211
'nativization' of the Holocaust, 203
Nazis: annihilations of Jews, 30–2, 85–8, 92,
    105, 167–8, 198, 204; Madagascar plan, 142;
    perception of Jews, 25, 94–5, 96, 102; pros-
    ecution of, 8; terminally ill, treatment of,
    96; unique intention of, 19–20, 93, 111, 204;
    Zionist leaders' collaboration with, 9; *see
    also* racism
'Necessity of Antisemitism' (Frederic
    Raphael), 115
'negation of Diaspora' doctrine, 88, 186, 216
Nekuda (journal), 139, 148, 149
neo-conservatives, 62, 166, 168, 230–1
neo-exilism, 135
neo-Nazism, 135
neo-Orthodox theory, 71
neo-Zionism, 138, 139, 140, 147, 150
Neusner, Jacob, 179–84, 200, 209, 214
New Republic (publication), 214
newspapers *see* periodicals
Ninth of Av, 111, 142, 146
Nolte, Ernst, 102, 111
Norden, Edward, 217
normalization, Jewish existence: and Arendt,
    43; assimilation process, 172, 173; and
    centripetal tendency, 229–30; dialectical
    approach, 162; Diasporism, 232; Elam on,
    153–4; general, 13, 226; and Holocaust
    Museum, 2; Holocaust–State nexus, 225;
    integration, 232; and Israel, 8; Jewish
    normalization, 13, 226–7; phases, 225;
    singular, 13, 226; strength, 59, 232; termi-
    nology, 13; 'vacillations', 227; and
    Wieseltier, 216; Yehoshua on, 159
Novick, Peter, 14–15
nuclear bomb, 65, 189
Nuremberg trials, 39

Olympic Games, murder of Israeli athletes
    (1972), 148
'Operation Haman', 87
Ophir, Adi, 118–20
Origins of Totalitarianism (Hannah Arendt), 86
Ornan, Uzi, 144, 145
Orthodox Judaism: fundamentalism, 107, 184,
    185; modern, 71, 72, 73, 74, 85; publica-
    tions of, 132; *see also* Ultraorthodox Judaism
Oz, Amos, 161, 163

Palestine: Arendt on, 40, 41, 43; ideological

debate, 130, 131; Palestinian question, 78;
    peace talks with, 138; self-determination,
    right to, 196; *see also* Jewish–Arab conflict
Palestine National Covenant, 137
Palestinian Jewry, 140
Palmah fighters, 130
particularism: academic discourse, 83, 84, 99;
    ideological discourse, 163, 169; and univer-
    salism, 13, 20, 45, 70, 84, 93–4, 95, 99, 108,
    169, 238; and Yad Vashem, 3
periodicals: *Al Hamishmar*, 129, 131, 134, 137;
    Aufbau, 37, 38; *Commentary*, 164, 165, 214;
    Davar, 129, 131, 132, 134; *Di Zukunft*, 164,
    165; *Forvets*, 164; *Ha'aretz*, 127, 130, 131,
    132, 134, 135; *Hatsofe*, 130, 132, 136, 137;
    Herut, 131, 132; *Jewish Daily Forward*, 164,
    165, 204, 211, 212; *Jewish Frontier*, 164, 165;
    Lamerhav, 132; *Maariv*, 41, 127, 136–7;
    Moment, 171; *Nativ*, 139, 149; *Nekuda*, 139,
    148, 149; *New Republic*, 214; *Politika*, 140,
    143; *Theory and Criticism*, 117, 118, 143;
    Tikkun, 186, 200, 209, 212, 214; *Washington
    Post*, 205
Petuchowski, Jacob, 72, 75–6
Podhoretz, Norman, 168
pogroms, 24, 235
Polish people, 96, 146; Jewry, 129
'political messianism', 88, 89
'politicization' of Holocaust, 76, 145, 231
Politika (journal), 140, 143
post-Zionism: and Berenbaum, 200; and Biale,
    187; and dialectical Zionism, 163; groups
    within, 184–5; and Israel–Holocaust relation-
    ship, 186; and Jewish nationalism, 147;
    Lerner on, 189, 190; nationalization of
    Holocaust, 146; and neo-Zionism, 138, 139,
    150–1
power, political, 59–60
Power and Powerlessness in Jewish History (David
    Biale), 186
*Preserving Memory: The Struggle to Create
    America's Holocaust Museum* (Edward
    Linenthal), 196
prisoners of war (POWs), 41
Proskauer, Joseph, 20–1, 25, 29, 30
public opinion, 24, 30, 206–7; media survey,
    18–19
'public thinking', 5, 12
publications *see* periodicals
pundits' discourse, 16, 196–219

qiddush ha-shem, 118
Quest for National Identity (Yosef Gorny), 12–13

Raab, Earl, 167–8
rabbinical era, 59
Rabin, Yitzhak, 149; assassination of, 145, 146,
    216
racism, 86, 204, 207